Dark Riddle

Dark Riddle

Hegel, Nietzsche, and the Jews

Y IRMIYAHU Y OVEL

The Pennsylvania State University Press
University Park, Pennsylvania

First published in 1998 in the United States by The Pennsylvania State University
Press, 820 North University Drive, University Park, PA 16802

ISBN 0-271-01781-3 (cloth)
ISBN 0-271-01794-5 (paper)

Library of Congress Cataloging-in-Publication Data

Yovel, Yirmiyahu.
    Dark riddle : Hegel, Nietzsche, and the Jews / by Yirmiyahu Yovel.
       p.   cm.
    Includes bibliographical references and index.   •
    ISBN 0–271–01781–3 (alk. paper)
    ISBN 0–271–01794–5 (pbk. : alk. paper)
    1. Hegel, Georg Wilhelm Friedrich, 1770–1831—Views on Judaism.
  2. Nietzsche, Friedrich Wilhelm, 1844–1900—Views on Judaism.
  3. Judaism and philosophy—History—19th century.   I. Title.
    82949.J84Y68   1998.
    296'.0943—dc21   97–49192
                                                                                    CIP

Typeset in 10½ on 12pt Meridien by Wearset, Boldon, Tyne and Wear.
Printed in Great Britain by MPG Books, Bodmin, Cornwall.

It is the policy of The Pennsylvania State University Press to use acid-free paper for
the first printing of all clothbound books. Publications on uncoated stock satisfy
minimum requirements of American National Standard for Information Sciences—
Permanence of Paper for Printed Library Materials, ANSI 239.48–1984

To the memory of my father
Zishe David Yovel (Freifeld)

Contents

Contents   ix

Preface

The last two centuries have seen momentous developments in Jewish history – from political emancipation to Nazi genocide, from
large-scale assimilation and secularization to the creation of a Jewish
State, and more – all linked to the tribulations of modernity, especially in Europe. However, Jews were not only the targets and victims of modern European upheavals; they also provided Europeans
with a mirror – a crooked, passion-laden mirror – in which to see a
reflection of their own identity problems. The "Jewish problem" was
basically a European problem: that is, not only a problem for Europe
but a reflection of Europe's own problem with itself – of how, in an
age of rapid transformation, Europeans were understanding their
own identity, future, and meaning of life.

The present study aims to make a specifically defined contribution
to this vast topic. We shall look at the image of Judaism as offered by
the two most important philosophers of the nineteenth century,
Hegel and Nietzsche. Both were German thinkers, one active in the
first half, the other in the second half of the century, the first a major
philosopher of reason, the second one of its severest critics. I should
point out from the outset that this is a study in philosophy, not in
the history of political ideology. I confine myself to treating Hegel
and Nietzsche as philosophers (hoping, thereby, to shed further light
on their general thinking as well). This means, first, that I center on
Hegel and Nietzsche themselves, discussing their own philosophical

ideas and terms rather than those of various ideological followers, disciples, users, and abusers. Secondly, I try to understand each philosopher's view of the Jews in relation to his other philosophical ideas and in light of his overall philosophical project. In each case I distinguish between two questions: (a) What is the role which the philosopher attributes to historical Judaism in the formation of the modern world? And (b) what is the place he assigns to the Jews of the present?

Hegel's philosophical project was a vast and ambitious one. It included the attempt to reach a philosophical understanding of the modern world, its essence and genesis, and thereby shape modernity still further, leading to its climax. Hegel saw European culture as the core of world history, and as essentially a Christian culture, which the philosopher must translate and elevate into concepts. Judaism was a necessary background for understanding the Christian revolution and era.

According to the Hegelian dialectic, every cultural form makes some true, genuine contribution to world history (and the world Spirit), after which it is sublated (*aufgehoben*) and disappears from the historical scene. Yet the Jews continued to survive long after their *raison d'être* had disappeared – indeed, after they no longer had a genuine history in Hegel's sense, but existed merely as the corpse of their extinguished essence. With the French Revolution, Jews were entering the modern world and claiming their rights and place within it. Hegel, despite his anti-Jewish bias, was perfectly disposed to grant these rights; but he did not know what to do with Jews in modernity as Jews, nor could he explain their survival in terms of his system.

Nietzsche too had an ambitious philosophical project, one which in many ways was opposed to Hegel's. A radical cultural revolutionary, his goal was not to bring the process of modernity to its culmination but rather to subvert and reverse it – more precisely, to divert it into a totally different course. The process which had started with Socrates, Moses, and Jesus, and which Hegel saw as creating truth, civilization, spirit, and even God himself (the Absolute), was for Nietzsche a story of decadence and degeneration. Nietzsche attributed this decadence to two main sources – rationalistic metaphysics and Christianity. The first stemmed from the Greeks, the second from the ancient Jews. He therefore needed an interpretation of Judaism (and also of Socratism, as he did in *The Birth of Tragedy*) in order to expose and disrupt the decadent culture of the present.

Given these projects, Hegel had seen the merit of ancient Judaism in its discovery – which led to Christianity – that God was spirit and that spirit is higher than nature; whereas for Nietzsche this was the great falsification which the ancient Jewish priests had brought about. However, as my analysis will show, Nietzsche did not recognize a single, permanent Jewish essence. He distinguished three different modes or phases in Judaism, and expressed admiration for two of them: for biblical Judaism and for the Jews of the later Diaspora. His harsh critique targets exclusively the middle phase, the Second Temple "priestly" Judaism (as he calls it) which began the "slave revolution" in morality – namely, Christianity. Nietzsche's true target is Christianity: so much so, that often he reads the ideas and even the phrases of the New Testament directly into what he derogates under the name of Judaism.

Another major difference between the two philosophers is that Hegel went on to see post-Christian Jewish life as a dead repetition of meaningless existence, whereas Nietzsche exalted Jewish life in the Diaspora as a great human experience. Having rejected Jesus and gone into exile, the Jews have schooled themselves in suffering and endurance, they have gained historical depth and existential power – which Nietzsche now wants to pour into his new Dionysian Europe, as an antidote to Christianity and its secularized forms (such as liberalism and egalitarianism). The Jews are thereby given a role in modernity as Jews. They are to mix with other Europeans, create new values and standards in all fields, and provide the power and potential virtue which are needed in order to revitalize the old continent which the Jews' forefathers had helped corrupt.

It has become a commonplace to say that Nietzsche was ambivalent about the Jews. Yet the word *ambivalent* is ambiguous and often creates an impression of depth where there is merely confusion. My aim in part II is to analyze the precise structure of Nietzsche's ambivalence regarding the Jews and bring to light its ingredients in their mutual relations. On the one hand, Nietzsche sees ancient Judaism as one of the main sources of European decadence; on the other, he assigns modern Jews, whom he admires, a leading role in creating the nondecadent, de-Christianized Europe he wishes for the future. As for modern anti-Semitism, Nietzsche repudiates it with the same passion he reserves for proto-Christian Jewish "priests" – and for similar reasons. These two human types, apparently so opposed to each other – the anti-Semite and the Jewish priest – are actually genealogical cousins: They share the same deep-psychological pattern of *ressentiment* which Nietzsche's philosophy diagnoses as the basis of human meanness and degeneration.

Hegel too was ambivalent about Judaism, but in a different way. His views shifted over time, sometimes reverting to older positions in a new form; and never, not even in maturity, did he fully come to grips with the problem. It is ironic that the notoriously unsystematic Nietzsche reached a fairly unified and coherent position on the Jews, however complex, and that Hegel, the great systematizer, never fully stopped wavering. The irony is enhanced when we realize that Nietzsche even displayed a quasi-dialectical pattern in this matter – a tense unity of supposedly preclusive opposites – whereas Hegel's position was never fully resolved. As a result, when Hegel is seen to be shifting his views (or emphases) about the Jews, most probably we have moved in time; but when Nietzsche does the same, he is moving synchronically from one zone of the same map to another – that is, he is stressing a different ingredient of the same complex position.

My aim is to follow Hegel's itinerary and to reconstruct Nietzsche's map. In presenting their views I try as much as possible to use the immanent approach, in order to do justice not only to them but to the historical issue at hand. My work is mostly reconstructive; it offers a picture, a conceptual portrait, and leaves much room for the reader to reach his or her own conclusions and final judgments. In a manner of speaking, I too am a reader of this study who draws his own conclusions from it, while not claiming a special privilege for them. My main effort and claims concern the description and the analysis; on their basis, I can well imagine other people making different evaluations.

Another aspect of my study addresses the question: To what extent did each philosopher overcome the anti-Jewish feelings imbued in him by his upbringing and milieu? Those feelings were of a different kind in each case. Hegel was raised in the Christian, theological, anti-Jewish tradition, primarily in the Lutheran version, to which he gave a conceptual form in terms of his philosophy. Nietzsche came to maturity amidst a raging new kind of anti-Semitism – secular, political, racist – that no longer depended on religion. As a young man Hegel denied the Jews any historical worth – they were responsible only for Christianity's defects, not its virtues – and used some biting, even venomous language against them. Later he overcame some of his negative attitudes, but in a mixed, incomplete, ambiguous way, incurring several regressions, and his mature system still contains many of his youthful prejudices – now raised to the dignity of the "Concept."

Nietzsche, the son of a Protestant minister, was also exposed to anti-Jewish feelings and stereotypes in childhood. As an adult living around the time of German unification, his environment seethed with the new secular and political anti-Semitism, which aimed at the Jews as persons – at their bare existence as a pariah group – rather than at their cult and beliefs. Through several anti-Semitic intimates, including Richard Wagner and Nietzsche's sister Elizabeth, Nietzsche for a while came into contact with this "disease" (as he later called it); but as his own genius and intellectual personality evolved, he broke with Wagner (and partly, painfully, also with his sister) and, in the early or mid-1870s, performed a powerful self-overcoming which made him an active and passionate *anti*-anti-Semite, a position that dominated his philosophy and writing from then on.

Despite some inevitable slips and lingering anti-Jewish stereotypes (which, in a dangerous rhetorical twist, he now turned against anti-Semites – see later), Nietzsche largely succeeded in this process of self-overcoming. Not so in the case of Hegel, who wavered back and forth, sometimes in the same act, and even in maturity systematized some of his early anti-Jewish prejudices. These prejudices, quite significantly, were reinforced by some Enlightenment ideas, including the old Kant's attack on all historical religions, particularly Judaism. Kant, the philosopher of pure reason and the epitome of the Enlightenment, denied that Judaism was a religion at all, because, he claimed, it had no moral content and message but was only an external political constitution. The best prospect Kant could offer the Jews was that they should convert nominally to Christianity (which Kant did not favor either) so as to gain social and political acceptance, but actually adhere to the universal (Kantian) morality of reason.[1] Kant dubbed this proposal "the Euthanasia" of Judaism. In another text the old Kant called the Jews "a nation of cheaters" and suggested that they were foreigners in the land who exploited its inhabitants.[2]

What should follow from here concerning Judaism and anti-Semitism? Does the negation of the Enlightenment necessarily lead to the persecution of Jews, and do liberalism and enlightenment always act as a guarantee against anti-Semitism? Many would like to think so, but this assumption is not supported by the historical material,[3] and my study too dispels it. We shall see the greatest philosophers of reason, Kant and Hegel, ennobling their anti-Jewish sentiments with a systematic form, while Nietzsche, the anti-liberal, defended the Jews and strove to use their superior qualities to create his "new man." Also, Kant and Hegel, the liberals, granted Jews, as individuals, merely a passive place in the modern world, whereas Nietzsche assigned them an active task – and specifically as Jews: that is, as bearers of their special experience, history, and "breeding," even though this is a temporary role that will eventually cancel itself.

Personally I am neither a Hegelian, nor a Nietzschean, though I have learned much from both. I have no particular ax to grind; nor did I write this book in order to condemn or rehabilitate anyone, but rather as a historian of concepts and ideas drawing a complex and sometimes fascinating picture. Of course, no description is neutral, yet some are fairer and more objective than others (usually because their dominant intentionality is descriptive rather than juridical).[4] An intellectual historian stands only to gain from recognizing the complex, unclassifiable, sometimes idiosyncratic element in notable intellectuals and abstaining from embroiling them immediately in some current polemics, or from making them what I should call "guilty by misappropriation." On the other hand, one should also abstain from apologetic writing (which was, and still is, current with respect to our two philosophers).[5]

Concerning Hegel there have been two kinds of apologetic writing: one trying to justify the Jews to Hegel (similar to what Herman Cohen did with Kant),[6] the other trying to justify Hegel to the Jews. Today, Hegel no longer evokes the stormy emotions he did in the past, when his views were misused by Nationalists, Socialists, Fascists, and Communists alike, as well as by their opponents.[7] But this is not the case with Nietzsche, whose critical force is still very fresh and who is still, for some people, the number one villain of modernity – especially because he wanted to uproot Christianity while also rejecting its secular substitutes, egalitarianism and democracy. For these reasons, and also because the Fascists and the Nazis misused him with fanfare, Nietzsche has incurred wrath and aversion and especially many misunderstandings. For example, in itself, as I argue, Nietzsche's thought was not political at all – but was, rather, politically sterile, which I take to be one of its weaknesses (and potential dangers).

In any case I must expect my analysis to anger some of Nietzsche's foes who might feel I have robbed them of a favorite villain. To them let me say: There is no contradiction in opposing Nietzsche's general philosophy and yet recognizing his true stand on anti-Semitism and the Jews. The reason is that the Jewish issue, as mentioned above, is not the best test case for determining the merit of a philosophy. Similarly, one can accept the plea for universal rationality (either in Kant's or in Hegel's form), while exposing the bias and inconsistencies of its pleaders on the matter of Judaism (or women, or other objects or victims of prejudice that was once considered obvious).

Few philosophers – especially when they were great – were faithful to their own philosophy, because their philosophical revolution ran ahead of what their all-too-human personalities could accept or accomplish. Descartes was no real Cartesian, nor Kant a true Kantian, nor Hegel a strict Hegelian. That Nietzsche, by contrast, was a Nietzschean – or came close to being one – does not necessarily speak in favor of his philosophical views, though it gives his philosophical person a more authentic and even a nobler appeal than that of some of the great thinkers against whom he rebelled.

This book started with an essay on Hegel and Judaism published in the seventies in several languages,[8] and with a public lecture on Nietzsche and the Jews given at the Israel Academy of Sciences and Humanities (1977) and repeated at the Paris Société des Études Juives (1979); a summary of that lecture was published in the *Revue des études juives*.[9] After writing the part on Nietzsche, I came to the conclusion that the part about Hegel left much to be desired in terms of scope and balance, and decided to rewrite and expand it, a task which was postponed year after year and only recently was completed. My compensation is that each of the two parts now offers a comprehensive study of its subject.

A number of papers prepared the ground for this book and contributed materials to it: (1) "Hegels Begriff der Religion und die Religion der Erhabenheit," *Theologie und Philosophie*, 51 (1976), pp. 512–37; (2) "Perspectives nouvelles sur Nietzsche et le judaïsme," *Revue des études juives*, 138 (1979), pp. 483–5; (3) "La Religion de la sublimité," in *Hegel et la religion*, ed. G. Planty-Bonjour (Presses Universitaires de France, Paris, 1982), pp. 151–76; (4) "Nietzsche ve-Zilleli ha-El ha-Met," Postscript to the Hebrew translation of Walter Kaufmann, *Nietzsche: Philosopher, Psychologist, Anti-Christ* (Schocken, Tel Aviv, 1983), pp. 426–38; (5) "Nietzsche, the Jews, and Ressentiment," in *Nietzsche, Genealogy, Morality*, ed. Richard Schacht (University of California Press, Berkeley, 1994), pp. 214–36.

In the meantime a few shorter studies on similar subjects have appeared, which I mention in the bibliography and from time to time in the notes. In a paper entitled "Nietzsche's Attitudes toward the Jews,"[10] Michael Duffy and Willard Mittelman attribute to Nietzsche a threefold division very much like mine, which they say they could not find in any former publication. Had they looked in the French literature, they would have found my summary paper in *Revue des études juives* mentioned above. Two recent books came to my attention after mine had already gone to the Hebrew publisher. One is the late Sarah Kofman's *Le Mépris des juifs: Nietzsche, les juifs, l'antisémitisme*,[11] which I found insufficiently structured and too apologetic; it practically suppresses Nietzsche's harsh texts against the ancient Jews, though these texts are crucial to understanding his overall position and must be quoted and read in its light. Weaver Santaniello's book, *Nietzsche, God, and the Jews*,[12] is more balanced and is well structured chronologically, though also on the apologetic side. Unlike Kofman, Santaniello quotes the anti-Jewish texts, but calls them "ambivalent," when *in themselves* they are not ambivalent but fairly univocal. Nietzsche's condemnation of "priestly" Judaism was straightforward and harsh; the ambivalence results, as we shall see, from his equally univocal condemnation of anti-Semitism and his complex admiration of Diaspora Jews – it is the conjunction of all three elements (together with equivocal uses of rhetoric).

Acknowledgments

I owe thanks to many people, including former teachers and students. Nathan Rotenstreich's work was the first to draw my attention to the importance of Hegel's coping with Judaism. With Walter Kaufmann, also a former teacher, I had some disagreement regarding his general presentation of Nietzsche (which I thought too tame), but not with his dispelling of the myth of the "anti-Semitic" Nietzsche. The late Jacob Talmon, whose anxious reading of Nietzsche's *Daybreak*, section 205, I contested, nevertheless graciously welcomed my work and presided over my Nietzsche lecture at the Israel Academy. My thanks go also to Mireille Hadas-Lebel and Gérard Nahon for the opportunity to address the Paris Société des Études Juives. Much earlier, Jacob Golomb, then my student and today an established Nietzsche scholar, helped me locate relevant source materials. The Memorial Foundation for Jewish Culture supported the initial stage of my work. Another former assistant, Tibor Schlosser, now at the Israeli Foreign Office, helped persuade me (I wish he had failed!) that I ought to revise the part on Hegel. During the long time this has taken, I have presented my ideas in lectures and seminars at the École des Hautes Études en Sciences Sociales in Paris, the Universities of Rome and Milan, the Free University of Berlin, and the New School for Social Research in New York, and got useful comments and objections. My old friend Yizhak Torchin has, as always, tended an attentive and well-informed ear to me, and he and his wife Suzanne were gracious hosts as always in splendid Barbizon (France). My further thanks go to my assistants in Jerusalem, Pini Ifargan and Tal Aviran, and to Kurt Leege and Morgan Meis in New York, who helped with the English translation. Jean van Altena copy-edited the manuscript with understanding and care, a quality manifested by everyone else at Polity Press. Special thanks are due also to my old-time associate Eva Shorr, Managing Editor of the Jerusalem-based philosophical quarterly *IYYUN*, whose quality editing of the Hebrew manuscript helped shape the English-language version as well.

The author and publishers gratefully acknowledge permission to reproduce extracts from the following works by Friedrich Nietzsche:

Daybreak: Thoughts on the Prejudices of Morality, translated by R. J. Hollingdale (1982); *Human, All Too Human: A Book for Free Spirits* translated by R. J. Hollingdale (1986); extracts reprinted by permission of the publishers, Cambridge University Press.

Beyond Good and Evil translated by Walter Kaufmann © 1966 by Random House, Inc.; *The Will to Power* translated by Walter Kaufmann and R. J. Hollingdale © 1968 by Random House, Inc.; *On the Genealogy of Morals* translated by Walter Kaufmann © 1967 by Random House, Inc.; extracts reprinted by permission of Random House, Inc.

The Antichrist, Thus Spoke Zarathustra, and *Twilight of the Idols* from *The Portable Nietzsche* edited and translated by Walter Kaufmann, translation © 1954 by The Viking Press, renewed © 1982 by Viking Penguin Inc.; extracts reprinted by permission of Viking Penguin, a division of Penguin Putnam, Inc.

Extracts from letters translated from the German by the author, Yirmiyahu Yovel, from *Briefwechsel: Kritische Gesamtausgabe* edited by Giorgio Colli and Mazzino Montinari (W. de Gruyter, 1975/1993) by permission of the publishers.

Every effort has been made to trace all the copyright holders, but if any have been inadvertently overlooked the publishers will be pleased to make the necessary arrangement at the first opportunity.

PART I

Hegel and the Religion of Sublimity

CHAPTER ONE

Hegel and his Predecessors

Judaism as a philosophical question

To some extent, Judaism has always interested Christian theologians. But only after Luther did this interest find a special impetus, because the renewed Protestant concern with the Bible brought into focus the relation between the two Testaments, the Old and the New. Still, Judaism was discussed only as a *theological* question.[1] Philosophers did not start reflecting upon it until a relatively late date. For that to occur, the modern *historical* outlook had to arise: namely, the view that world history is not an arbitrary empirical story or a mere aggregate of facts, but a comprehensive, meaningful process whose pattern, at least in its broad lines, can better be deciphered by rational philosophy than through the old theological terms of Fall and Redemption, Incarnation, Providence, Revelation, a chosen people, and a sacred history leading to the establishment of God's kingdom on earth. In other words, two developments had to occur: First, history had to be *secularized*, released from the universe of theology and subsumed under the laws of nature and reason; second, reason *itself* had to manifest such patterns as might give secular history meaning as a totality – that is, as a system possessing an overall rational significance.

For thinkers like Kant and Hegel, the goal of history no longer consisted of God's other-worldly kingdom but of human freedom,

rational self-awareness, and (for Kant) universal morality and inter-
national peace. This overall goal allows the philosopher to assign
meaning to distinct historical eras and to draw a line of ascent
through human affairs. Although this view translates some Christian
themes into rational philosophy, it also profoundly changes their
meaning – and this change itself, seen as both correction and purifi-
cation, was considered further proof of historical progress. Kant and
Hegel observed a process of growing clarity and self-purification in
human culture. Whereas myth and religion contain a nucleus of
rational ideas which they express sensuously, under the veil of
images and metaphors, higher forms of culture make these dim ideas
more explicit, until they start assuming a conceptual form, first in
dogmatic philosophy and theology, and later in the more coherent
form of critical-systematic thinking. The ongoing effort to extract the
latent rational seeds from the religious tradition and to raise them to
clear, coherent consciousness is what much of history is about; it testifies to the historicality of human life and to reason's power of self-
elucidation.[2]

The rise of the philosophy of history

The secular philosophy of history was born from the rationalism of
the Enlightenment, seemingly as its opposite, but actually as a marriage of principles. Its founding idea was that reason itself has a history. Even the eternal principles of reason require a process by which
they arise in the human mind and gradually become explicit – and,
no less essential, become realized in the scientific, moral, political,
and religious products of culture. The most current metaphor was
the growth and maturation of the human person. In principle, reason is "pure," and we are all potentially "rational beings"; yet for
our rationality to become actual and fully known to itself, we need a
long, hard evolution, in which irrational factors play a necessary role
– sensuality, imagination, passion, accident, obscurity, and also suffering, conflict, and violence. This is the necessary substrate within
which reason evolves, breaks into consciousness, externalizes itself,
returns to itself on a higher level of awareness, and gradually realizes
its pure, genuine essence in human life, institutions, and cultural
products. In this way the philosophy of history has grown within
rationalism itself.[3] It reached its mature expression in the school of
German idealism, starting with Kant and culminating with Hegel.

What enabled reason to discover an overall, meaningful pattern in

history was an offshoot of the Kantian idea known as the "Copernican revolution." When reason observes human history, it does not
see an external, accidental reality completely alien to reason, but
sees itself there. The true subject (and subject matter) of history is
reason itself. Embodied in all varieties of human life, reason is the
essential human feature which penetrates everything we do, feel,
think, and desire. Yet reason has diverse manifestations, most of
which are still obscure and wrapped in sensibility and imagination,
so their form and medium are incompatible with the rational message they are said to contain. Still, a philosopher penetrating beneath
the profusion of deeds, events, and cultural forms which history presents will observe the work of human reason as it assumes diverse
forms and shapes and strives in all of them toward greater clarity,
explicitness, self-knowledge, and (thereby) actuality.

In a word, the way by which reason can discover an intelligible
overarching pattern in history is to view human history as reason's
own evolution – as the history of reason. When we observe history
philosophically, reason is both the subject and the object, the investi-
gator and that which is investigated. In a more popular idiom (used
by Lessing and Herder), reason is humanity's process of self-
education and maturation (which also means liberation).

A Kantian paradox

Kant was the first major philosopher to start systematizing this idea.
But it was only with Hegel that historical rationalism reached its full-
grown expression. Thereby a framework was also provided for interpreting Judaism in *philosophical* rather than theological terms.
Judaism is not just another revealed religion competing with Christianity and opposing the religion of reason: Judaism was now conceived as a specific figure in the history of reason (or of the human
spirit), and as such had to be assigned a place in the overall process.
As long as the philosophy of the Enlightenment maintained a rigid,
abstract opposition between reason and historical religions (or
between philosophy and revelation), it had to present all religions –
Judaism, Christianity, Islam, etc. – as superstition, the antithesis of
reason. Yet this sweeping negation became impossible when the
matter was treated historically. One had then to take seriously the
specific differences separating one religion from another, study and
characterize each of them from within (rather than simply rejecting
them from without), and determine the relative contribution each

religion made to the overall history of reason, together with its flaws and limitations.

Given this historical approach, it would seem that Judaism too would receive its place and role within the evolution of human reason. But what role? This question will occupy us for some time when dealing with Hegel. But first we should take a brief look at the historical background. How was Judaism depicted by three of Hegel's predecessors – Spinoza, Mendelssohn, and Kant – whose views are partly linked to, and influential for, those of Hegel?

Kant, religion, and the metaphysical interest

Kant attributes a metaphysical interest to human reason, which takes different shapes. It appears first in myth and primitive religion, then in the higher religions (especially in their theology), then in "dogmatic" metaphysics, and finally in Kant's own critical metaphysics. The evolution is marked by crises, contradictions, and revolutions in the way of thinking, the last of which is Kant's own Copernican revolution. Kant saw his philosophy as bringing the Enlightenment phase of human reason to its climax, by deciphering the true structure – and limits – of human reason, and giving it a conclusive systematization. Henceforth there will be metaphysics as *science*, not as mere opinion, and thereby the history of metaphysics will come to an end – just as the histories of geometry, formal logic, and physics has ended in principle[4] when these disciplines attained the conclusive form of science. Thus the history of reason has an *end* in Kant which excludes relativism; but the end cannot be reached until a long process of evolution and crisis has been consummated.

Kant insisted that no religion had made a valid contribution to knowledge; religion's only contribution was to the history of *morality*. Kant's critique of reason refuted all claims to know such matters as God's existence, the freedom of the will, and the immortality of the soul. Of these supreme matters we can know nothing, and there is no valid content which cognitive philosophy borrows from religion. The rational seed of all religions is the moral consciousness latent and arising within them. All the rest – the ceremonies, customs, "statutory commands," and historical tales told by the various religions (including their accounts of the world's creation, shape, and early history) – belong to the "sensuous cover" in which the rational seed is wrapped and from which moral consciousness gradually breaks out.

In Kant's terms, the history of religion exhibits the transformation of reason's *practical*, rather than theoretical interest. Religion concerns the practical commands of human reason. What evolves through the various religions is human respect for the moral law, which even the lower religions contain in some dim form that rises toward greater explication and self-awareness. What will be Judaism's place in this framework?

Here we are struck by a paradox. Placing the essence of religion exclusively in practical commands is an old Jewish view made explicit (though overstated) by Spinoza and Mendelssohn which also has adherents today (the followers of the late Y. Leibowitz). True, Kant understood practical commands as moral decrees, rather than as the commands of God and part of a ceremonial tradition; morality for him was based on the purity of the will, as opposed to acting in conformity with an external law. However, although Kant recognized in every other religion a moral kernel hiding under the cover of external, God-issued laws, he refused to see the same pattern in Judaism. The Jewish religion stood out for Kant as having no moral content at all; it was merely legalistic, a *political* constitution only. As such it was *not even a religion*, since religion is defined by this moral kernel.

As the irony of Jewish history often has it, these ideas reached Kant by way of two great Jews, Spinoza and Mendelssohn: the first a Jewish heretic who abolished all the laws of the Torah, the other a rationalist Jew who observed all the *mitzvoth* (religious commands). Kant's direct source was the observant Jew, Mendelssohn; he probably knew of Spinoza's views through Mendelssohn, and also by way of learned rumor. Kant, in any case, drew from these sources what he wished and corralled them in his own direction.

Since this is the background with which Hegel coped, we must take a short look at it.

Spinoza: Judaism as a political religion

Spinoza's view of Judaism has two main components. First, he makes Jewish history – and, following it, human history at large – a thoroughly *secular* phenomenon determined by rational and natural causes alone. Second, Spinoza construes the Mosaic religion as the *political constitution* of the ancient Jews (the Hebrews), created by a social contract in which the Jews decided to make God their political sovereign. The first component abolishes the notions of miracle, providence, the "chosen people," and *historia sacra* (sacred history) in general; the second component leads Spinoza to view Jewish life in the Diaspora as outdated because it has lost its political *raison d'être*, and explain the Jews' continued survival – even their eternity, in which he still believes – as the result of perfectly natural causes: the other nations' hatred toward the Jews (caused by the Jews' willful seclusion and disdain for Gentiles) and the power of the Jews' religious faith (which Spinoza, who left the Jewish community in a scandal, calls their "superstition"[5]).

Taking the Bible's own point of view, says Spinoza, we must admit that the election of the Jews had no supernatural implications; it concerned only "dominion and physical advantages."[6] The Jewish "election" is a metaphoric expression which connotes only a successful political existence. In the same way, Spinoza's strong belief that at some future time "God may a second time elect them"[7] also means that the Jews will some day reestablish their worldly, political State, and this will occur by natural causes alone. This is Spinoza's version of the old Jewish saying (reiterated by Maimonides) that the sole difference between the present day and the messianic era is the Jews' subjection to foreign powers.

Spinoza's view of Judaism's place in history is derived from his immanent metaphysics, which denies transcendent forces and entities. The Jewish people were formed by a natural process – the making of a political contract in Hobbes's style, with the added peculiarity that instead of some mortal person, the Jews chose God himself to be their political sovereign. Rather than God choosing the Jews as his people, it was the Jews who decided that God – or whoever they deemed to be God – should be their earthly ruler. By this act they established a theocracy in the true sense (where *theos*, God, is also the governor) and primordially identified religion with the State: God's commands are those of the political ruler, and the Jews' *religious* laws are actually the political constitution which organizes their life and determines their identity.

This view has major implications for Jewish life in the Diaspora. If the Jewish religion is essentially the state constitution, then after the destruction of the Jewish State, the Jewish religion became obsolete and has no place in the Diaspora. Nevertheless, Diaspora Jews continued to adhere to their religion many centuries after going into exile. With the destruction of their real state, they created an imaginary, phantom state embodied in their religious decrees (including the oral law). The laws of religion which formerly governed a real, terrestrial state have become the fictional substitute for a state that exists no more, and this fiction has become so powerful that the Jews forfeit their lives for their religion as if they were sacrificing it for the fatherland. The laws of the non-existent state have become the Jews' spectral fatherland, independent of time and place, which they carry with them wherever they go in their exile.

This is also Spinoza's interpretation of the fact (to which he strongly objects, but can offer no alternative), that Judaism demands of a person strict observance of the *religious* commands as a condition for admitting him or her as a citizen in the Jewish *nation*. As a result – as Spinoza knew from bitter personal experience – "whoever fell away from religion ceased to be a citizen and was, on that ground alone, accounted an enemy."[8] Spinoza saw this as a catch, a trap for a free-thinking Jewish person, and certainly considered himself as having been trapped by it.

It is doubtful whether Spinoza saw a solution *within* Jewish life to this problem. His thesis about the Jews was intended primarily as a basis for reforming European life in general. His goal was to secularize the modern state and purge it of allegiance to religious belief. While his theory of Judaism helped him, perhaps, to explain his personal fate (and also to get even with the Jewish leaders who had expelled him), its chief purpose was as a basis for criticizing the relations of state and religion as they existed in *Christian* Europe. The argument's covert point is aimed at Calvinist theocracy, the Pope's claims, the Iberian Inquisition, the principle that "state religion goes after the ruler" (*cuius regio eius religio*) which ended the wars of religion, and against the very notion of "state religion" itself.

To Spinoza, European theocracy was even worse than its ancient Jewish model. In Jewish theocracy religion *itself* was political – it acted as the state's direct expression – whereas in Christian Europe religion functioned as a "realm within a realm" and as superior to the state. In other words, the balance in the Hebrew state shifted in the state's favor – a situation Spinoza preferred.

Like Machiavelli (and unlike Kant), Spinoza saw nothing pejorative in a religion that functions as a political constitution. He wished to reduce all historical religions to a popular "universal religion" whose only content consisted of justice and solidarity (or "charity"), two social and political virtues. The universal religion requires no cognitive beliefs as a condition for salvation; nor does it command its adherents to participate in any ritual. Its sole demand is to "obey the true word of God": that is, to practice justice and help neighbors. To the inevitable questions, What do these virtues mean in practice?

Who is to interpret them in detail?, Spinoza answers: the secular political authorities. The civil government is thereby anointed the only legitimate interpreter of the universal religion, that is, of God's true word.[9]

It follows that Spinoza does not separate the state from *any* religious forms but only from the *historical* religions (Judaism, Catholicism, Calvinism, etc.). They are to be replaced by a religion of reason that assumes a political role and is subject to the secular legislation of the state.

How did this *positive* view of "a political religion" find its way in to Kant and come to be assigned negative significance? To answer this question – which will also set the ground for understanding Hegel – we must see what Kant found, or wanted to find, in the work of another famous Jew, Moses Mendelssohn.

Mendelssohn: Judaism as revealed constitution

Mendelssohn was both a major spokesman for the German Enlightenment (*Aufklärung*) and the proponent of Jewish *haskala*, the movement toward rational learning and Europeanization. The two tasks were intrinsically linked for him. As a Jew who had turned toward European culture and tried to excel in it without renouncing the religion of his fathers, Mendelssohn wanted to prove that a Jew can also possess the highest religious consciousness, which is founded on universal reason rather than some special revelation, and is therefore open to every person. Mendelssohn actually helped the German Enlightenment attain one of its peaks, thereby proving his point and, in so doing, making use of the intellectual climate which the *Aufklärung* itself made available to him.

The German *Aufklärung* differed from the French *Lumières* in that it did not oppose religious truth but tried to make it as rational as possible. Whereas French deists attacked religion in the name of reason, German Enlightenment thinkers tended to *reconcile* reason with revelation, and did so mainly by having reason prove of itself, on its own authority, the existence of God, free will, the immortality of the soul, and a moral order governing the world. At the same time – this was the movement's historical importance – religion was to be purged as much as possible of absurdity and superstition, and especially of excessive particularism – like its dependence on politics. The knowledge of God was to consist mainly of universal, human faculties, and every one had the capacity to share the truths of reason.

Writing in the vivid style that made his *Phaidon* an all-European bestseller, Mendelssohn reformulated proofs of the immortality of the soul. He thereby represented a central trend of the *Aufklärung*, which Kant called "dogmatic metaphysics" and set out to destroy. Kant's *Critique of Pure Reason* made obsolete the whole philosophical culture of which Mendelssohn was a chief spokesman. But, although the two men opposed each other in metaphysics, they agreed about the relation between religion and practical commands – agreed, that is, until it came to the question of Judaism.

Mendelssohn, who sought a legitimate place for both universal reason and the religion of his fathers, followed a strategy learned from Spinoza. Jewish religion, he argued, neither demands belief and opinion as conditions for salvation, nor teaches any metaphysical or theological truths; it only commands the Jews what to do and how to live. In Mendelssohn's words, Judaism is not a revealed *religion* but a revealed *law* ("constitution"). Knowing the truth and observing religious law are two absolutely separate domains. The knowledge of truth is open to every person through the power of rational evidence and is not a matter of *duty*; yet Jews are distinguished in that they have been commanded, and agree of their own free will, to observe a special set of statutes and ceremonies which have determined their historical identity and preserved the purity of their monotheism throughout the ages.

Mendelssohn also accepted Spinoza's idea that Judaism had been a political religion, but claimed that this changed in the Diaspora. So long as the Jewish State existed, its authority was indeed the same as that of religion; but the destruction of the Temple brought an end to the Jewish identification of politics and religion. Religion then took on a voluntary character in Judaism, losing the coercive power it had in antiquity and depending only on the individual's heart and inner will – as Christianity too ought to do in the age of the Enlightenment. Consequently, Mendelssohn denounced the weapon of excommunication and other coercive means employed by the clergy. However, observing religious law should continue to bind the Jews and ought to determine their lives – though not their beliefs – even without coercion. Judaism as both norm and a system of laws must shape the Jewish private and collective life in *all* circumstances. When the Jews had an actual state, the law of Moses served as its political constitution; after the destruction of their state the Jews are still required to keep the laws of the Torah, at least until a new revelation occurs. The Torah is a super-temporal constitution which does not depend on time and place. Although it must not be imposed by force, it is sufficient for a Jew to observe it in order to realize his or her identity and belong to his people and religion, regardless of his beliefs in science, metaphysics, history, and other cognitive domains. Spinoza too, Mendelssohn says graciously (while extending a Spinozistic principle to the banned philosopher), would have been admitted as a legitimate Jew had he only agreed to normally observe the Law.

Thus the two main thinkers announcing Jewish modernity, Spinoza and Mendelssohn, separate the Jewish religion from the truths of the intellect and make it a purely practical, even political constitution: Spinoza does so as part of his attack on historical religion and the principle of revelation, while Mendelssohn, on the contrary, does this in order to *defend* his ancestors' religion and its revealed foundation.

Mendelssohn's solution was designed to perform in one stroke his dual task as a propagator of German *Aufklärung* and an ideologue of Jewish *haskala*. To his Christian colleagues Mendelssohn presented an original Jewish solution to a vital concern: how to relate reason to revelation. The thinkers of the Enlightenment ran into insoluble problems when trying to reconcile reason and revelation, because they saw them both as sources for some kind of *knowledge*. Can a rational thinker accept a double concept of truth? How is the relation between them to be determined, and can they contradict one another? Above all, which of the two authorities is superior? Mendelssohn, who shared these worries as an Enlightenment thinker, offers an original solution from the sources of Judaism. Of course, he says to his coreligionists, an enlightened Jew must recognize the unshakable authority of revelation – that is, of our own, Mosaic revelation, which does not disclose any truths to us, but only lays down a code of behavior, a set of laws by which to organize our lives. For us Jews, he goes on, the compatibility of reason and revelation does not depend on some problematic relation between two sources of knowledge, but is an agreement between the intellect and the will, more precisely between knowledge and a legal constitution. In what concerns knowledge, the Jews are subject only to the authority of universal reason; we possess no special, particular knowledge of our own, and our religion contains no dogmatic beliefs which the Jew must accept on the strength of revelation, and as a condition for salvation. Our peculiarity as Jews resides wholly in the practical commands we have been given and which we accepted – above all the ritual commands.

From the standpoint of the Enlightenment – as follows from

Mendelssohn's claim – Judaism has an advantage over Christianity, because it is free of the contradictions between science and religion, and reason and revelation, which plague the Christian Enlightenment. Jews hold many cognitive beliefs, of course, but these derive from reason, not from prophetic revelation; that which was strictly *revealed* to the Jews (that is, according to the meaning of "revealed religion" at the time, what the Jews are supposed to accept on the basis of a historical authority) are only the commands.

This cutting and rather practical division was also designed by Mendelssohn to transmit a message to his fellow Jews. On its basis he can tell them: Don't be afraid of science and learning, there is absolutely nothing in our religion that hinders us from devoting ourselves to "external" studies (meaning science, philosophy, and other secular studies). Let us get out of our physical and mental ghetto and adopt the secular learning and culture of Christian Europe. This culture is based on reason, and reason does not endanger our Jewish uniqueness, because our religion contains no truths which were specifically revealed to us which rational learning might threaten. All we have to do in order to be Jews is to follow our ancestors who accepted the laws of the Torah with the saying: "we shall do and we shall listen." Apart from that we may indulge in secular learning, science, and the other achievements of European culture, adopt the mores and civilities of Europe – and both claim and obtain our political rights within it!

There was much oversimplification and wishful naiveté in Mendelssohn's approach. Ultimately, it took a bitterly ironic turn, when most of the Jewish sage's descendants converted to Christianity.[10] His attempt to save Judaism from the challenge of modern rationalism, to present it as immune to the threats which the Enlightenment posed for traditional religion, was artificial and doomed to failure. The Enlightenment endangered *all* religions, Judaism included, because rationalism stresses universality and tends to blur uniqueness, and because Judaism – Spinoza and Mendelssohn notwithstanding – *does* involve a world view and popular metaphysics (in the plural), as do all other Western religions. This is no accident: Religion is meant, among other things, to respond to people's cosmic wonderment and anxieties. It is easy for the quibbling philosopher to tailor religion to his or her needs by expelling all metaphysical concerns from it; but life and the popular mind will hardly follow such unnatural representation and in the end will rebel against it.[11]

Mendelssohn, who wanted to believe in his own ideology, could not sustain it without some self-deception. Leibowitz, in our day, has suggested the same idea as a way of *reforming* religion: This is how Jewish life *ought* to be. Spinoza, more profound than both, knew he was neither describing an empirical fact nor offering a full-fledged reform. His expulsion of knowledge from religion was intended for the popular domain of politics – to ensure free thought and speech; yet for those capable of true philosophy, Spinoza took the opposite road (following Aristotle and Maimonides): true philosophical religion, which alone can liberate and unite the person with the eternal and the infinite, is necessarily based on metaphysical truths and does provide "salvation" through knowledge. The equation of "true religion" with practical life refers only to lower religious forms, which include the historical religions and the popular religion of reason to which they are to be reduced. No such reduction applies to the upper, philosophical religion, where justice and solidarity are the products of knowledge rather than obedience.

There is another major difference between these two Jewish thinkers. Mendelssohn admits the authority of revelation, which he then tries to reconcile with reason; whereas Spinoza, who recognizes the authority of reason alone, rejects revelation *as a philosopher*, but uses the public's belief in it to solve the political problem of the multitude, and to build a social and political framework for the less-than-philosophical human majority – a problem that, perhaps for the first time in modern thought, is treated as a philosophical problem in its own right.

Another of Mendelssohn's flaws, perhaps the most consequential, is the contradiction between viewing Judaism as a particular constitution and the endeavor to emancipate the Jews politically. Emancipation demanded the Jews' political assimilation, their entry as equal citizens into the European nations (as Frenchmen, Germans, etc. in their nation, and as direct citizens of the French or the German state, unmediated by an interim body like the Jewish community). This required the abolition of autonomous Jewish communities with their own laws and the political integration of Jews as individuals into the host society. This is not a formal contradiction, but a practical and historical one; it is the opposition between the medieval and the modern situation of the Jews. To continue Jewish existence in Mendelssohn's way, as a special legal community, required extending into modernity the medieval ghetto situation in which the Jews were enclosed in their autonomous community; but this contradicted another Mendelssohnian principle, which required religion to be voluntary and the Jews to modernize, to get out of their enclosure and become integrated into European society. Jewish assimilation was in large measure the result of this contradiction – a reaction to it, rather than its resolution.

We cannot discuss here Mendelssohn's position in itself; I have invoked it only as a background for the young Hegel. But this requires passing again through Kant.

Kant: Judaism as a nonreligion

Kant had read carefully Mendelssohn's *Jerusalem* and praised it to their mutual friend, Marcus Herz. He had also absorbed some basic ideas from this book, including those which came from Spinoza. All religion (not only Judaism), says Kant following Spinoza, is based on practical commands and makes no claim on knowledge. The only valid source of knowledge is the rational intellect, which is, however, impotent in the highest metaphysical matters and unable to determine whether God exists, man is free, or the human soul immortal. This shortcoming has its reward, for it liberates the human person from the dominion of a transcendent God (whose very existence is put in doubt), and makes possible an immanent, autonomous morality, based on the rational human will as the unique source of moral value and obligation. Furthermore, obeying the autonomous commands of morality is also what religion is all about. The religion of reason is not only independent of God's external will, but in order to practice true religion, we must rid ourselves of the idea of God as lawgiver and follow only the commands of free, universal, human reason.

Kant says that there is only one (true) religion, though there are many churches and historical faiths. He defined religion as viewing all "our duties as divine commands."[12] The definition is deliberately equivocal and allows for two opposed readings which divide the religious space in two – a rational religion versus all the historical religions. One reading says: "In order to know that something is my moral duty, I must first know it is a divine command." This is the principle of the religions which Kant calls "statutory": that is, unfree, repressive, heteronomous. It ranges, in different degrees, over the entire spectrum of historical religions, including Christianity in its various forms. The other reading of the definition is quite the reverse: "In order to know that something is a divine command, I must first know that it is my moral duty." Here autonomous morality takes precedence and defines what is divine. If something is required of us by free, self-legislating human reason, then we ought to experience it as a divine command: that is, as expressing and bearing the attributes of sanctity, veneration, divinity, and sublimity which traditional religion ascribes to its image of God and his commands. In this new version of religion, the noun *God* has no place, but the adjective *divine* does. The moral law issued by free human reason is raised to divine status: It inherits the elevated qualities and states of mind associated with religious experience.

Needless to say, the equation of rational morality with true religion is subject to all the conditions of Kantian ethics, above all the crucial distinction between acting in mere *conformity* with the moral law and acting out of *respect* for the law. Only the second act is moral, since everything in morality – and therefore in religion – depends on the nature of the motive. Egoism, prudence, and self-serving utility may often lead to an act which conforms to that which morality recommends, yet, when judged by its motives, is immoral. External conformity to the law satisfies the requirement of legality, but not the genuine demand of morality. Legality, says Kant, can be maintained even in a kingdom of intelligent devils who understand what maximizes their aggregate utility. The spirit of morality, on the contrary, resides in the inner heart, in the intention, in the purity of the motive which makes us obey the law, and not in the content of our action; only pure respect for the law – that is, its disinterested recognition as a value in itself – counts as a moral incentive.

A moral act, in other words, is an act performed from no other motive than our will to fulfill our duty for its own sake. When several persons are united by the permanent disposition to do their moral duty for its own sake and to treat one another as autonomous moral agents (as "ends in themselves"), they overcome the "ethical state of nature" and constitute an "ethical community," internal and invisible, which is also the true *religious* community. (In Kant's equivalent metaphor, they found an "invisible church" within the religion of reason.)

This is why Kant must distinguish between inner morality (in which religion resides) and the political and juridical domains which, even at their rational best, are but an external imitation of the moral idea, its translation into the language of external actions and institutions. The realm of "legality" has no inherent moral or religious value. This is an issue on which Kant conflicts with Spinoza (and also with the mature Hegel) and which helped him condemn Judaism.

Kant, as we have seen, also has a historical outlook which takes the religion of reason as the latent essence of all traditional faiths, each of which shapes the seed of moral essence in its own distorted way. One can, in consequence, draw a scale of ascending stages, depending on how clearly or dimly the moral consciousness resides in each religion. The criterion must evidently derive from Kant's principles: The more external decrees a religion contains — the more legalistic or statutory it is – the lower its place on the historical scale; the more it expresses inner and universal morality (two independent demands), the higher it stands on the religious ladder.

Kant's religious ladder

In a short but important section of *Religion within the Boundaries of Reason Alone*, Kant sketches the evolutionary scale of religions. The lowest is Judaism, then come Catholic and Byzantine Christianity, then Protestantism, then a higher spiritual variety deriving from Protestantism which Kant leaves unnamed. From all these statutory religions – and their revolutionary overcoming – there finally emerges the pure, universal religion of reason, which receives its form in Kant's system and thereby attains philosophical self-consciousness.

Though we cannot elaborate here,[13] there is one fact which ought to catch our eye and perhaps surprise us: Kant puts Judaism not only at the bottom of the scale, but actually outside it. Judaism is not only the lowest religion; it is not a religion at all, but merely a political constitution. What Spinoza and Mendelssohn held to be the unity of a political and a religious constitution here becomes a merely political affair, devoid of any religious content and significance.

Kant means this in a pejorative sense. "Religion" for him has the connotation of spirituality and human value. In denying Judaism a religious content and reducing it to political law, Kant deprives it of any spiritual value, even of the minimal moral significance that we would expect a historical view like Kant's to recognize as latent in every past religion. Kant graciously acknowledges the obvious: that Jewish *individuals* – he clearly thinks of his friends, Mendelssohn, Marcus Herz, Lazarus Bendavid (everyone has Jewish friends) – can have a developed – even an intense – moral mind, since they are rational beings, but this applies to them as individuals; as Jews, they possess only a political constitution, devoid of moral and spiritual value.[14]

This is a conspicuous inconsistency from Kant's own standpoint. The radical opposition – and watershed – in Kant's system does not occur between Judaism and the other religions, but between *all* the historical religions, Judaism included, (which are all to some degree statutory), and the pure religion of reason. Therefore, by Kant's own logic, the existence in a religion of *some* statutory element is not a sufficient ground for denying it *any* moral value. Since Kant's evolutionary scheme assigns every religion a hidden moral-rational kernel, and since every historical religion is, to some degree, statutory, it follows that Kant has no valid reason for denying a moral kernel to Judaism just because it may be *more* statutory than other religions. Kant cannot ride this horse at both ends: either he must give up the historical approach and return to a strictly dualist position, which recognizes moral value in the religion of reason only and dismisses all historical religions, including Lutheranism, as irrational and counter-moral; or he must maintain the model of historical evolution, which allows for a rational content to persist while assuming sensible, distorted forms in the various religions. Kant decided on the latter course – yet made one conspicuous exception: Judaism falls outside this rule, it does not even belong to the infancy of the moral consciousness, to its first twinkling, but stands completely outside its boundary.

Since no reasonable ground exists in Kant's system for this view, we must conclude that *pre*-systematic prejudices were at work here. Kant was a liberal of reason; his civil treatment of Jews came from a sense of propriety and perhaps of moral duty; yet on a deeper level he never overcame his strong anti-Jewish bias. Rather, he let it sometimes burst out into the open, both in disguised "philosophical" form and even in blunt ejaculations. His relations with Mendelssohn make a particularly fascinating story. One cannot avoid the impression that Kant was not particularly sorry that, of all people, it was his Jewish rival-friend who supplied the chief conceptual weapon (viewing Judaism as political) which Kant, perhaps not in full awareness, was able to turn against Mendelssohn's own people and religion.

It was not until his old age (a telling fact[15]) that Kant's pen ejected blunt anti-Jewish utterances. In a letter to Reinhold (28 March 1794) he says: "Jews always like to do such things, acquiring a semblance of importance at other people's expense." Kant is referring to Solomon Maimon, who suggested improvements in the critical system; but subconsciously he may have been aiming at Mendelssohn, too. Reinhold was Mendelssohn's enemy, and Kant may have wanted to cater to him somewhat; yet his sweeping language ("Jews *always* ...") and the rhetorical context in which two non-Jews are gossiping between themselves about Jews (just as, no doubt, two Jews might be gossiping about the "Goy") testify to Kant's deeper feelings. Incidentally, in a letter to Marcus Herz five years earlier Kant had praised Maimon as one of the rare persons who had fathomed his thought (26 May 1789).

I conjecture that the "Jewish" feature Kant finds in Maimon – the wish to make a name for himself at other people's expense – may be an unwitting generalization of Kant's relation to Mendelssohn. Mendelssohn's career was marked by the effort to prove Jews capable of acquiring European culture and excelling in it even more than non-Jews (which Mendelssohn had actually been doing as a senior spokesman for the *Aufklärung* – until Kant's *Critique* came along). In the early days of their acquaintance Mendelssohn even took first prize to Kant's second in an essay contest declared by the Prussian Academy. In old age, after Kant's great critical achievement had completely eclipsed Mendelssohn, another Jew arrived (Maimon) and tried to repeat what Mendelssohn had done in the past – surpass Kant in what belonged to him; and what was most irksome, Maimon did it with evident talent (as Kant was honest enough to recognize). So, with honesty and irritation, Kant both praised Maimon to his Jewish patron, Herz, and denounced both Jews, Mendelssohn and Maimon, to Mendelssohn's Christian rival, Reinhold.

The euthanasia of the Jewish people

Four years later Kant used still harsher words, in public. In his book *Anthropology from a Pragmatic Viewpoint* he flatly called the Jews "a *nation* of cheaters." He also referred to them as "the Palestinians living among us" – an appellation to which President Arafat would probably object, though Kant used it to suggest that the Jews were foreigners who did not really belong to the land and who were exploiting their German hosts, a claim that any xenophobic extremist might still make today. Kant went on to describe the Jews as an unproductive merchant-people who use cunning tricks (*Überlistung*) against their hosts. To be sure, this behavior was caused by the lowly state to which the Jews had been driven, but the result was that the Jews renounced honor and civil status and compensated themselves by fraudulent behavior.[16] It is only fair to add that Kant was reproducing an image of the Jews that was prevalent in the Christian world. Even Christian Dohm, in a famous tract pleading for the Jews' political emancipation, said that because they had been discriminated against, they were driven to become a people of cheats (see next chapter).

Kant had Jewish friends whom he held in high esteem and even loved. If his relations with Mendelssohn were strained and ambivalent, Kant maintained a warm, intimate friendship with Marcus Herz, a friend of both his and Mendelssohn's (and a sometime patron of Maimon). As a young student Herz had studied under Kant in Königsberg, and after moving to Berlin (where he became a well-known physician and intellectual, and husband of Dorothea Herz, who hosted one of the leading literary salons), he continued to correspond with the famous master, who trusted Herz so much that he confided in him the most intimate things concerning his body (Kant consulted Herz about indigestion, diarrhoea, etc.) and especially concerning his mind. The only documents which tell us anything about that crucial period in Kant's life, and in the history of the human spirit – in which the *Critique of Pure Reason* was evolving and ripening, the 11 years in which Kant kept silent, publishing nothing – are the occasional letters he wrote to his Jewish friend and admirer in Berlin. These give an inkling of Kant's new philosophical project and the progress he had made.

Another Jewish friend of Kant's was Lazarus Bendavid, an early convert to the critical system who wrote popular books about it in German. In *The Strife of the Faculties*, written in old age (1798), Kant offers the Jews a plan which he mistakenly attributed to Bendavid ("One of the better heads of this nation"). The Jews should publicly adopt the "religion of Jesus" and study the New Testament in addition to the Old, but interpret them both in the spirit of modern morality and the Enlightenment, and thus actually transcend both religions.[17] Only in this way, said Kant, could the Jews acquire civil rights and at the same time overcome historical religion in favor of the religion of reason. Kant called this move "the euthanasia of the Jewish people" – a striking appellation. Though Kant could not have known the future resonance that this term would come to have, and his words were greatly misinterpreted, they nevertheless testify to the cool distance, not to say aversion, which Kant felt toward historical Judaism.

Yet Judaism, after all, was a relatively marginal matter for Kant. It was neither central to his philosophy nor very important in his emotional life. This was not the case with Hegel, nor with Nietzsche, the two major German philosophers of the next century. For both of them, Judaism was far more pressing and consequential than meets the eye – probably because each of them was intensely preoccupied with a reinterpretation, or critique, of Christianity. In both cases we shall find a far more complex and profound – also ambivalent and at times convoluted – relation to Judaism than we have met in Kant.

CHAPTER TWO

The Young Hegel and the Spirit of Judaism

The riddle of Judaism

"Judaism was a dark riddle which both attracted and repelled Hegel," said his early biographer, Karl Rosenkranz, one "with which he coped all his life."[1] Hegel was a Christian thinker, but very heterodox. He placed Lutheran Christianity at the height of the world Spirit, yet as philosopher, he negated it dialectically.[2] Religion is based on images; as such it falls short of philosophy and must be elevated to it through rational concepts. The young Hegel believed that Judaism represented only the negative aspects of religion, everything that must be rejected in it. In maturity, he revised his view and attributed to Judaism a crucial positive role in the history of religion and the human spirit, but a role that has long since been consummated and left behind the train of history. Even then, Hegel ascribed to Judaism all the ills he had found in it as a young man. Inconsistency? Not necessarily: a dialectical thinker is supposed to stress the flaws and contradictions in every positive phenomenon. Yet, quite remarkably, the *specific* flaws which the mature Hegel found in Judaism were the same ones which the Enlightenment, and critics of religion since Epicurus, had found in the religious phenomenon *in general*. This suggests that, consciously or not, the mature Hegel continued to assign a negative role to Judaism, to the point of making it a theoretical scapegoat for the ills of *all* religion; and unlike

Nietzsche, he was unable to completely overcome the anti-Jewish prejudice of his youth.

Religion and philosophy

Judaism represented a broader problem with which Hegel had always coped: the relation between philosophy and religion. Hegel started his philosophical career as a sharp critic of religion; but later, when shaping his mature system, he reached a heterodox reconciliation between historical religion and philosophical truth. Hegel was educated at the theological seminary in Tübingen where, as often happened in those days (even in seminaries), he was caught up with the new ideas of freedom, reason, and the Enlightenment, including its critique of religion. Together with a few friends (some of whom became well known in later years) he followed with great enthusiasm the events on the other bank of the Rhine, where the French Revolution was in progress. France was the theater of great upheavals which, to them, announced a new historical era. And when, observing the political backwardness of Germany, Hegel wondered who had laid the ground for Germany's participation in propagating the spirit of the Enlightenment, he thought mainly of three people.

First and foremost was Lessing, the celebrated humanist who had written a free, rational theology which bordered on Spinoza's pantheism. Lessing's popular play, *Nathan the Wise*, had given the ideas of toleration and the universality of the human race a vivid artistic expression. The young Hegel was profoundly influenced by *Nathan the Wise* and quoted this work more than any other. Second was Moses Mendelssohn, the extraordinary Jew and chief spokesman for the Berlin *Aufklärung* (Enlightenment), whom Lessing used as the model for *Nathan*. The young Hegel was particularly inspired by *Jerusalem*, Mendelssohn's book on religion, though he used it selectively. He adopted the first part in which Mendelssohn argued for religious toleration, but rejected the second part which implied that Judaism, because it is free of religious dogma, was more suitable for the Enlightenment than Christianity. Like Kant, but with more aggressive zeal (perhaps because Hegel was then 25, while Kant was over 70), Hegel turned Mendelssohn's idea into convicting evidence *against* Judaism (see below).

The third and most influential, and the only one still alive, was of course the old Kant. Kant's book *Religion within the Boundaries of*

Reason Alone had appeared two years before the young Hegel started scribbling philosophical essays. He seems to have read Kant's *Religion* even before the *Critique of Pure Reason*, Kant's major masterpiece. Kant, as we have seen, advocated a universal moral religion based on reason and the inner will. Kant's rational religion was the same as his morality, extended into a world-historical project of moral educa tion. It rejected the external authority (including revelation), the power structure of the Church, the irrational, historical modes of religious cult, and the rigid legalism which Kant saw as the legacy of Judaism. The young Hegel was so affected by these Enlightenment ideas that he imagined Jesus as a cultural hero of the Enlightenment and an early precursor of Kantian morality, whose message was falsi-fied by the later history of Christianity.

Nevertheless, the Kantian overtones of the young Hegel's anti-religious radicalism should not mislead us. At bottom there was a fundamental difference separating the two men. Kant, even in matur-ity, had no religious temperament or affinities; he was flatly hostile to historical religion and saw its replacement, the religion of reason, as subservient to the demands of humanistic morality. By contrast, Hegel, despite his Kantian beginnings, and even while attacking Christianity, displayed a genuine religious spirit, albeit in a dialectical and unorthodox way. Religion was essential to Hegel's spiritual world and a foundation of metaphysical truth; but this refers to reli-gion not as traditionally given, but as the object of criticism, of trans-formation and *Aufhebung*. In order to unveil the deep truth to which religion points, one must go beyond religion – that is, in a sense, *abandon* religion and do something quite different with it than what religion itself demands. But what is this something else? Where and how should religion be transcended?

In his youth Hegel looked for the answer in a Kantian-like critique of religion that would dispose of religion's historical shell but main-tain its inner moral kernel. The mature Hegel, on the contrary, looked for the answer in the historical religion itself, as the substrate which alone allows reason to develop and spirit to become absolute. These two answers, so different from one another, are nevertheless linked by a common goal: to extract the essential content of religion so as to have it match philosophical reason, and to use philosophy's concepts hermeneutically, as a means to re-interpret religion and raise it to a higher level.

The mature Hegel believed that this could be accomplished with-out losing religion's historical basis and without abolishing its link to imagination, myth, and the life-experience of ordinary people. But his early view was far more one-sided. "Pure reason, incapable of any limitation, is the deity itself" – declared the youthful Hegel in one of his earliest fragments.[3] Divine reason negates all the values and institutions sanctified by tradition. It rejects religion's claim that men should obey heteronomous commandments and believe in "historical" (narrative) truths which lack rational justification. Reason also negates the many cults and ceremonies whose moral content, if it ever existed, has long since become a meaningless external convention. At first, therefore, Hegel's philosophical project assumed a Kantian intent: One must negate religion's "positive" shell in order to unveil the true religious spirit, which is the spirit of rational, moral autonomy. This is what defines philosophy's first task. In order to philosophize, one must first deal with religion; that is, one must reveal its inwardness through a critique of its externality. This explains why Hegel's early essays constantly deal with Christianity, and therefore also with Judaism.

The "enigma" of Judaism

In Christian eyes, which Hegel secularized but never abandoned, Judaism's transformation into Christianity is one of the major events in the history of salvation. This is the moment when the redeemer appears on the historical stage and is rejected by his own people. Thereby the Jews depose themselves from their divine mission in favor of Christianity, which absorbs their message while negating its flaws and raising it to a higher, more universal level.

Hegel internalized the pattern of this Christian metaphor. He even made it a model of his concept of *Aufhebung*, a concept which means that something is negated but not annihilated; rather, its essential content is preserved and raised to a higher level of expression. For the mature Hegel, this is a basic pattern of reality and history. Every cultural form makes some genuine contribution to the world Spirit, after which it is sublated (*aufgehoben*) and disappears from the historical scene. Yet the Jews continued to survive long after their *raison d'être* had disappeared – indeed, after they no longer had a genuine history in Hegel's sense, but existed merely as the corpse of their extinguished essence. But how could it be that Judaism evaded the fate (and defied the model) of which it was itself the prime example?

The classic Christian answer – that the Jews survived in order to bear witness to the truth of Christianity – is too mythological for Hegel. History does not polemicize with people and need not convince them by proofs. History justifies or refutes various cultural forms by its very course. Historical necessity is the external expression – full of deviations, to be sure – of the inner, rational necessity governing human evolution. Hegel says in the preface to the *Phenomenology* that there is an inner rational necessity in the advent of a new historical need or life-form. Similarly, the decline of cultures, empires, and human communities indicates that their message has been exhausted and absorbed into history's new stages.

Of all the great historical figures, only Judaism seems to violate this rule – indeed, so blatantly that it cannot be dismissed as a merely "accidental" leftover.[4] Thus, in Rosenkranz's words, Judaism remains a "riddle" for Hegel. From every important standpoint it has become obsolete, yet it perseveres, a degenerate, persecuted – but stubborn and persistent, and therefore powerful – relic of antiquity which survived the Middle Ages, the genuinely Christian age, and now enters the modern world and claims its rights within it. Hegel was perfectly willing to grant those rights; but he did not know what to do with the Jews in modernity *as Jews*, nor could he explain their survival in terms of his system.

Hegel saw the new era that was beginning as the ripest, and probably the last, historical era, one in which the human spirit would eventually realize its essential potential. This vision of modernity took different forms in different periods of Hegel's life. In his youth he viewed modernity through the glasses of the Enlightenment and the French Revolution. Later, in the *Phenomenology*, his view of modernity became dialectical, but it was still vigorously optimistic until the Restoration dealt it a severe blow. Even then, Hegel's basic optimism, though sobered, was not extinguished: only now he was looking at a more distant horizon and understanding the conflict between liberalism and reaction to it as a mark of the necessary setbacks that every dialectical process must undergo. As for the Jews, since they had made it into the modern era, Hegel assigned them a place too, though not specifically as Jews (as Mendelssohn had demanded) but as individuals and human beings "in general." In that he reverted to a typical Enlightenment position.[5]

The early historical approach

In other matters, however, the young Hegel went beyond the Enlightenment to a point which starts to announce his later position. Here are a few examples.

First, the essence of religion cannot be understood by a formal definition or by merely analytic categories. A spiritual essence must be grasped through its manifestations and the exhibition of its sources in previous forms of the spirit. Hence, understanding the essence of religion requires both a genetic and a historical explanation expounding its origins.

Second, as key to this exhibition, the young Hegel had already begun to use the concept of "the spirit of the people" (in this he was influenced by Herder[6]). The historical approach does not investigate the human spirit directly, or "in general," but through its manifestations in specific cultural and ethnic configurations.

The young Hegel was seeking a concept of reason that would not oppose, but rather concord with, the other mental powers – feeling, imagination, etc. – and would thus do justice to the human being in its totality. Hegel was influenced in this respect by Goethe, and particularly by Schiller, who both sought a fruitful balance between the different human powers. Even Hegel's early Kantianism differed from Kant in its color and temperament. Kant expelled emotion and feeling from morality. Even religion, founded on morality, was based by Kant on a cool, self-sufficient rationality, which did not need warmth of heart to move a person to action, whereas the young Hegel sought a warm morality nourished by feeling and love. Kant's "purity of intention" expelled all feeling and pathos from religion, whereas the young Hegel's "purity of the *heart*" required feeling and love, and expelled from religion only external ceremonial and authority. Against this backdrop the spiritless legalism which Kant attributed to Judaism looked even worse to Hegel.

What really interests Hegel, however, is not Judaism, but Christianity. To him, Christianity is the European world's overall culture; its many faces and transformations constitute the history of European spirit since the decline of antique paganism; and Hegel, who at that period saw himself as a critic and reformer of European culture, started by scrutinizing the origins and fate of Christianity. This is what makes him turn repeatedly to Judaism, as one of Christianity's origins and as a (primarily negative) clue for grasping and revising it.

"The Positivity of the Christian Religion"

Hegel investigates the "positive" element in Christianity, which opposes its "natural" element. According to the linguistic convention of the time, "positive" is everything in a religion that derives from (is "posited" by) an external authority rather than from reason. This includes all the historical, inessential facts and stories associated with religion: myth, ritual, ceremony, miracles, beliefs in a special revelation, and the "statutory" laws (Kant's word) – and also the official theology, the intolerance, the power structure of the Church, and the clergy's meddling in politics. These "positive" factors had dominated religious life not only in Catholicism but in the Protestant world which had tried to purge itself of them but failed. Philosophical reflection must understand that fact and expose its sources, so that it can now be truly overcome.

This leads Hegel to Judaism. In one of his early texts, a fragment written in 1774 (at the age of 23–4) and not intended for publication, Hegel says: "It cannot be denied that the Jews had twisted and immoral notions of their Yehova – His anger, sectarianism, the hatred to other peoples, intolerance – and these notions have unfortunately passed over to the theory and practice of the Christian religion."[7] This quote sets the tone for the essays which followed. First was "The Positivity of the Christian Religion," which the 25-year-old Hegel wrote while serving as a private tutor in Bern. In a typical passage, influenced by Kant's attack on Judaism as a religion of merely statutory laws,[8] he says:

> [The Jewish Spirit at the time of Jesus] was overwhelmed by a burden of statutory commands which pedantically prescribed a rule for every casual action of daily life and gave the whole people the look of a monastic order. As a result of this system, the holiest of things, namely, the service of God and virtue, was ordered and compressed in dead formulas, and nothing save pride in this slavish obedience to laws not laid down by themselves was left to the Jewish spirit, which already was deeply mortified and embittered by the subjection of the state to a foreign power.[9]

No wonder, Hegel goes on, that "in this miserable situation there must have been Jews of a better heart and head who could not renounce or deny their feeling of selfhood, or stoop to become lifeless machines." These dissident Jews refused to have their life "spent in a monkish preoccupation with petty, mechanical, spiritless, and trivial usages." They felt the need for "a virtue of a more independent type" and a "freer activity than an existence with no self-consciousness." From these people Jesus arose, the revolutionary who, quite miraculously (but isn't religion built on miracles?), "was free of the contagious sickness of his age and his people."[10]

These words convey a harsh judgment. The Jews have not

produced a great new religious idea, not even in a false form. They are presented from the outset in their negative aspect only. The Jews contributed nothing to Christianity's spiritual content, they are responsible only for its "positivity": namely, for the irrational and authoritarian elements in it. Jesus' spiritual message was born not from Judaism, but as a reaction against it.

On the other hand, Jesus preached this message from above, in the name of a superior authority, and thereby damaged the principle he was propagating. Jesus' message was spiritual, true, anti-"positive," yet he gave it a positive form by imposing it upon his listeners using his authority as prophet. To this extent Jesus was negatively influenced by the religion of his people and the spirit of his time.

As in other matters, Hegel again relies here on *Nathan the Wise*. In Act II Sultan Salah-a-Din speaks with his sister Sita, who says of the Christians what Lessing himself wants to say, but prefers to put it in the mouth of someone watching Christianity from outside:

> SITA: You do not know the Christians, you don't want to know them.
>
> They are proud of being Christians, not of being human. For
>
> Even that humanity, by which their Founder seasoned superstition,
>
> They love not because it is human
>
> But because Christ teaches so; because He did so.
>
> How fortunate for them [*Wohl ihnen*] that he was such a good man
>
> How fortunate they can accept his Virtue
>
> On trust and faith! But what Virtue?
>
> Certainly not his; it is only his Name
>
> That must be propagated everywhere;
>
> His Name must devour and demean the name of all good people;
>
> It's the name, only the name that interests them!

The young Hegel quotes Sita's opening remarks with agreement. In an earlier fragment he had unfavorably compared Jesus with Socrates, the true philosopher. Socrates did not preach from the hilltops, he did not speak *ex cathedra*, nor did he have 12 mobilized apostles to spread his word; he had only a diverse group of disciples, "or rather, he had no disciples at all" because, unlike Jesus, Socrates did not teach any truth from above. He invoked in people what they had in themselves, their superior interest; therefore, each of his listeners remained what he had been. Hegel, with more than a tinge of sarcasm, goes on to say that "Socrates did not live in his disciples, he was not the root from which, like branches, they drew the essence of life."[11] Hegel is undoubtedly alluding to the *hostia* – the sacrament of eating Jesus' body, which he takes to be the ground of the authority attributed to Jesus' words.

This critique evolves in "The Positivity of the Christian Religion" into a daring and original position. If Christianity has degenerated, it is because of its own founder. Christian reformers usually praise Jesus and blame his followers for distorting his message: the young Hegel blames Jesus himself. Christianity's founder has himself sown the seeds of its "positivity," in that he has given his rational message an authoritative form which opposes its content.

At this point the young Hegel demonstrates the quasi-dialectical pattern that was to characterize his future writings – namely, the opposition between content and form, between an essence and its actual shaping. Here we observe the ironic opposition between Jesus' intention and what it had produced. Such incongruity of intention and meaning was typical of what the mature Hegel saw in the pattern of history.

"Is Judea the Teutons' fatherland?"

Elsewhere Hegel paraphrases an idea he borrowed from the pre-Romantic poet Klopstock (and partly also from Herder). Every nation has its cultural fatherland located in a fantasy world of its own. The product of the people's creative imagination, this fatherland is inhabited by heroes, angels, demons, and saints who continue to live in the people's traditions, nourishing them through children's fairy tales and public festivities. This world of fantasy is born from that nation's unique reality and historical climate. The Germans in the pagan era, just like the Gauls and the Scandinavians, had their own mythological heroes – they had *Valhalla*. Yet, says Hegel,

> Christianity has emptied Valhalla, felled the sacred groves, extirpated the national imagery as a shameful superstition, as a devilish poison, and given us instead the imagery of a nation whose climate, laws, culture, and interests are strange to us and whose history has no connection whatever with our own. A David or a Solomon lives in our popular imagination, but our country's own heroes slumber

in learned history books, and, for the scholars who write them, Alexander or Caesar is as interesting as the story of Charlemagne or Frederick Barbarossa.[12]

As a result, Germans do not have "a religious imagery which is homegrown or linked with our history."[13] This forces Hegel to ask sarcastically: "Is Judea then the Teutons' fatherland?" This paraphrases Klopstock's question: "Is Achaia, then, the Teutons' fatherland?"[14] Klopstock had complained that the German Olympus was mainly inhabited by Greek gods, and Hegel transfers the complaint from the pastures of Achaia to the hills of ancient Judea.

A superficial reading might lead one to conclude that Hegel blames the Jews for having stolen the Germans' spiritual fatherland and creative imagination. Such charges have been voiced by modern anti-Semites: the Jews drain our forces, they corrupt our souls, etc. – up to the Nazi slogan "The Jews are our misfortune." But a careful reading shows that it was not the Jews, but Christianity, which robbed the Teutons' imagination-world. Christianity emptied Valhalla of its gods and filled it with the heroes of a foreign culture. The Christians also did this to the Jews – took their great kings, David and Solomon, and planted them in European soil. In that respect, Jews might feel the victims of usurpation no less than the young Hegel or Klopstock. The usurper in both cases is the Christian religion which proclaimed itself "the true Israel" and adopted the Jewish holy books and gave them to the Teutons.

Hegel further complains that Alexander and Julius Caesar have also expelled Charlemagne and Frederick Barbarossa; thus, between the Greco-Latin and the Jewish heroes there is no fundamental difference: all, to the Teutons, belong to a foreign mythological universe.

Again, a superficial reading might suggest that Hegel is an early Wagnerian calling for the romantic revival of German mythology. But this is not the case. Hegel insists, *contra* Wagner, that the situation cannot be reversed. "It has become totally impossible to ennoble these remnants of [Teuton] mythology and thereby refine the imagination and sensibility of the common people."[15] Attempts in this direction (Hegel mentions a few authors, now forgotten) can no longer affect the popular consciousness, which is irreversibly cut off from its mythological infancy.[16]

We see that despite being somewhat inspired by the romantics, Hegel already opposes them on their main point. The attempt to regress in history will not do. This recognition anticipates Hegel's mature system. Nostalgia over a lost past must serve as a spur to go *forward*, to produce something new that has meanwhile ripened and will lift the old essence to a higher level of expression. The mature Hegel continued to value the people's creative imagination, mythology, and spirit, not as the focus of nostalgia but as a force that could nourish the new rational society and preserve its vitality. The intellect breaks the popular imagination and kills primary intuition, it creates a rupture in life and severs the different life-forces. Therefore intellectual understanding causes malaise and suffering. Yet this suffering is the condition of progress. One cannot attain spirit and create civilization without passing through the intellect, which severs and ruptures, but also gives valid shape to human knowledge, experience, and life. The longing we feel for the lost unity of the past must drive us onward, toward the third stage in which Spirit attempts to restore the original unity – not in the world of popular imagination and intuition, but within the domain of rational thought itself. The same power that has caused the rupture – rational reflection – must now provide the means by which to restore unity of a higher, more developed type. This is the project of modernity (and also what distinguishes "reason" from mere "understanding").

The young Hegel does not yet possess this theory in full; but one can already detect the strong qualifications with which he absorbs the German national spirit. Hegel shared its intense feelings, but not its direction.

The anti-Jewish style

Hegel's anti-Jewish language in "Positivity" is harsh; but to put it in context we should remember that this was the customary tone of his day. Jews were ordinarily described with disdain. A special anti-Semitic genre developed within the Enlightenment movement itself (Voltaire, Reimarus, Holbach, and others). Jews were referred to negatively even by their best friends. The philo-Semites of the time (like the later Zionists) wanted to "cure" the Jews by changing their degenerate conditions, but they did not deny they were degenerate. A prominent advocate for the Jews, Abbé Grégoire, describes them as sunk in moral and physical degeneration.[17] Lessing defended not Judaism as such, but the Jews' capacity to *overcome* Judaism and manifest the nobility of their "universally human" soul. The Templar knight in *Nathan the Wise* shows admiration for Nathan as a person, without retracting the disgust he has just expressed for Nathan's nation. And another well-known philo-Semite, Christian Wilhelm Dohm, a friend of Mendelssohn, in a book calling for Jewish emancipation, says:

> I may concede that the Jews may be more morally corrupt than other nations; that they are guilty of a proportionately greater number of crimes than the Christians; that their character in general inclines more toward usury and fraud in commerce; that their religious prejudice is more antisocial and clannish; but I must add that this . . . is a necessary and natural consequence of the oppressed condition in which they have been living.[18]

If this is how defenders of the Jews were writing, one can imagine how Jews were being discussed by others. From here a special strategy arose (that we shall meet again with Nietzsche). Since Judaism was taken to be depraved, one could attack other cultural forms – even Christianity itself – by partly identifying them with Judaism. The more one strikes at the Jews, the more one is attacking one's real target. Hegel did not create this strategy, but used it with acuity.

The young Hegel did not spare Christianity either. In an earlier text we saw him blaming Jesus for his authoritarianism; now he also mocks the holy sacrament of the *hostia*, the act of consuming Jesus' body and blood. In this custom, which ought to be the feast of universal brotherhood, "many are afraid that through the brotherly goblet they might be infected with a venereal disease by someone who drank from it before."[19] In particular, Hegel denounced the "spirit of mourning" in which the Christians conduct this celebration. The Greeks celebrate with joy, whereas Christianity cultivates suffering and is plagued by a peevish spirit. For the Greeks, "misfortune was misfortune, pain was pain," whereas Christianity has, "for the sake of suffering humanity . . . piled up such a heap of reasons for comfort in misfortune, . . . that we might be sorry in the end that we cannot lose a father or a mother once a week."[20]

Read in rhetorical context, Hegel's style in "Positivity" does not yet manifest the anti-Semitic venom that his pen was to sprinkle a little later. That was to come in "The Spirit of Christianity and its Fate," the most abusive text Hegel ever wrote against the Jews.

"The Spirit of Christianity and its Fate"

Hegel wandered between many cities. Born in Stuttgart, he studied at the seminary in Tübingen, then served as private tutor in Bern until his friend, the poet Hölderlin, found him a better job in Frankfurt. Hegel received his first academic appointment at Jena, where he wrote *The Phenomenology of Spirit*; then he went to Nüremberg as director of a Gymnasium (academic high-school), and after a short stay at the University of Heidelberg was finally appointed professor in Berlin, where he stayed until his death. Hegel scholars, especially his editors, tend to divide his work according to the cities he inhabited, a somewhat artificial custom that confuses biography and geography. Actually, the most important intellectual shift in Hegel's career occurred when he was residing in one place (Jena). At the same time there were changes in his views, not only in his addresses, and sometimes it is convenient to use such designations as "Bern" or "Nüremberg," bearing in mind that their significance is more chronological than thematic.

Thus in 1797 we move with the young Hegel from Bern to Frankfurt, where he wrote "The Spirit of Christianity and its Fate."[21] Hegel has now become concerned with the issue of "religion and love,"[22] and consequently started – only started – to distance himself from Kant and make peace with Jesus. Kant had argued that duty and love cannot be united in a single concept, because love cannot be commanded; yet Jesus, in the single dictum, "love God above all and love thy neighbor as thyself," knew better. The religion of love makes it possible to live morally and maintain a sense of emotional plenitude rather than be torn, as in Kant, between one's life and one's duty. Kant had banned all natural drives and human needs from morality, whereas Jesus' religion of love expressed human needs in their noblest form, and is capable of restoring the unity between man and his Other, his feelings, and the world.

Thus we find Hegel in Frankfurt praising the Sermon on the Mount which he had scoffed in Bern. The basic document of the religion of love, the Sermon on the Mount, exposes Jesus' spirit as it "surmounts mere morality": that is, a morality based on the chasm between life and the "Ought." This is an early occurrence of the idea of "going beyond morality" which philosophers like Nietzsche and Kierkegaard later proposed in their different ways. The mature Hegel would revert to this idea when presenting *Sittlichkeit* as going beyond mere morality (*Moralität*).

The religion of love clearly makes Judaism look even worse to Hegel, since he shares the tradition which saw Judaism as built on seclusion and hatred of all other nations. Judaism also lacked the element of beauty, the essence of Greek religion which Christians learned to absorb but Jews rejected fanatically. Opposing the unity and harmony of the Hellenic spirit, Judaism is severance, the fissure between man and everything else, including himself.[23]

It is interesting to see how Hegel used his critique of Judaism as a lever for distancing himself from Kant. Jesus' principle of love is now set against the Kantian "Ought." All human legislation that mediates between contradictory interests is based upon an Ought, says Hegel; as such, the law is not part of nature but is imposed upon nature as a command.[24] This is true of Kantian moralism and Jewish legalism alike. In the morality of love, by contrast, a person performs his or her duty out of a natural drive and a sense of communion, thus bridging the chasm which the Ought introduces into the world.

Thus, by means of his new text on Judaism and Christianity, a major event in Hegel's intellectual biography starts taking place – his rift with Kant. Hegel now attributes to Kant the source of the "positivity" he had previously ascribed to Jesus. Kant's morality is so abstract that all particular acts of duty must take their content from occasional circumstances: that is, from empirical accident; therefore, a residue of "positivity" remains in Kant's morality that is ineradicable.[25] Thus a moral system which claimed to be pure and universal is affected by contradiction between its form and its content. Hegel says that this contradiction "shocks us," because it makes it possible to stamp all kinds of arbitrary, occasional actions with the seal of absolute morality, while disqualifying as immoral – or at least as morally irrelevant – "all human relations which do not unquestionably belong to the concept of [Kantian] duty," be they love, solidarity, familial links, etc. "Woe to them all," says Hegel ironically, from the morality of the Ought![26]

This is not only criticism, but a program. In *Philosophy of Right* Hegel would, under the rubric of *Sittlichkeit*, offer a new moral framework which attempts to unite the historical world and the Ought. It would incorporate real human relations within the family, society, and the state. It would not reject peoples' drives and feelings but accept them as the necessary substrate of moral life. The role of social and legal institutions would be to reshape this substrate and draw a rational significance from it. Thus our text sheds early light on the concept of *Sittlichkeit* which the late Hegel is to distinguish both from Kantian *Moralität* and from its classic Kantian opposite, *Legalität*.

In *Sittlichkeit* as embedded morality we find the "surpassing of morality" toward love which the young Hegel attributed to Jesus. Because morality is a matter of the inner conscience and the heart, the mature Hegel viewed it as a lower stage of practical philosophy.

Sittlichkeit is higher than *Moralität* because it elicits practical rationality from the real, historical world with all its passions and sensuality, and embodies that rationality in actual institutions.

Fairness demands that we respond to an erroneous charge which Hegel (possibly following Schiller) makes against Kant. Schiller claimed that only an action performed against one's heart's inclination can have moral value for Kant. A moral act must hurt one's feelings and frustrate all natural inclinations. This fairly common view derives from a misunderstanding of Kant's moral psychology. In fact, the rational will in Kant has a self-sufficient motivational power which, of itself, regardless of a person's inclinations, is capable of producing a moral decision followed by an action. This capability is the precondition of morality implied in the concept of freedom. If so, it is possible for a pure moral motive to produce of itself the same behavior that a natural inclination would recommend under the same circumstances. What counts is not the content of the act but its source and motivation. Kantian morality demands that we ignore – that is, neutralize – motives coming from natural inclinations and adopt our reverence for the moral law as our sole motive. We may at times wonder which of the two motives has actually determined our action, but this shortcoming is cognitive, not ontological: the act itself might still have been purely moral.

In short, the moral conflict in Kant is not between alternative contents of action, but between alternative motivations, or modes of decision. Nothing therefore excludes a possible agreement between reason and inclination. But I have no intention of proceeding in this debate; my aim was to point out how Hegel's early text on Judaism and Christianity serves to incubate some of his later ideas. Beneath the Enlightenment crust, a dialectical ferment was stirring which eventually led Hegel to the *Aufhebung* of his early thinking.

Abraham, Moses, and the robbers of Marseille

"The Spirit of Christianity and its Fate" is the fiercest anti-Jewish text ever written by Hegel. His aim, here too, is not Judaism as such but Christianity and European culture. Hegel opposes Judaism to Hellenism. The Hellenic spirit unites love and nature, while Judaism signals man's break with and severance from both love and nature. In this respect, says a French commentator, Hegel sees the spirit of Judaism as the source of Western history, and also as the source of its negativity.[27]

Hegel defines spirit as the "unity" and "soul" of a certain people or culture, which is constant throughout the ages, but takes on different shapes according to the forces with which it struggles. Sometimes the spirit assumes "an alien nature" which assaults it: Hegel calls this its "fate" (anticipating the future concept of alienation). At this point Hegel still understands spirit undialectically, as an unchanging essence whose forms alone are altering. We are still far from the revolutionary concept of *The Phenomenology of Spirit*, according to which the spirit's *very essence* is constituted by the process of its becoming.[28] The concept of "fate" too, or alienation, is seen as deviation only; it is not the spirit's *self*-alienation which helps to develop it, but merely the result of its clash with external circumstances, and therefore an accidental factor.

The spirit of Judaism is represented by the patriarch, Abraham. Abraham is an unrelenting wanderer, who severs all his ties to life, nature, a particular place, family, and love, in order to be absolutely free, but thereby becomes alienated and dehumanized – "a stranger on earth, a stranger to the soil and to men alike."[29] This multi-faceted severance is the first, constitutive act by which Abraham becomes the father of the Jewish nation; and Abraham's spirit lives on as "the unity, the soul, regulating the entire fate of his posterity."[30]

To Abraham the world depended on a God who was absolutely Other, alien. His battle against idolatry introduced an infinite chasm between the creator and his creation. Since nothing in nature can participate in the divine essence, God's relation to the world is one of absolute difference, not participation but *domination*. Abraham cannot relate to nature directly, only through God's mediation. Thus God is the lord and owner of the land, the crops, and his people, for whom he remains the absolute Other and also the absolute Master, who instills fear and trembling in his servants.

Following the anti-Jewish vein of the Enlightenment, Hegel now embarks on a hostile, biased exegesis of the Old Testament. If Abraham insists on paying Ephron for the Makhpela cave, it is because he is arrogant and refuses to recognize Ephron as his equal. After Dinah's rape, her brothers take a horrible revenge on the people of Shechem despite a generous compensation that was offered them. Hegel concludes: Jews become brutal when they have power. The most grotesque Hegelian midrash refers to Jacob's son, Joseph. When Joseph rose to power in Egypt, he used the many years of famine to impose his boss, the Pharaoh, as absolute lord and tyrant, in imitation of the Jewish God's relation to his slave-people. Hegel's bias makes fun of history. The Israelites did not come to a political culture which preceded them by over a millennium; they *imposed* that culture on the land of the Nile!

Later the situation was reversed, and the Jews became Pharaoh's slaves, in addition to being enslaved by God. Their spirit was passive and resigned – a mental disease and corruption, says Hegel, which continued even when the Jews broke away from Pharaoh's rule. Hegel refuses to see the exodus as liberation. The Jews continued to have a slavish spirit even as they were leaving Egypt, an act for which they were not responsible and which Moses had to impose upon them.

Then came the ten plagues. Egypt is in agony for the Jew's sake, but they themselves remain passive; everything happens *to* them through an other's action.

> Amid general lamentation they withdraw, driven forth by the hapless Egyptians, but they themselves have only the malice the coward feels when his enemy is brought low by someone else's act; ... they go unscathed, yet their spirit must exult in all the wailing that was so profitable to them. The Jews vanquish, but they have not battled. The Egyptians are conquered, but not by their enemies; they are conquered (like men murdered in their sleep, or poisoned) by an invisible attack, and the Israelites ... look like the notorious robbers during the plague at Marseilles.[31]

Who are the robbers of Marseille? A study of Hegel's life by Jacques D'Hondt allows us to answer that question.[32] It turns out that the young Hegel had read a book by one Jacques d'Entrechaux which gave a "shattering account" of a plague in southern France in the year 1720. When the source of the plague was discovered on an island where contaminated goods from the Levant had been stored, thieves in the region started looting these goods, thus spreading the plague to other places, first of all to their own families and villages. Hegel saw an analogy between those thieves and the Jews leaving Egypt: both had profited from other people's agony, and both drew advantage from an act that was not theirs; freedom had fallen to the Jews from heaven, like the loot to the thieves; both had acted meanly, as cowards.

Nor is this all. Like the thieves who contaminated their family and neighbors, so the Jews, Hegel insinuates, also carry a disease. That disease is "the slavish spirit that was retained within freedom and corrupted it," a passivity that later entered the Jewish messianic hope.[33] The Jewish messianic hope expects a new exodus from Egypt involving the same impotence and passivity.

One might add a point which the French scholar has not noticed. Jews in the Middle Ages were accused of contaminating the water wells. Hegel does not go that far, but gives this charge a more refined version. The Jews did not cause a physical plague, though the Marseille robbers did, and the Jews resemble them in spirit.

Jewish history – an early dialectic

The Jewish nation was thus constituted in three stages, each of which displayed an opposition between essence and appearance, or intention and result. In the first stage Abraham cut himself off from the world and the life of feeling in order to attain absolute freedom, but ended up in complete submission to God. The reason for this – the mature Hegel, the philosopher of *Sittlichkeit*, would say – is that true freedom cannot be gained in seclusion but requires one to be involved in life and the actual world. In the second constitutive act, the exodus from Egypt, the Jews were God's passive object, and their servitude deepened. Freedom manifested itself as its opposite. The relation's inner essence was servitude, with freedom serving as its outer appearance, even as a veil that concealed it.

In the third stage, the receiving of the Torah (the divine teaching, or law) we see how Moses "who had freed [his people] from one yoke laid on it another."[34] Freedom was again transformed into servitude. Hegel draws a sharp line between Moses, the active, commanding man and the rest of the Jews. The Jews were not autonomous, they did not give their laws to themselves, since "a passive people giving laws to itself would be a contradiction" (ibid.). Moses had to impose the Law on the Jews as an external legislator, acting on behalf of a despot who left his slaves nothing but absolute dependency.

This should qualify the common view that the young Hegel's writings "are not yet dialectical." Actually we discovered a budding dialectical pattern in all three stages of Judaism, and also in the figure of Jesus. Though Hegel does not yet extend the dialectic to a whole system of reality and history, his treatment of Judaism and Christianity enables us to identify an early form of dialectical thinking, which later will dominate the Hegelian system at large.

God as master and tyrant

Between the Jewish God and his people there is a permanent relation of master and slave. In view of so immense a God – "the
absolute subject" – human life and the whole world look totally
insignificant; therefore "in every enjoyment, in every human activ
ity" there must be some reminder "of the nullity of man and the lit-
tleness of an existence maintained by favor."[35] The signs Hegel
mentions include God's ownership of the people and their property,
as expressed in the laws of dime and *teruma*, and the years of *shemita*
and jubilee in which fields sold to others were returned to their historical owners. Hegel refuses to recognize a similarity between the
Jewish jubilee and Greek laws against the accumulation of wealth
enacted by Solon and Lycurgus: the Greeks made laws for free men,
whereas Moses made laws for slaves. "The Greeks were to be equal
because all were free, self-subsistent; the Jews equal because all were
incapable of self-subsistence."[36]

Moreover, among the Jews there was no civic body (*Staatsbürger-
schaft*) at all; what looked like an interdependence of citizens was
actually a series of dependencies upon their invisible master and his
agents, the priests. Nothing like the Greek rule of law (*Staatsrecht*)
was possible among the Jews; individuals were tied to each other by
family links or by external coercion, but not through identifying
themselves with a larger ethical community.

Hegel offers a particularly hostile exegesis of Jewish customs that
would normally count as merits. The laws of bodily purity are
another sign of the Jews' slavery, since "the human body, which was
only lent and did not properly belong to them, must be kept
clean."[37] The weekly day of rest, the Sabbath, is a day of emptiness
and "inactivity," which a people of slaves finds desirable, yet free
men will refuse to devote to God so empty a time.[38] Hegel mentions
favorably only the three holy festivities, perhaps because they resemble the Greek popular celebrations.

Another tortuous example is Hegel's use of Josephus Flavius' story
about Pompey's entry into Jerusalem. The Roman general broke into
the inner sanctuary of the Temple in order to find out who the mys-
terious God of the Jews was – and was amazed to find the place
empty. An unbiased monotheist, whether Christian or Jew, would
be edified and flattered by this story which elevates monotheism
above paganism; yet Hegel presents this merit too as a flaw: the
empty sanctum indicates that the people's *spirit* is empty and cut off
from God and life.[39]

Jewish materialism: servitude without overcoming

As a result of their passivity and servitude, "there remained to the Jews, beyond the testification of their servitude, nothing save the sheer empty need of maintaining their physical existence and securing it against want."[40] This echoes an old charge: Jews are materialists, they have no spirit. Proof: the Old Testament does not recognize the next world. Jewish rewards and punishments were merely this-worldly, and their highest prize was a *land*, breeding milk and honey.[41] This, to anti-Semites, was crude materialism worthy of the Jews' later reputation as money-lovers and usurers. But a reader familiar with *The Phenomenology of Spirit* will notice here something else which is rather interesting.

A central chapter of *Phenomenology* deals with master–servant relations. The servant (or slave) has shunned a struggle of life and death with the master and has opted for mere physical subsistence: this choice *makes* him a slave, in contrast to the master, who was ready to risk his life for something he values more. But this is not the end of the story, only its beginning. The slave serves the master with his labor, and thereby stands in direct relation to nature – the world of needs – which he changes and reshapes according to human intentions. Meanwhile the master lives in isolation from nature and cannot relate to real existence except through the slave's mediation. Now it is the master who leads a life of mere existence, without development and self-realization – that is, without real history – a life enclosed in its own circle and getting nowhere; whereas the slave leads a real life which engenders history, because by his labor, the slave imprints his needs and intentions – and those of the master, as included in his work-goals – upon raw external nature, and thereby is able to rediscover his own image embodied in the external world. Hence the slave evolves, his subjectivity is enhanced, his humanity gradually develops, until he reaches self-consciousness followed by the overcoming of his slavery. The slave even liberates the master, by reversing the system in which they are both locked.

I cannot go into the nuances of the master–slave issue; but a comparison with the text of "Positivity" shows again how Hegel's struggle with Judaism yields the beginning of a major future idea. But notice that the young Hegel denies Judaism the merit which in the *Phenomenology* he will grant the slave – of being the active, creative agent who liberates both himself and his master. Rather, the portrait of Jews in "The Spirit of Christianity" is built from the defects of both the slave and the master. The Jew is the slave who clings to merely material existence, and *in addition* lives an empty passive life, severed from nature – just as the master does in the *Phenomenology*. Is this an inconsistency? Perhaps not. It can be argued that Hegel did not know in Frankfurt what he was later to write in Jena. But the anti-Jewish bias breaks out from this text in effulgent colors.

The Jewish tragedy – Macbeth or Carthage?

Even the Jews' suffering does not evoke the young Hegel's empathy, but rather his revulsion. Discussing tragedy, Hegel insists that the Jewish spirit, unlike the Hellenic, lacked beauty, and goes on to say:

> The great tragedy of the Jewish people is no Greek tragedy; it can rouse neither terror nor pity, for both of these arise only out of the fate which follows from the inevitable slip of a beautiful character; it can arouse horror alone. The fate of the Jewish people is the fate of Macbeth who stepped out of nature itself, clung to alien Beings, and so in their service had to trample and slay every thing holy in human nature, had at last to be forsaken by his gods (since they were objects and he a slave) and be dashed to pieces on his faith itself.[42]

These infamous words conclude Hegel's discussion of the Jews in "The Spirit of Christianity." In a less sordid moment Hegel might have explained that he did not mean to say that the Jews have committed an *actual* murder (although many others, over the centuries, did and do mean that); he used "murder" as metaphor for a spiritual act – corrupting religion; and that he was driven (as many authors are) by a *literary* temptation – to exploit the concept of tragedy in order to stress the lack of an ideal of beauty among the Jews.[43] In any event, this is not the only case in which an author speaks of revulsion and provokes it himself.

But, in fairness, Hegel's pendulum "between attraction and repulsion" has swung also in the other direction. On an earlier occasion (in "Positivity"), Hegel had flown into great admiration of the Jews' resistance to Rome during the great revolt, when, he said, they overcame their passivity and took to arms.

> So long as the Jewish state found spirit and strength enough in itself for the maintenance of its independence, the Jews seldom, or, as many hold, never, had recourse to the expectation of a Messiah. Not until they were subjugated by foreign nations, not until they had a sense of their impotence and weakness, do we find them

burrowing in their sacred books for a consolation of that kind. Then
when they were offered a Messiah who did not fulfill their political
expectations, they thought it worth toiling to insure that their state
should still remain a state; they very soon discarded their ineffective
messianic hopes and took up arms. After doing everything the most
enthusiastic courage could achieve, they endured the most
appalling of human calamities and were buried with their polity
under the ruins of their city.[44]

This too is an account of tragedy – but how far it is from the venomous comparison with Macbeth! Hegel had read Josephus on the
Jews' revolt against Rome, a daring, active moment in their history,
and was impressed by the Jews' instinct for *political* survival – that is,
independence, which even explains their rejection of Jesus. The
Jews have been expecting a national liberator, a political Messiah,
and were deeply frustrated when Jesus told them that he had come
to liberate the Jews not from Rome but from their own spiritual
bondage. Any sane people would have felt the same, Hegel suggests.
(Is he also suggesting that Jesus' extradition to the Romans was a
justified act of *raison d'état*, equally motivated by national survival?)
The disappointment which Jesus created had liberated the Jews for a
while from their messianic illusion and forced them to discover hidden forces in themselves which led to the Great Revolt – an event
which the young Hegel, clearly thinking of Germany, extols with
great admiration:

> In history and the judgment of the nations they would stand along-
> side the Carthaginians and Saguntines, and above the Greeks and
> Romans, whose cities outlived their polities, if the sense of what a
> nation may do for its independence were not too foreign to us, and
> if we had not the impertinence to order a nation not to manage its
> affairs on its own but to follow our opinions and live and die for
> them, though we do not lift a finger to uphold them ourselves.[45]

The first sentence betrays the young Hegel's patriotic fervor (which
cooled off in later years), and the ending is a sneer at intellectuals
which would fit most times and places. Ironically, the subtext shows
that Hegel too, like those he criticizes, goes on telling the Jews how
they should live and die. He sees the revolt as a great apotheosis in
which Jewish existence reached not only a climax, but also its *end*.
Had the Jews followed the example of the Carthaginians and left the
world stage at the tragic moment of their state's demise, they would
have been remembered with awe and admiration by generations to

come. But they did not. They defied the young Hegel's order – or his
logic and theology – so that he was left to ponder the scandal and
enigma of their continued existence, and shift between attraction
and repulsion.

"The scattered remnant of the Jews have not abandoned the idea
of the Jewish state."[46] Henceforth, this is characteristic of Diaspora
Jews, whose messianic hopes express the same passive spirit and
spiritual "disease" which we encountered in the exodus.[47]

A similar criticism was made by the first Zionists, who also saw
Jewish existence in the Diaspora as defective, because it relied passively on the Messiah. The Zionists called on Jews to discover their
true selves and to "supplant" the Messiah – that is, take their fate
into their own hands. No wonder the revolt against Rome (and the
Masada story) play a major role in Zionist mythology today. Hegel
was neither a Zionist nor an anti-Semite,[48] though both camps could
have found some support in his early utterances.

Hegel and Mendelssohn

"From his student period onwards," says Otto Pöggeler, a major
Hegel scholar and editor, "Mendelssohn's *Jerusalem* became one of
his key books, which he used to explain his own ideas."[49]
Mendelssohn, indeed, was one of the young Hegel's heroes. In "Positivity" he discusses the relation between religion, state, and morality,
in the spirit of Mendelssohn's theory of toleration, as developed in
part I of *Jerusalem*. Yet part II, which discusses Judaism, was read by
Hegel with the hostile eyes of Kant, for whom Judaism was spiritless
legalism and a merely political religion. This enabled Hegel to hint –
delicately, at first – that the Jewish sage's ideas were incompatible
with his religion.

Mendelssohn argued there is no greater absurdity than imposing
religious belief or morality by state laws. The young Hegel agrees: A
political legislation requiring citizens to be moral is absurd and
grotesque.[50] The same is true with regard to religion, which can be
useful to morality only when operating as a voluntary, nonstatutory,
and nonpolitical educational instrument. But did not Mendelssohn
himself, as a Jew, adhere to a religion based on legal coercion? If so,
Hegel implies, Mendelssohn cannot hold on to both his theory of
Enlightenment and the religion of his fathers. Judaism and Enlightenment are incompatible.

Mendelssohn, now dead, had been accustomed to polemical

dilemmas devised by his opponents. One vocal opponent was
Johann Kaspar Lavater, a Swiss priest and tactless bore, who chal-
lenged Mendelssohn to convert to Christianity or else prove by the
force of reason that Judaism is superior to Christianity. Years later,
the anti-Enlightenment religious philosopher Jacobi, who saw
Spinozism as the necessary outcome of rationalism, presented
Mendelssohn with a different dilemma: Either admit you are an
atheist like Spinoza, or abandon reason in favor of faith. Both attacks
endangered Mendelssohn only rhetorically, in the outer arena of cultural politics. Essentially, *in foro interiore*, Mendelssohn had no problem denying both Lavater's Christianity and Jacobi's philosophy of
faith. But the dilemma implied by Hegel – either Judaism or Enlightenment – was much more serious. Mendelssohn could not abandon
either of the two, since his life project consisted in demonstrating
that it was possible to.combine them.

It was in order to meet such claims that Mendelssohn had written
the second part of *Jerusalem*. There, he made two claims (which we
met in the Introduction): first, that the Jewish religion was never a
separate power structure – in ancient times the authority of religion
coincided with that of the state, and after the state's destruction it
took on a voluntary character, no longer based on coercion;[51] and
second, that Judaism imposes no dogmatic belief as a condition for
salvation. In Judaism there are no revealed truths, only a revealed
constitution, or basic laws.[52] Kant, abusing this idea, read Mendelssohn as testifying that his people's religion was merely political
and devoid of moral content.[53]

The young Hegel follows Kant in that technique too, turning a
great Jew he admired into a witness against his people. Mendelssohn
had seen Judaism's merit in that it had no dogmas and was free of
the contradictions between the truths of revelation and those of reason which afflict Christian rationalists. Hegel turns this merit into a
defect. "What deeper truth is there for slaves than that they have a
master?," he asks sarcastically.[54] If the Jews have no truths, it is
because a people of slaves is incapable of grasping truth. Truth
requires freedom, but the Jews are unable to live outside the master–slave relationship. They understand only commands, so truth too
had to take the form of a command for them. The claim that there is
only one God appears in Judaism as a commandment, even as the
supreme law of the state.

Because truth eluded the Jews, Hegel says contemptuously, of
course they did not make a dogma of it. But what advantage does
this give them? The Eskimos on their icy steppes did not impose

taxes on the wine they did not have. Does this make them superior to the Europeans?[55]

Hegel as the Templar knight: the logic of the duality

With these words we take leave of the young Hegel.[56] His harsh style and venomous comparisons (the robbers of Marseille, the plague, Macbeth, etc.) clearly go beyond the ordinary anti-Jewish convention of his time. They reveal the writer's deep personal aversion to the Jews, which goes together with rare but distinct moments of admiration. Can some logic be found in this duality? Especially, how can the aversion to Judaism be reconciled with the reverence which Hegel felt for great Jewish figures, and his support of civil equality for the Jews?

Again we turn to *Nathan the Wise* for a clue. In Act II, scene 7, Nathan meets the young Templar knight who has saved his daughter from a fire and wants to get closer to the noble young man. When starting to say "noble Franc," the knight cuts him short scornfully: "What, Jew, what?" Nevertheless the knight agrees to start a conversation, first impatiently and later with growing interest. Then, after some personal contact has been established, a moment comes when the knight says: "But Jew – your name is Nathan? – but Nathan. . . ." The knight has by now established a personal relation with his interlocutor, so he shifts from designating him by his contemptible nation to calling him by his proper name, as an individual. Suddenly the knight discovers a real person regardless of his nation or religion. Later he even compliments him:

> TEMPLAR KNIGHT: I must confess you know how Templar knights
> should think –
> NATHAN: Only Templar knights? And only should?
> And only because these are the rules of the Order?
> I know how good people think, know
> There are good people in all lands.

The concept of "universal humanity" has now entered the background. Yet the knight explains frankly that his heart abounds with hatred for the Jews. He attacks their alleged arrogance, their sense of religious superiority. The young Hegel could have been this knight.

And what is Nathan's/Lessing's answer?

> NATHAN: You can loath my people as much as you like. Neither of us has chosen his people. Are we our people?
>
> What does people mean, then?
>
> Is a Christian or a Jew more Christian or Jew than a man?[57]

This is Lessing's Enlightenment view which the young Hegel fervently endorsed. The Jew's humanity must be discovered and acknowledged, not through the mediation of his or her Jewishness, but rather by *ignoring* that Jewishness and uncovering some "universal man" beneath it. Similarly, a person's human worth is also recognized by the Enlightenment "as man" rather than as German, Jew, Christian, woman, etc.; that is, it is not mediated by the particular identity which that person assumes and by which she may want to interpret her humanity. Implied in this abstract liberal approach is the demand that the individual renounce his specific identity as a condition for his humanity to be discovered and acknowledged, a condition that was imposed on the Jews as the price of their political emancipation, first in Napoleonic France and later in other countries as well.[58]

If we see the young Hegel as the Templar knight and Lessing as Nathan, we can start to understand the duality already mentioned. Nathan (= Lessing = the Enlightenment) does not demand of the knight (= the young Hegel) that he stop hating Judaism ("You can loath my people as much as you like"). He demands only that he *abstract* from Judaism when relating to an individual person and recognize the latter's "universal" humanity. In concurring with this demand, the knight signals the victory of the Enlightenment; but the victor's view sees no contradiction between accepting a person and rejecting his or her specific identity, or between loathing the Jews as a people and admiring individual Jews like Spinoza or Mendelssohn, or supporting the Jews' political emancipation.

Hegel liked to quote another bit of *Nathan the Wise*. Nathan is telling the cloister-brother how years ago he saved and adopted a Christian girl after his wife and children had been murdered in a pogrom. To which the good friar responds: "Nathan! Nathan! You are a Christian! By God, you are a Christian! A better Christian has never existed!" And Nathan answers: "What makes me a Christian for you, makes you a Jew for me."[59] Again, we have the same idea: peoples and religions are external shells. True religion – universal humanity – can hide under many names but needs none. This too could have taught Hegel that he may hate the shell while loving the person beneath it.[60]

And so, despite the great difference between Lessing's philo-Semitism and the young Hegel's abomination of Judaism, on this point they share a common deep structure. This explains why, in terms of the Enlightenment, for which Lessing set the example, there was no contradiction between the two trends that coexisted in the young Hegel. Later in life, Hegel rejected the Enlightenment as too abstract, demanding that rational freedom be embodied in a person's specific community and the particular ingredients of his or her identity. Even then, he did not see Judaism as the medium of some future liberation, but only as a contingent remnant of the past. As the following chapters show, even after he became a dialectical thinker, Hegel's Enlightenment past is most clearly visible in his relation (negative and positive) to the Jews.

CHAPTER THREE

Jena and the Phenomenology: *A Telling Silence*

Of all Hegel's places of residence, Jena is where his mature system emerged. In Jena he wrote his most original work, *The Phenomenology of Spirit*, a rich, profound, at times puzzling work of genius, which left a deep mark on modern European philosophy.

Hegel conceived of the *Phenomenology* both as an introduction to his new system, and as its first part. The reason is explained in the preface: In philosophy, "the true is the whole,"[1] and the whole must contain its own genesis as part of itself. Philosophical truth cannot emerge timelessly from someone's head. It depends on the process of its own becoming, which depends on the social, political, and cultural history of mankind. Truth emerges as the result of that history; it undergoes a process of self-generation which is retained in the result, and which the final system of philosophy expresses in concepts.

This conceptualization starts with *The Phenomenology of Spirit*. Spirit is the underlying subject of human culture, and the *Phenomenology* expounds the structure (and thereby the "logic") of Spirit's self-becoming through its historical manifestation.

Although human history seems chaotic, an irrational disorder devoid of meaning, philosophy can, in retrospect, find a meaningful rational structure underlying its evolution. Looking back on history from the vantage point of its last phase (which Hegel, writing in 1806, felt had just begun), the *Phenomenology* tries to reconstruct the major phases of the evolution which made modernity possible. Hegel finished writing the *Phenomenology* sometime before Napoleon's troops marched into his town of Jena, after beating the Prussian army in the famous battle of Jena. For a fleeting moment Hegel had a glimpse of the emperor riding in town, and is reported to have said that he had just seen the world Spirit on horseback (a joke of course, but very Hegelian, for it is a jesting, secular version of the Incarnation). At that time Hegel held Napoleon in higher regard than the original French Revolution, which he criticized as abstract. The emperor was both a soldier and an administrator; he spread the ideas of freedom and equality throughout the European continent and, above all, institutionalized them in concrete political bodies and legislation, including the legal code that bore his name (*Le code Napoléon*). The mature Hegel preferred ideas that have been given (some) concrete existence, even at the price of losing their original purity, to great edifying abstractions.

Personally he was full of expectations. In the preface to the *Phenomenology* he sees himself living at a historic "birth-time" (p. 6). Spirit has torn itself away from its past world and is ready for a "qualitative leap" that will bring forth a new world – which Hegel describes as childbirth, playing with associations of the Nativity (which we shall meet again later). For a long time it had been difficult to notice the disintegration of the old world except by the "frivolity and boredom" which were biting into its flesh; now, "this gradual crumbling is cut short by a sunburst which, in one flash, illuminates the features of the new world" (pp. 6–7).

Hegel's enthusiasm about the new world was as vigorous in 1806 as it had been a decade earlier. In the meantime, however, he had transcended his Enlightenment views and adopted a more complex (and dialectical) historical outlook. Reason cannot emerge ahistorically, it requires the "work, the labor, the suffering" of generations; yet that process is almost done. Now Hegel sees the last historical stage looming on the horizon, the era when freedom can be realized in its various aspects – as personal, political, and metaphysical freedom – and when philosophy will be able to renounce its name as *love of* wisdom and become *actual* wisdom ("absolute knowing").

Hegel's early optimism sobered up considerably in later years, following the imposition of the conservative Restoration's iron grip on Europe, but it never vanished completely. Hegel was also logically committed to *some* version of the "end of history," because his system can overcome historical relativism only by stepping out of history into a supra-historical standpoint, which becomes available only at the end. As long as we are immersed in history, our view of the process is inevitably fragmentary and partial, and relativism takes over. If Hegel is to maintain his claim to understand history from an "absolute" nonrelativist standpoint, he must assume that the end of history is already in sight – at least on the far horizon. He must see himself living at the threshold of the new era, even if it will be a very long and difficult era, and even if he, personally, like Moses looking out on the Promised Land from the height of Mount Nebo, will never get there himself.

The dialectic: basic features

Henceforth we shall have to consider Hegel's view of Judaism in light of his dialectical system, which the *Phenomenology* introduced; so let us take a cursory glance at some features of the dialectic.

The structure of truth and actuality in the *Phenomenology* is dialectical in at least the following senses:

1 Although Spirit is essentially rational, it needs its "other" – empirical existence, phenomenality, error, contingency, suffering, etc. – as means or medium through which alone its essence can develop and eventually become realized. Spirit's rational essence must become other-than-itself in order eventually to return to itself on a higher level, as actualized.

2 The rational essence is actualized only at the end – as its own result. At the outset it is not actual but only latent and abstract; it needs a long, complex, diversified development in order to actualize itself and thus become what it is.

3 Hegel's so-called dialectical logic follows the dynamic structure of mental, or subject-like, systems. In such systems, self-consciousness (and self-identity) are gained only at the end of the road. This (as Kant and Fichte had already said) presupposes a process in which consciousness ascribes to itself a variety of predicates – contents, situations, mental states, etc. – and recognizes them as its own. At the same time it recognizes and identifies itself as the subject of all this diversity.

4 In a system expressing the life and evolution of the mind, acts of negation do not erase the preceding stages but, rather, preserve them as a kind of organic memory in the texture of the new stage. The collapse of a mental position drives the process onward, toward a new position which serves as a specific, if temporary,

answer to the specific flaw that arose in the previous stage and caused its collapse. Thus all affirmations, negations, growths, and collapses are retained in Spirit's organic memory – that is, in the texture of every new phase.

5 Contradictory positions in the domain of the Spirit do not necessarily cancel one another out, they can complement and modify each other in the framework of a higher totality ("the true is the whole"). Truth and falsity are not a binary matter, an either/or option. Rather, in all philosophical systems, in all rival religions, in all divergent political institutions and competing artistic schools, there is a kernel of truth which they express in a partial, one-sided manner. Some of these cultural forms are higher than others, because they express truth in various degrees of fragmentation and distortion – but none of them is absolutely false. Falsity resides in the attempt of a particular cultural form to express the whole truth and to exclude its opposite (its "other") as a nullity, when actually it *needs* that other – and all the others – to modify and complement it within the totality.

6 Hegel pictures the Spirit's evolution as a spiral in which "the end is the beginning." This means that the actualized end (goal) is also the abstract beginning. In the middle lies the main body of history – a series of figures and phases which Spirit assumes and abandons according to its inner logic, and in which it is partially realized. Because of inadequacies and contradictions arising at every historical stage, the process is driven onward through further contradictions, distortions, and partial realizations, until all opposites are reconciled (that is, integrated, accepted as constructive) within the actualized goal.

7 Given the previous points, the dialectic rejects the common view that a dual negation must return the process to its point of departure (not-(not-P) = P). The principles of formal logic expressing this view – the laws of noncontradiction and excluded middle – cannot hold true in the "organic" domain of Spirit and philosophy. They are valid only for "inert" systems, in which fragmentary, self-identical items (sentences, sense-data, mathematical values, etc.) are arranged and manipulated according to external rules. Yet these laws are inadequate for dealing with "a complete whole" endowed with organic memory and with an inherent movement of self-actualization.

Religion – a reappraisal

In Hegel's order of things, religion is the "other" through which philosophical truth has to evolve. Religion represents in images, symbols, metaphors, and stories what philosophy expresses better in concepts. Although philosophy is the higher of the two, this does not make of religion a false superstition, as in Spinoza and the radical Enlightenment. Rather, historical religion with all its contingent, irrational elements – including those features which the young Hegel had denounced as "positive" – is now recognized as a necessary, vital medium of truth's evolution and of the human spirit.

In principle, every historical religion makes some genuine contribution to Spirit's long process of development. Specific religions express fragmentary aspects of truth in a form that is inadequate to their content. Even the highest religion (to Hegel, a kind of reformed Lutheranism) is locked within a universe of stories and metaphors which oppose its "absolute" content. Historical religions must therefore be transcended twice: first, toward a higher form of *religious* expression, and secondly, outside religion altogether, toward the philosophical concept.

Hegel calls this transcendence *Aufhebung*, a key term in his dialectic. *Aufhebung* has a triple meaning: (a) negation, (b) preservation; (c) elevation. For any given cultural formation, the act of *Aufhebung* negates (cancels) its inadequate form, preserves the seed of its true content, and elevates this content to a higher medium or form of expression. Eventually the new figure will also become ridden with incongruities, and they too will have to be *aufgehoben* in turn. This process will continue until the form of truth is compatible with its content, giving rise to "absolute knowing."

A common mistake is to present the Hegelian dialectic as a march of thesis–antithesis–synthesis. Hegel only once used this formula, which comes from Fichte. Hegel's dialectics are far more flexible than Fichte's and do not conform (at least, not in the *Phenomenology*) to the rigid "trinities" into which some disciples and interpreters have tried to regiment his system. For, precisely as dialectician, Hegel had to recognize that some degree of freedom and contingency is necessary for the rational move itself. The dialectic is not some frozen a priori formula or airtight method, but the structure resulting from "the subject-matter's own evolution," which precludes rigid formulas and requires, as a matter of dialectical necessity, that some measure of contingency (and unpredictability) be involved in the process.

Religion in the Phenomenology

Religion has a strong presence in the *Phenomenology* in two ways. First, the *Phenomenology* is not only the conceptualized story of the human race, but, implicitly, also the story of *God's* self-becoming through the mediation of human history. This idea translates the Christian notion of the Incarnation which is latent in (the deep-structure of) Hegel's system. The infinite, absolute God is not actual from the start, but becomes actual through his "other" – the finite human race in its evolution. The *profane* history of humankind is thereby also the history of God's own becoming (and thus a secular version of *sacred* history, *historia sacra*); this explains how *The Phenomenology of Spirit*, a book full of profane matters such as politics, science, art, morality, sense perception, etc., acquires a theological background and an implicit religious sense.

Second, religion also has an overt place in the *Phenomenology*. Two crucial stages in Spirit's evolution have a religious form. In one of them, the so-called unhappy consciousness, Spirit becomes split, torn between the finite and the infinite. It is thereby alienated from its divine essence, God, whom it experiences as a transcendent and utterly unreachable absolute, the object of painful, insatiable yearning. Hegel, in the *Phenomenology*, associates this stage with medieval Christianity (but actually alludes to a broader mental figure that also fits Judaism). The second is the penultimate stage, from which Spirit is said to rise to complete actuality and self-consciousness. Hegel conceives this stage as a reformed Protestantism which consummates Christianity as "manifest religion." The next stage sublates religion altogether and leads to systematic philosophy as "absolute knowing" whereby the divine Spirit itself becomes actual and knows itself through human knowledge. This signals the end of the historical process – but not necessarily the end of religion; for even after philosophical knowledge has become absolute, people will continue to need its sensual schematization in metaphor and ritual symbols; this will satisfy their hearts and imaginations while knowing that, henceforth, the philosophical meaning of these images is also available to them.

Judaism in the Phenomenology

What is Judaism's place in this grand scheme of things? Strangely enough, the question cannot be answered. Judaism is hardly ever mentioned in the *Phenomenology*. Hegel discusses a whole procession of cultural forms – Hellenism and paganism, Stoicism and skepticism, the Reformation, the *ancien régime* and the French Revolution – but not Judaism. On this subject, which was so prominent in his early essays, Hegel now seems to be completely silent.

Hegel's omission becomes all the more striking when we examine his account of religious history (in the chapter on religion): here Christianity arises directly from Greek and Roman paganism, while Judaism seems to disappear completely. Remembering that religion is the medium by which Spirit is realized and reaches absolute knowledge, it would appear that by omitting Judaism from religious history, Hegel has reverted to Kant's radical view that Judaism is not a religion at all and embodies no spirituality.

What can explain such a roaring silence? At first glance we might think that Hegel continues to assign Judaism only a negative role. But that should not have prevented him from including it as a figure in the *Phenomenology*. A dialectician should be the first to know that negation has a positive role to play. Moreover, Hegel's new system maintains that every cultural form contributes *some* specific ingredient to Spirit's evolution. How then, of all cultural formations, can Judaism alone have played so marginal a role that even its name is not mentioned?

A more probable explanation is that Hegel's view of Judaism had indeed changed, but that this change was out of pace with the transformation of the rest of his philosophy. When writing the *Phenomenology*, he was still reluctant to express overtly his new appreciation of Judaism, and was perplexed as to exactly where to place it, and this conflict paralyzed his pen. If, as Rosenkranz said, Judaism was a "riddle" to Hegel, then in Jena and the *Phenomenology* Judaism became the most enigmatic of all religions – to the point of producing the most telling silence.

Holes in the veil of silence?

Is Hegel's silence as impenetrable as it sounds? Is there indeed no reference to Judaism in the *Phenomenology*, either explicitly or implicitly?

On two occasions Hegel mentions Judaism by name, albeit briefly, in passing, and when discussing something else. One occasion may be significant. The context is "Observing Reason," a special formation of knowledge which Hegel claims must abort itself in attaining its peak. To illustrate this, he uses the Jewish people as an analogy: "Just so, it may be said of the Jewish people that it is precisely because they stand before the portal of salvation that they are, and have been, the most reprobate and rejected: what that people should be in and for itself" (p. 206). The Jewish people reached the gate of salvation but refused to go through it; therefore they will be locked out of the gates of salvation forever, with no further evolution and no real hope. In other words, *they will no longer have a history.* As the most reprobate (*verworfene*) people, all that remains for the Jews is an ongoing fossilized existence. Hegel adds that had the Jews been able to give their object (namely, their product: Christianity) back to themselves, they might have risen to a higher state and regained a historical (spiritual) existence. However, they clearly cannot do so. Unlike Kant and those who recommended that the Jews convert to Christianity to facilitate their entry into European society, Hegel understood this to be impossible, because what maintains the Jews as such is, above all, their fidelity to their original refusal. The implied conclusion is that the Jews' dehistoricization is irremediable. Jewish history has not only been *aufgehoben* (sublated) by Christianity; it has also dried out and become frozen and drained of all spiritual content.

Despite its unfriendly tone and conventional anti-Jewish polemic, this passage already implies a favorably changed attitude toward the Jews, since it draws a sharp line between Jewish history before and after Christ. Prior to Christ's appearance the Jews *did* have a history – that is, a role in shaping the world Spirit; theirs was actually a decisive role, since they led humanity "to the portal of salvation": that is, to Christ as Messiah. Yet Jewish history aborted itself just when it was about to yield its highest fruit, Christianity, since the Jews refused to recognize themselves in their product, to view it as their own essence and highest form of existence. Instead, they made their refusal their most characteristic mark. Thus the third dialectical stage was missing, the return to self on a higher level. Jewish history got sidetracked, turned off, and the Jews were thrust outside the dialectic of world history, to become a dead remnant of their own past which merely exists, with neither role nor future, and therefore without significant hope.

This is harsh and haughty. Yet Judaism is treated here as having its "product" and true essence in Christianity – a change from the early essays. Incidentally, the image of Judaism waiting without prospect outside the gate of salvation brings to mind Kafka's famous story "Before the Law." Kafka probably had not read the

Phenomenology, yet he seems to have generalized its view of the Jews into an allegory of the common human condition.[2]

The unhappy consciousness

So much for the overt reference to Judaism in the *Phenomenology.*[3] But what about its subtext? Some commentators (Hyppolite and Pöggeler) believe that Judaism is implicitly referred to in the chapter entitled "Unhappy Consciousness." This view is certainly plausible. The way Hegel characterizes the unhappy consciousness recalls his description of Judaism in other works. Unhappy consciousness is the experience of extreme duality, of tornness and alienation; it is the pain and yearning for a God who is infinitely remote, a God whom one confronts in fear and trembling and absolute dependence. However, the *Phenomenology* associates the unhappy consciousness explicitly not with Judaism but with medieval Catholicism, which therefore needs the Reformation to overcome its defects. Hegel's anti-Catholic bias shows through his scientific style: and it is interesting that in the *Phenomenology* he attributes to medieval Catholicism the same flaws which he usually finds in Judaism. If so, Judaism *does* appear in the *Phenomenology,* though under another name: it serves the familiar polemical strategy of denigrating something by attributing "Jewish" features to it.

The birth pangs of Christianity

Another tacit allusion to Judaism occurs toward the end of the *Phenomenology,* where the history of religion is discussed as the lever to "absolute knowing." Overtly, Christianity seems to be born directly from paganism; but on closer reading we find Judaism lurking under the surface.

Hegel divides the various religions according to how they relate to the Absolute. This yields three main categories: natural religion (Asia), the religion of art (Greece and Rome); and "manifest religion" (Christianity).[4] In natural religion, the Absolute is not a self-conscious Spirit, but a thing, a natural element or substance such as light (Persia), animals (Egypt), and so on. In the Greco-Roman world, natural religion becomes the religion of beauty, since art supplants nature as the embodiment of the divine. Both these forms are pagan, because they deify natural phenomena and human artifacts, and, especially, because in them Spirit has not broken away from nature and become self-conscious. This crucial step is attributed by the older Hegel to "the religion of sublimity": namely, Judaism. But in the *Phenomenology* it seems to occur within the Hellenic world itself. The category of a religion of sublimity is missing in the *Phenomenology*, and Christianity seems to arise directly from paganism.

Here is how the process is described. At a certain point the Greco-Roman culture starts declining, its spirit dwindles, and nature becomes drained of the divinity which characterized it in the past. "Trust in the eternal laws of the gods has vanished, and the oracles ... are dumb." "The statues are now only stones," and the works of art, formerly full of religious meaning "have become what they are for us now – beautiful fruit already picked from the tree" (p. 455). Nature has become a secular, "prosaic" object, lacking the kind of objectified spirituality that formerly resided in it. The mind experiences this dramatic loss with pain, similar to the pain of the unhappy consciousness – which now arises as the awareness of that loss. Hegel does not explain how this loss is incurred. In later works he attributed it to the penetration of the Jewish idea of sublimity into the pagan world. But in the *Phenomenology*, which recognizes no religion of sublimity, Judaism is not alluded to as the *cause* of nature losing its divinity, but as the unhappy *awareness* of this crisis. This is rather odd, since it is improbable that Judaism would react with unhappiness to the crisis of paganism. We must conclude that Hegel's inhibitions with regard to Judaism are displayed not only in his overt text, but also in the hidden subtext. His incomplete recognition of the role of Judaism caused him to be incoherent.

In the next stage the gods are stashed away in the Pantheon, and tragic art takes over. Greek tragedy (like Roman Stoicism) is dominated by the concept of Fate, which, says Hegel, introduces a rudimentary form of self-conscious Spirit (p. 456). The absolute as Fate is already a self, an individual, if only as a "shade" (p. 410). In the next stage Christianity makes its appearance, and the absolute changes from substance to full-fledged spirit.

Thus in the *Phenomenology*, the absolute-as-spirit makes a first, rudimentary appearance in Greek tragedy and Roman Stoicism – and then emerges in full in Christ, the God-man. Judaism is not mentioned and plays no role – at least, not overtly.

But let us take a second look at the crucial text. The account of the rise of Christianity reaches a climax on pages 456–8. Hegel is again playing with the metaphor of the Nativity. He even uses the metaphor of "place" (birthplace), but instead of the stable in Bethlehem, he speaks of the "center" and the "periphery" of the event. The "periphery" includes the cultural phenomena which preceded Christianity and prepared its place of birth, such as Stoicism, skepticism, the unhappy consciousness, and the spirit of Greek legal right discussed in the foregoing chapters. The "center" is the act of giving birth itself, around which all these forms are now gathered.

Hegel proclaims that "all the conditions are now present" for the delivery of Spirit as consciousness of itself (p. 456) and goes on to describe the climactic act:

> These forms, and on the other side, the world of person and the law, the destructive ferocity[5] of the fixed elements of the content, as also the person as *thought* in Stoicism, and the unstable restlessness of the sceptical consciousness, constitute the [audience or] periphery of shapes which stand impatiently expectant [*erwartend und drängend*, which can be translated "expecting and pushing," an allusion to the act of childbirth: the mother pushes, and everyone waits in tense expectation and pushes with her] round the birthplace of Spirit as it becomes self-consciousness [i.e. round the manger at Bethlehem]. The grief and longing of the unhappy self-consciousness which permeates them all is their centre and the common birth-pang of its emergence – the simplicity of the pure Concept, which contains these forms and its moments. (Ibid., pp. 456–7).

Hegel draws this nativity scene in vivid, physical brush strokes: the figures surrounding the mother's bed, the expectation, the pushing, the pain and the birth pangs which everyone present is sharing empathetically. On the level of metaphor, assuming a common denominator for Judaism and the unhappy consciousness, Judaism is thereby seen as the "birth pangs of the Spirit" (and Christianity). Judaism is the pain and sorrow from which the Messiah, Christ, was born and from which Spirit emerges as a self-conscious subject. So Judaism is, after all, assigned a major role in the *Phenomenology*. However, it is not the *content* of Judaism which contributes to the rise of Christianity, but the kind of experience which it involves. Judaism is not one special form among others (on the "periphery") but is the "center" which permeates all the rest. Judaism's unhappy, transcendent spirit penetrates the totality of the Roman-Hellenic world which has been drained of its divinity; and although it cannot offer compensation (rather, it emphasizes and amplifies the loss), the pain and yearning which Judaism provokes make it the birth pangs of Christianity and of the absolute-as-subject.

This reading presupposes, of course, that the unhappy consciousness is not attached to one single historical period but manifests itself
in several periods. It cannot belong to medieval Christianity alone,
since it (the unhappy consciousness) had already appeared in antiquity, when the immanent gods of nature and art were dwindling
and ancient Judaism penetrated that world while experiencing pain
and yearning for a transcendent world.[6]

Since Judaism is only the birth pangs, not the *content* of the new
phase, the absolute-as-subject does not draw its actual figure from
Judaism, but emerges from the start in the Christian figure of the
Incarnation – as a God-man whom everyone can see and touch. This
is what a "revealed" religion basically means to Hegel – an odd
meaning which excludes Judaism and Islam, although they too are
based on prophecy and a text revealed by God. To stress his point,
Hegel refers to revealed religion by the unusual term *offenbare Religion* ("manifest religion"), instead of the more standard *geoffenbarte
Religion*, implying that true revelation does not come about through
words alone, but by an actual incarnation of the divine. A truly
revealed (= manifest) religion expresses the absolute as a spiritual
totality in which man and God, the finite and the infinite, are reconciled and mediate each other. This is the core of Christianity, but not
of Judaism and Islam (which have no Incarnation). A subtler critical
slant is directed at the Catholics, for whom the word of God is
revealed but not manifest. Catholics require authoritative interpretation by the clergy, whereas for Protestants, God's word has become
accessible and manifest in the divine texts.[7]

To conclude, there is no special Jewish form in which the absolute
appears: to that extent the *Phenomenology* remains silent on Judaism.
The absolute-as-spirit makes a rudimentary appearance in pagan culture, and then emerges in full in the Christian figure of the Incarnation, the God-man. However, Judaism has the role of "birth pang" of
Christianity, the pain and yearning that spurred its rise from the
pagan world. *To that extent, Judaism does contribute to the world Spirit –
and at its most critical moment.* Hegel was still too inhibited to spell out
his new view – and insofar as his silence is a *talking* silence, it tells
more than it conceals.

Even so, post-Christian Judaism remains locked outside the gates
of the salvation it offers. Judaism's own project is aborted, and the
Jews are ejected from history at the moment of their highest
achievement.

CHAPTER 4

The Mature Hegel: The Sublime Makes its Appearance

During the next decade Hegel still did not write much about the Jews, though no longer because of inhibitions. The reason, I think, is that his works during that period were mostly systematic and not historical.[1] Later, however, especially after moving to Berlin, Hegel embarked on the great lecture series in which he expounded the historical side of his system, and there again Judaism appears as a clear, explicit subject. Reversing his youthful position, Hegel, in most of these lectures (on the philosophy of history, aesthetics, and – most important for us – the philosophy of religion), explicitly recognizes Judaism as a crucial phase in the evolution of the world Spirit, though he also criticizes it with shifting emphases and varying degrees of severity.

The Philosophy of History: the Jewish overcoming of nature

The most striking tilt of the pendulum is found in his *Lectures on the Philosophy of History*. Instead of his former waffling and silence, Hegel here speaks his mind clearly and decisively.[2] The old reproving tone gives way to a balanced appreciation of Judaism, perhaps the most objective in the Hegelian corpus. And although Hegel is still critical of Judaism, there is no more malice, no negative passion. Hegel now shows feeling toward, and empathy with, aspects of Jewish life and suffering that had formerly repelled him.

In a section entitled "Judaea," Hegel reiterates his general dialectical principle, now with specific reference to Judaism:

> Every form of Spiritual force, and *a fortiori* every religion, whatever its peculiar nature, has an affirmative element necessarily contained in it. However erroneous a religion may be, it possesses truth, although in a mutilated phase. In every religion there is a divine presence, a divine relation; and a philosophy of History has to seek out the spiritual element even in the most imperfect forms.[3]

Applying this principle to Judaism (as he failed to do explicitly in the *Phenomenology*), Hegel makes a major break with his earlier writings. Unequivocally, Judaism is now attributed a major role in world history and the evolution of Spirit. Judaism effected a radical break with nature, allowing Spirit to replace and oppose nature. Thereby Judaism, though hailing from the "Persian" cultural zone, made possible the rise of the West – Christendom – and created the break between the East and the West.

The supremacy of Spirit over nature which the Jews achieved had a crucial civilizing effect. Although nature and Spirit are dialectically related, their opposition must endure for a long time – until, after many transformations, they can be reconciled within Spirit's own domain – that is, within culture and history.

In a passage that, in retrospect, illuminates the obscure "nativity scene" of the *Phenomenology* analyzed above, Hegel declares that the Jews' "world-historical importance and weight lies in their unhappy consciousness" (p. 321) – the painful yearning for a transcendent God before whom the individual feels insignificant. This insatiable thirst for God is expressed "most purely and beautifully" in the Psalms of David and in the Prophets. It could *not* have arisen within the Roman world itself (says Hegel now, reversing his view in the *Phenomenology*[4]). Jews long for God as a *spiritual* entity, as a person, not as a natural substance; and when God is grasped as spirit, nature loses the self-sufficiency it had in paganism and is reduced to something created. Nature becomes subservient, reified, desacralized – and God, its creator, is elevated to the status of the sublime.[5]

Nietzsche would later denounce the Jewish break with nature as a source of Western corruption (see part II). Hegel, however, extols it as a great leap forward – indeed, as the origin of self-conscious spirituality. Because Spirit prevails over nature, "true morality and righteousness can now make their appearance"

(p. 196), as do freedom, choice, and the ego as a separate principle (p. 321).

Hegel's new position contrasts sharply with that in his early essays, where Judaism was merely external, ceremonial, and lacking moral content – as in Kant. Now he perceives a true "subjective feeling" in Judaism, based on "the pure heart, repentance, devotion" (p. 197), and the religious yearning expressed in great poetry. Although Hegel is still very critical of the Jews, this recognition of an exalted interiority in Judaism (which in Protestant culture signifies spirituality and freedom) is nothing short of sensational when compared with Hegel's early Enlightenment essays and, even more so, with Kant. One need only remember the story of Pompey finding the Jewish Temple empty, which indicated to the young Hegel the emptiness of Judaism. Now he praises Judaism for precisely the same feature: namely, that "the Spiritual speaks itself . . . absolutely free of the Sensuous" (p. 196).

The flaws of Judaism are still numerous, however. The individual is not really free, but bound by the family and the community. In front of the divine One who unites the Jews, the individual vanishes. This is expressed in the "rigid cult" and "harsh law" to which the Jews are bound, which makes the law of Moses look as if it had been given to them as punishment. Another serious incongruity exists between the essential universality of the Spirit and its limited and particular appearance in Judaism, due to the idea of the Jews' election.

Perhaps the most astonishing defect which Hegel now finds in Judaism is its alleged nonpolitical character! "The State is an institution not consonant with the Judaistic principle, and it is alien to the legislation of Moses" (p. 197). Judaism was created by the patriarchs and is tied to the family, not the state. "Properly speaking, no political union existed" among the Jews (ibid.), because their nation was an extension of the family. This will surprise anyone familiar with the more usual charge: that Judaism is *nothing but* a political constitution (Kant) or is basically a theocracy (Spinoza and others). But Hegel distinguishes between a mere state and a true political union (*Rechtsstaat*) whose laws express the citizens' spirit and rights, rather than simply being imposed upon them. Such a union, Hegel stresses in several works, existed in Greece under the laws of Solon and Lycurgus, but not under the laws of Moses.

Yet, despite all this criticism, Hegel now shows empathy with the Jews' suffering in the Diaspora, and even sympathizes with their messianic hope to regain "the lost plenitude of their existence" (that is, their land and state). This contrasts with the young Hegel's denunciation of the messianic hope as a passivity and a "disease." Hegel now extols Jewish hope and suffering as "active" attitudes and as superior to Stoic resignation to fate. The Stoics endure suffering by imagining that it is unreal; the Jews know that suffering is real yet strive to overcome it. Thereby the Jews show a better understanding of history; they know suffering to be both real and a central agent of historical evolution.

Had Hegel developed this idea, he might have found Diaspora Judaism, when secularized, a role within the modern world, since according to Hegel, modernity involves the human will's attempt to reshape reality in its image, as opposed to conforming to the limits of a static, unchanging world. Hegel also saw the modern state as secularizing religious (Protestant) culture while retaining its spiritual meaning. This conforms to the goals of many modern Jews in the last two centuries, who, driven by an active will and a secularized version of Jewish messianism, have been involved in political movements to change the world. If so, Hegel might have seen a role for secularized Judaism in building the modern world as *he* understood it. However, as we shall see, Hegel (unlike Nietzsche) did not take this road.

The poetry of the sublime: the *Aesthetics*

The tone of empathy recurs in Hegel's *Lectures on Aesthetics,* in which he views Judaism through the Psalms of David – its religious poetry – rather than exclusively through the laws of Moses. Thereby, once again, he recognizes depth in Judaism, a rich inner world to which he had been blind in his youth.

Aesthetics was a new, lively subject in German thought before Hegel. From Baumgarten and Mendelssohn to Kant, Goethe, Schiller, the Schlegel brothers, Schopenhauer, and Hegel himself – to cite the better-known names – German thinkers in the golden age discussed beauty and art with the freshness of a new discovery. Hegel's *Lectures on Aesthetics* combined a theory of art with a critical history of art forms. Although in his youth he excluded Judaism from the realm of beauty (remember "Macbeth"), now he includes Jewish religious poetry in his aesthetics – though not under the category of the beautiful, but under that of the sublime.

The old distinction between the beautiful and the sublime, made by Longinus, was revived in modern times by Burke and, in Germany, by Kant. Hegel follows Kant, but places the sublime in art, whereas Kant had placed it in natural phenomena. The art of the sublime is "the attempt to express the infinite, without finding in the sphere of phenomena an object which proves adequate for this representation."[6] Implicitly, this definition makes the art of the sublime essentially non-Christian. The sublime – invisible, shapeless – "soars above any finite expression"; it defies all distinct forms, especially plastic and narrative forms, and is incommensurable with anything finite – including the God-man. This should exclude the bulk of Christian art (nativities, cathedrals, crucifixions, chants, cantatas, etc.), except the work of a few esoteric mystics.[7]

Hegel distinguishes further between a "positive" and a "negative" sublime. The positive variety is pantheistic art, which expresses God's immanence in all of nature, as illustrated, Hegel thinks, in Indian Brahmin and Persian Muslim (Sufi?) poets. The negative sublime is found in the Old Testament. The Hebrew poets severed the pantheistic link between God and nature. God was powerfully withdrawn from nature and elevated to become nature's infinite master and creator. Thereby pantheism was replaced by sublimity. God as infinitely remote from the world became sublime, while nature became God's mere "creation," a contingent entity lacking justification of its own.[8] As a result, says Hegel, "nature and the human form confront us as prosaic and bereft of God" (vol. 1, p. 374). Man becomes insignificant, and nature's whole glory, its plenitude and immense diversity, becomes a mere instrument of God's glory. Hegel cites Psalm 90 which treats a thousand years as "yesterday" and calls human life a dream: "In the morning it flourisheth and in the evening is cut down and withereth" (vol. 1, p. 376). He also cites Psalm 104 where all the mighty elements – the sea, the wind, the light, etc. – bow to God's dominion and serve his glory. It is God who makes water flow in rivers, who plants the cedars of Lebanon, who makes the grass grow and provides man with food and, most importantly, the wine that cheers the human heart. Thus all of nature, from the mighty elements to the simplest daily events, tells of God's immense power and wisdom and its own nullity and absolute dependence. In this way, Hegel says, "the [Jewish] Psalms supply us with classic examples of genuine sublimity set forth for all time" (vol. 1, p. 375).

But here we must ask: How sublime is sublimity? Is the fact of expressing sublimity an advantage for a religion? The full (negative) answer is given in Hegel's *Lectures on the Philosophy of Religion*, where sublimity is linked to the notion of a false self-consciousness. But before considering this crucial text, we need to look at the historical background, especially at Kant.

Kant discussed sublimity mainly in his aesthetics,[9] but mentions sublimity also with reference to religion. In both areas, the experience of the sublime involves a kind of mystification; for it hides from man his true relation to the infinite. This state is corrected by Kant's "Copernican revolution" for which the analysis of the sublime serves as a paradigm case.

Kant and the sublime

Few readers of the *Critique of Judgement* have noticed that Kant discusses the sublime on two levels: (a) the level of the consciousness which *experiences* sublimity and (b) the level of the consciousness which *investigates* that experience. It is as though the philosopher observes a person who has undergone the experience of sublimity and asks two questions: (1) What does that person feel, what is the structure of her experience in her *own* eyes? And (2) what is the *actual* structure of that experience, and what does it really reveal? As the philosopher discovers, the experience of sublimity recalls something profound about ourselves and our standing in the universe; yet the consciousness experiencing sublimity misinterprets that disclosure – inverts its meaning, in fact – and shapes itself as a deceptive self-consciousness. To properly investigate the experience of sublimity is therefore to correct the false self-consciousness it entails.

The person experiencing sublimity stands before an immense object – the starry heavens, outer space, a great tempest, an imposing mountain range, a glacier, or whatever, whose power and enormity seem incommensurable with human capacities. This object instills fear without actually endangering the spectator, who feels herself negligible and totally insignificant before that tremendous object. Because no actual danger is involved, the spectator's fear is aesthetic rather than practical. We might call it "disinterested fear" (parallel to the disinterested pleasure which lies at the root of beauty).[10] Indeed, despite the fear, sublimity produces a kind of "negative pleasure."[11] The negative element in this pleasure derives also from the spectator's experience of himself as worthless, whereas all power, reality, and value seem to belong to the object.

A similar experience is known in religion and metaphysics. Pascal gave it a modern form when exclaiming: "The eternal silence of these infinite spaces frightens me" (*Pensées*, para. 206). And Kant said in a famous dictum: "two things fill the mind with ever new and increasing admiration and awe . . . the starry heavens above me and the moral law within me."[12] Kant's feeling of sublimity differs, I think, from Pascal's dread, in that it involves a kind of pleasure (*wohlgefallen*), even if its ground is negative.

The difference deepens when we move from the *experience* of sublimity to its *analysis* by the observing philosopher. Gradually, Kant's analysis leads to the discovery that it is our own mind, or something fundamental *in us* which actually possesses the power and the value. Why does our attraction to sublime objects increase the more dreadful they look to us? Because they bring out an extraordinary power from within our soul and give us courage to oppose nature despite its apparently unlimited dominion.[13] Moreover, not only does the experience of sublimity arouse us and heighten our power, it also hints that the human being, as a moral-rational creature, has a special *advantage* over nature with its infinite vastness. Sublimity is in this respect a *reflective* experience, turning our glance back from the object to something fundamental in ourselves. A deep metaphysical truth is disclosed in this experience, something which we are in the habit of hiding from ourselves and projecting onto the external object. To the person ready to see this, the experience of sublimity reveals that he or she is not standing before nature as a base, insignificant creature; rather, as rational beings, humans are superior to the whole of nature – though not because of our scientific, cognitive powers, but only by virtue of our moral reason and the moral-historical project it prescribes for the human race: to embody the laws of morality within the actual natural world and thus reshape it as a *moral* world. Thus it turns out that, "Sublimity, therefore, does not reside in any of the things of nature, but only in our mind, in so far as we may become conscious of our superiority over nature within, and thus also over nature without us."[14] And again: "Therefore nature is here called sublime merely because it raises the imagination to a presentation of those cases in which the mind can make itself sensible of the appropriate sublimity of its own being."[15] Sublimity (and the value it entails) is not an attribute of the natural object but belongs to man – though neither to man as merely existing nor to human reason as a mere unused faculty; rather, sublimity attaches to what the human race must still do and become by means of its reason. In Kant's formula, it resides in the moral "destiny" of the human race.

Elsewhere[16] I have interpreted this destiny as advancing moral history and creating "the highest good in the world." The task which elevates the human being above mere nature demands that he use his rationality to reshape given, existing nature and gradually to create a new world within it – a social, political, spiritual universe embodying the laws of morality. This goal is to be achieved through social action, politics, education, the legal system, and other ingredients of human culture.[17]

This moral-historical destiny, says Kant, gives the human being power and prominence which surpass nature with all its fright and splendor. The human being does not stand before nature as miserable and insignificant but undertakes a semi-divine role – as a kind of demiurge who creates a moral universe and imprints its laws upon nature (including social and political nature).

This, in summary, is the hidden metaphysical truth which critical analysis unravels in the experience of the sublime. What we discover in that experience is not an object but ourselves, and what we revere as sublime is not something external but our own moral destiny. Yet by a kind of "subreption" (Kant's word) the mind reverses the (true) order and falls victim to self-mystification.

Sublimity and the Copernican reversal

Herein lies the Kantian seed of the concept of self-alienation as later developed by Hegel and his successors. And the mental revolution which corrects the situation is a paradigm of Kant's "Copernican revolution" in its several domains.

For example, all past philosophers have been mystified by the (notion of the) "thing in itself" – which the human mind must duplicate in order to know it, and to which all statements must conform in order to be true. Enter the Copernican reversal, which states that, on the contrary, in order for the external object *to be* objective, it must conform to the norms laid down by the human intellect. In moral theory, too, the ordinary person and the dogmatic philosophers representing him believe that there are preestablished virtues and values to which the human will must conform in order to be morally good. Enter the Copernican reversal, which states that, on the contrary, it is the (rational) human will which legislates the laws of morality and serves as the source of all moral value. Even religion undergoes a similar revolution. The uncritical person thinks that she must first believe that there is a distinct infinite entity, external and separate, which created the world and issued moral commands – and that only on this assumption can she be religious. Enter the

Copernican reversal, which says that, on the contrary, one must first recognize the validity of those moral commands which one's own rational will legislates, and then revere them as sacred – this is true religion. Moreover, Kant's religion requires that we *abstain* from belief in an external divine legislator and admit God only as guarantor of our *own* capability to create a moral universe.

In all these cases the philosopher finds that ordinary consciousness has cast, thrown, or projected the origin of truth, objectivity, moral value, and sublimity upon some external object – and then bowed before it. This is the origin of the self-alienation involved in traditional metaphysics and in the morality, religion, and politics based upon it. Reversing that situation is the core of Kant's "Copernican" outlook and the essence of his philosophical revolution.

Hegel and several of his disciples, like Feuerbach and Marx, developed the seed of self-alienation found in Kant's analysis of the sublime. In all varieties of this concept we see the human essence turned upside down or externalized in a way which opposes its humanity. Feuerbach attributed alienation to the structure of religious consciousness: God is the imaginary projection of man's own "divine" essence, which turns against itself as an oppressive power. With Marx, religious alienation became economic: man's externalized essence, work, becomes alienated under capitalist conditions and, instead of expanding his humanity, impedes and distorts it. As for Hegel, he links sublimity, alienation, and false self-consciousness specifically to the Jewish religion. True, there are in Hegel other manifestations of alienation (like medieval Christianity, or the rococo culture of externalities) and, more generally, alienation becomes a dialectical necessity of spirit itself, since spirit must become "other than itself" in order to be realized. Yet Judaism remains the prime example.

This is particularly manifest in Hegel's *Lectures on the Philosophy of Religion*, to which I now turn.

CHAPTER FIVE

Sublimity is not Sublime:
The Philosophy of Religion

In the last decade of his life Hegel delivered four series of lectures on the philosophy of religion (1821, 1824, 1827, and 1831, the year of his death). Hegel spoke slowly, which allowed his listeners to take extensive notes. However, efforts to reconstruct an integral, reliable text of these lectures have not been completely successful. Student transcripts differ, and some have meanwhile been lost. Hegel's own lecture notes (which survived from 1821) are fragmentary and incomplete, and differ from what he ended up saying in class. Since all editorial options have been tried (the latest, by Jaeschke, is the most up to date), it seems that we can no longer expect to have an integrated and critical single text of Hegel's lectures on religion.[1]

Still, all versions agree on the basic ideas and exhibit the same outline. Part I discusses the general concept of religion; part II, entitled "Determinate Religion," the most detailed part, examines each religion's image of the deity (the Absolute), its cult, and the relation between man and the divine as implied in this cult; and part III deals specifically with Christianity, the "consummate religion," to which all the others are said to lead in a dialectical hierarchy.

Hegel makes clear that he is offering not a theology, but a philosophy of religion – that is, of the religious *phenomenon*. It is not the business of the philosophy of religion to offer rational proofs of religious doctrines such as God's existence, providence, or the immortality of the soul. This scholastic project, which the early German

Enlightenment had revived and Kant had demolished, Hegel views as irrelevant to philosophy – an "external reflection" that misses its object. The philosophy of religion works with the real, living materials of the religious phenomenon – with myths, stories, cults, prayers, images, and the rest – in order to extract the fragmentary and partial philosophical significance which hides in each historical religion under the veil of images (*Vorstellungen*).

As for Judaism, the Berlin lectures class it invariably as "the religion of sublimity", but offer two somewhat different accounts of it. Roughly speaking, the lectures of 1821 and 1824 give a harsher, but also a richer and more complete, account of Judaism than the later lectures. Before examining these accounts, a word is needed on Hegel's concept of religion and its relation to philosophy.

Philosophy and religion

Unlike modern philosophers, who severed philosophy from religion, Hegel sees them as intimately linked. Both share the same object – namely, the actualized unity of being and knowledge – which Hegel sometimes calls Truth, sometimes the Absolute. Philosophy is the conceptualization of religious truth. As such, it is higher than religion. Yet, in order to understand itself, philosophy must first understand religion, both in its general essence and in its diverse historical manifestations. The difference between philosophy and religion lies in the form or medium by which each of them expresses their common object. Religion uses *Vorstellung* – particular images, symbols, metaphors, rites, and stories, produced by the imagination – whereas philosophy uses the medium of the *Begriff* – the universal, structured power of concepts.

The affinity of religion and philosophy is stressed in most of Hegel's works. In the *Phenomenology* they both appear at the uppermost stage of Spirit. In passing from the highest religious form into pure philosophy, "absolute knowing" is accomplished. The content of absolute knowledge is first expounded in *The Science of Logic*, of which Hegel says metaphorically that it exhibits "God as He is in His eternal essence before the creation of nature and a finite mind."[2] Logic thus expounds God's eternal "thoughts" and is a kind of philosophical gnosis. *Contra* Kant, who barred the human intellect from knowing God by attributing him predicates, Hegel saw the categories of ontology as God's inner predicates which must be systematically attributed to him.

When summarizing his mature system in the *Encyclopedia of the Philosophical Sciences*, Hegel further stresses the unity between the content of religion and speculative philosophy:

> The objects of philosophy, it is true, are upon the whole the same as those of religion. In both the object is Truth, in that supreme sense in which God and God only is the Truth. Both in like manner go on to treat of the finite worlds of Nature and the human Mind, with their relation to each other and their truth in God.[3]

The *Lectures on the History of Philosophy* interpret the above idea as follows:

> So religion and philosophy have a common subject-matter [or object – YY], namely, what is absolutely true – God inasmuch as He is absolute, in and for himself, and man in his relation to him. . . . Now philosophy has the same subject-matter [as religion]. . . . But while religion accomplishes this reconciliation in devotion and cult, i.e. by way of feeling, philosophy wishes to reach this result in thought, in a knowledge achieved through thinking.[4]

Philosophy deals with truth – more precisely, with God. It is a permanent "worship of God." Philosophy and religion differ, therefore, in form, but not in content. Yet the difference in form is so great that it often makes them appear as contradictory and mutually exclusive. "Thus religion has a content in common with philosophy, and it differs from philosophy only in form; and the only point for philosophy is that the form of the concept shall be so far perfected as to enable it to comprehend the content of religion."[5]

Finally, our own text, the *Lectures on the Philosophy of Religion*, summarizes the issue as follows: "The object of religion, like that of philosophy, is the eternal truth, God and nothing but God and the explication of God. Philosophy is only explicating itself when it explicates religion, and when it explicates itself it is explicating religion."[6] And: "The different forms of determinations of religion, as moments of the concept, are on the one hand moments of religion in general, or of the consummate religion. . . . On the other hand, however, they take shape by developing on their own account in time and historically."[7]

Since philosophy is higher than religion, one might wonder why religion is necessary at all. In Hegel's view, this is due to Spirit's dialectical necessity – to actualize itself through its "other." Philosophy must take the form of religion, and religion too must appear in a dialectical hierarchy of higher and lower forms, in which its (abstract) essence becomes embodied in diverse historical religions and assumes a distinct shape in each of them. The many religions are stages in the absolute Spirit's evolution, as it discloses itself through images. Parallel to that, Spirit manifests itself also conceptually, in a series of philosophical systems or outlooks which culminate in "absolute knowledge."[8]

The opposition between form and content is first expressed as the incongruity between the clear, rational concept (*Begriff*) and the confused images, metaphors, and so on which purport to express it. A second incongruity is between the *absolute* essence of religion in general and the limited form in which each historical religion expresses it. What limits these religions is not only the confused and partial manner in which they present their content, but also their dialectical *falsification* of it. The content appears as its own distortion, an "other" which frustrates the essence instead of helping to actualize it.

Herein lies another important distinction, between externalization and self-alienation. Externalization is a necessary moment of the dialectic; every essence must manifest itself in the empirical or historical world as a precondition of being actualized. But this externalization can be either adequate or inadequate; it can either promote the actualization of the essence or impede and distort it. The latter is a case of self-alienation, as distinct from simple externalization. (This will be pertinent to Judaism.)

Hegel stresses that the concept of religion must externalize itself in empirical history. The Berlin lectures (the text we shall henceforth be using) puts this idea in strong terms: "What is *necessary* through the concept must have *existed*, and the religions, as they have followed one another, have not arisen in a contingent manner. . . . It is not a work of chance. . . . When we consider the sequence of the determinate religions under the guidance of the concept . . . the sequence of the historical religions emerges for us from it."[9]

Because the essential moments of religion are said to be present, however partially, in all its finite configurations, it follows that every religion has *some* rational justification within its own time and historical form. No religion can be dismissed as the direct opposite of reason; rather, says Hegel, "we must do them this justice [of recognizing their basic rationality], for what is human and rational in them is also our own, although it is in our higher consciousness as only a moment." He goes on to say that we must be reconciled even to what is horrible and insipid in previous religions, not because we accept it as the rational in itself, but (presumably) because it is the contingent aspect of a process that we recognize as *essentially* rational. In this sense, the philosophy of religion is at least a weak kind of theodicy.[10]

Secondly, it follows that a religion's rank on the historical scale depends on how aware (and demystified) it is of God's true nature, of his relation to man, and of its own role as a religion. "The rank of the religious spirit," says Hegel, "is higher or lower, richer or poorer to the extent that such knowledge exists [in it]."[11]

Elsewhere in the lectures Hegel declares that "the image man has of God corresponds to the image he has of himself, of his freedom." Accordingly, two questions determine the measure of truth in a given religion: "(1) How God is known to man, how He is determined; (2) how the subject is thereby known to himself."[12]

Thus, the religions of nature picture God as a finite object; in Judaism God is pictured as infinite spirit, infinitely remote from man; and in Christianity God is infinite spirit residing within the finite world and man. Judaism stresses God's spirituality but immediately distorts it by interpreting it as "sublime"; Christianity, on the contrary, stresses the mutual mediation between man and God, a principle which Catholicism again distorts and only Lutheranism starts to realize.[13]

When, in the quote above, Hegel says "*our* own" religion, the underlying "we" can be understood as "we philosophers" and also as "we Lutherans." Speaking to his students as a Lutheran to other Lutherans, Hegel insists that their "consummate" religion does not rigidly oppose other religions. When dealing with another religion, Lutherans are not dealing with something utterly alien, as they may at first think, but with something of their own. This recognition makes it possible to reconcile one's own "true religion" with the "false religions" of others, and thus provides a theoretical basis for tolerance in the Hegelian system – a patronizing, hierarchical tolerance to be sure, but tolerance all the same.

Natural religion

By his nature, God is spirit; yet the religion of nature conceives him as object, a tremendous substance (rather than subject). God does not appear as actual spirit, but as spirit's externalization: that is, as nature. In Eastern religions – Chinese, Hindu, Persian, Egyptian – nature is not, however, the profane, "prosaic" object it has become in the West, but a hallowed object, emanating a sacred property. The veneration of substances like light or the sun indicates that they are not seen as neutral objects of observation or action. The "prosaic" Western attitude requires, according to Hegel, a *higher* degree of development (which Judaism made possible).

Also, the flaw in the religion of nature is not yet alienation, but one-sided externalization. Alienation becomes possible only in a relatively high religion, which already contains the principles of freedom and rational purpose, and whose God appears as subject or person; for only then can God's intended role contradict the role he actually plays in that religion.

The higher phase is called "the religion of spiritual individuality,"[14] and is further divided into the religions of sublimity (Judaism), beauty (Greek religion), and expediency (Roman religion). We shall focus on Judaism, using first the more complete lecture materials of 1821 and 1824, and then those of 1827.

Sublimity as false self-consciousness

As in the *Lectures on Aesthetics*, it might at first appear that "sublimity" indicates some admirable feature of Judaism; but that is not the case. Hegel does not say that the Jewish religion is sublime; he says only that it is the religion *of* sublimity: namely, it pictures God as sublime and man as his opposite. God is an infinite power which subdues and overwhelms man, and in front of whom man experiences himself as meek and despicable. Yet, as Hegel hints, we philosophers know that this self-humiliation is inappropriate. The opposition between an insignificant man and an overpowering God is not the truth of the matter but a deficient idea shaped by the human mind – in this case, by the Jewish mind. Therefore Judaism is a form of false self-consciousness, representing man's alienation from himself and his true essence.

The new point in the Berlin lectures is that alienation is made possible not only by Judaism's negative features, but primarily because of the *progress* Judaism brings forth. Only because it perceives God as spirit, and no longer as natural object, can Judaism produce alienation, for it presents its new principle in opposition to its essence.

The meaning of sublimity: alienation, fear, and servitude

Hegel presents Judaism as the first *Aufhebung* of natural religion. We already know what that means. The absolute is seen as subject, spirit;

the seeds of freedom and meaningful purpose make their first appearance in religion; and the ground is laid for a *potential* reconciliation of the finite particular and the infinite universal. As long as the absolute is a natural object which man faces from without, humans cannot rediscover their own selves, interests, and spirit in the supreme principle of reality, and their only salvation consists in being sunk within the overpowering "One."[15]

A philosophy of substance, therefore, does not allow the individual to be truly free. Freedom entails the individual's ability to rediscover his or her spirit and true essence embodied in the outer world – in the customs and institutions of the society through which the individual reconstitutes him- or herself as an actual, free person.

This analysis of freedom requires a dynamic, subject-like totality.[16] Substance is a false totality, because it submerges the individual instead of rebuilding him or her. By contrast, Hegel's system understands the absolute as subject too. This, says a famous aphorism, is the distinctive outlook of modernity and the most important turn in his philosophy.[17] And since a similar turn had been effected, historically, by ancient Judaism, *it follows that the mature Hegel draws an implicit parallel between Judaism's historical role and the most important turn in his own philosophy.* The Jewish revolution did not announce Christianity only, but also the fundamental principle of the Hegelian system. We have gone a long way indeed since the youthful essays!

The image of Judaism that evolves from here is nevertheless very negative. The Jews have made alienation possible, because when God is conceived as spirit, we may expect to see ourselves reflected in him. Yet Judaism frustrates this expectation. The Jews introduced a revolutionary principle – spirit, freedom, purpose – but falsified it from the start. There was no process of degeneration here, as when an idea is first announced and then distorted; rather, the Jewish idea was introduced from the outset as its own falsification. This can be seen from several viewpoints.

Although in natural religion the Absolute appears as externalized (as object), it is not yet alienated. Only when God is conceived as spiritual can we, in principle, recognize our human image and our various goals and meanings as being either reflected or distorted within the (meaning of the) totality. A subject is, among other things, a purposive activity; it sets goals for itself and assigns some teleological significance to things around it. Therefore, whoever demands a rediscovery of his or her goals and spirit in the objective course of the world – and whoever worries about the purpose of the world itself and the way it goes – tacitly presupposes the subjectivation of the absolute. If the absolute had been a blind natural object, we would be asking in vain – that is, senselessly – about its goal or complaining that no such goal can be found. We shall then have to agree with Spinoza and Nietzsche that the whole problem of teleology originates in the self-delusion of a person who projects his or her own wishes and modes of thinking upon an indifferent world. But if the absolute is a spiritual entity, we may wonder about its own *inherent* purpose, complain about its apparent conflict with our human goals, and work toward the dialectical reconciliation of that conflict.

The conflict is particularly apparent in Judaism, where God is viewed as a person, but no use is made of the dialectical notion of subject. God is a separate person residing beyond the world and ruling it from without. He is an "abstract" universal, which does not depend on the particular in order to be what it is and contains nothing that can explain the particular's existence; if a particular entity exists, this is mere chance, a contingent fact which should be attributed to God's grace or arbitrary will. The contingency of all being is expressed by the image of the world's creation, which the Jews must imagine as merely an act of grace.[18]

The same pattern characterizes the individual's relation to God. Because God's spirituality is not mediated by the *human* spirit, God and man stand in unilateral dependence and are separated by an insuperable gap. No reconciliation between the finite and the infinite is possible. In experiencing God as sublime, I stand before him in fear and trembling, servility and self-effacement. God's power transcends my grasp and is therefore terrifying, overwhelming, and inscrutably remote.

Wisdom and purpose

Sublimity is further analyzed in terms of wisdom and purpose. Only with respect to a God who can think and set goals can one inquire about the purpose of human life, of particular events in history, and of creation in general. But in Judaism, because of God's infinite distance, an insuperable abyss separates his wisdom from human goals and interests. A contingent world which depends totally on God's grace cannot, of course, have an *immanent* purpose exclusively. The Jews are therefore forced to see the world as existing exclusively for *God*'s purpose – which must remain inscrutable to the human mind. Indeed, says Hegel, in Judaism the only purpose that creation can have is to worship God, aggrandize his name, and fulfill his wishes in every detail.

Equipped with his new concept of sublimity, Hegel now returns to the Jewish legalism he denounced in his youth. Just as God's aims are inscrutable, so his commands are arbitrary. The Jews are condemned by God's sublimity to look in vain for a reflection of their own goals and concerns in the laws they are required to obey. The Jew's private interests are arrogated in favour of alien goals which must appear meaningless to him.

Thus again, Judaism introduces a master–slave relation into religion. A God conceived as a thing cannot be a master; a master–slave relation requires two subjects or consciousnesses. It exists only where there is a possibility of freedom too. But God's appearance as a person – infinite and tremendous, as in Judaism – makes him a master and the human being his slave. Herein lies the dialectic of the Jewish God: he emerges as a principle of liberation which immediately becomes an oppressor.

Slavery is compounded by fear. In the first place this is metaphysical fear and trembling before a tremendous object which shatters the bounds of our comprehension. With psychological finesse Hegel explains that this is fear not of some *finite* violent force but of the unseen, the absolutely other "standing infinitely in-itself against me as undetermined, infinite power."[19] This brings to mind the famous distinction (also made by Kant, Kierkegaard, Heidegger, Rudolph Otto, and others) between a definite utilitarian fear and an indefinite ontological dread. In the second place, the Jews also conceive of the transcendent God as intervening in the affairs of the world and as a master ruling over his slaves. As such, God evokes not only awe, but ordinary, terrestrial fear, the kind which arises, says Hegel, when I imagine myself losing property, or my interests being damaged, or something being ripped from me. Because of this fear, the Jew's relation to God consists mainly in obedience.

In both respects, fear is the most characteristic trait of Judaism. It even becomes a religious duty. Hegel writes in his notes for the 1821 lectures: "The overall command in Judaism is fear before the absolute master"; I have the duty to "see myself as nothing, to know myself as absolutely dependent: A slavish consciousness before the master."[20] In this quote Hegel deliberately confuses the two kinds of fear.

Again we see the dialectical paradox in Judaism. Only when the absolute is conceived as spirit can human beings rediscover themselves in God; but just when Judaism makes this possible, it (immediately) also makes it impossible, and man ends up as God's slave. While man bows to God's sovereign and independent status, God does not recognize human freedom. All men and women are bound by a web of arbitrary commands to which they owe blind obedience but in which they can perceive neither reason nor freedom.

Another negative emotion affecting the Jews is their hatred toward other nations – that *odium generis humani* which has been attributed to them since Tacitus.[21] The Jews' hatred of other nations stems from their notion of the Chosen People which Hegel criticizes on several counts. First, it is contradictory, because the universal (God) is said to be manifest only in a particular nation, which indicates that no true totality has been achieved. Second, the Jews became God's people through a contract which subjected them to fear and submission as the price of their election: "God gives *himself* a people on condition that it fear God," Hegel's notes read; fear is "the basic feeling of its dependence, namely its serfdom."[22]

I have mentioned already that the Jewish God, by becoming a person, acquired special interests and entered the material world – hence his image as a demanding, vindictive master who runs the affairs of the world and hands out punishments and rewards. Also, because God is absolute master, there is no room for authentic *property* in Judaism. Everything belongs to God; the slave has nothing of his own, not even his own body. Hegel distinguishes between genuine property (*Eigentum*) and mere holding of property (*Besitz*). Property expresses recognition of the owner's freedom and person,[23] whereas *Besitz* ("holding") is contingent, something at my disposal which I merely occupy, but which does not express recognition of my person. This is how land is held in Judaism, where its true owner, as the laws of *shemita* and jubilee make clear, is God. Hegel reverts here to his youthful essays. The law which frees Jewish slaves every seventh year – a social achievement in the eyes of many – proves to Hegel, on the contrary, that the Jew was God's absolute property and had *no* independent personality.

As proprietor, God provides food and shelter for his slaves; indeed, it is he, not the human laborer, who grows the grain and draws bread from earth. This alienates the Jew from nature even further. Not only is the land not his property, even the land's cultivation is not his real and direct doing but requires the owner's grace and support. Hegel's notes read: "[Jewish] man is unable to relate to nature as something at his service according to his will; he cannot approach it directly and take what he wants, but must get it through an *alien mediator*. Everything is in the master's hands and from him everything must be acquired."[24]

The Jew's relations with God assume an earthly, commercial character. All reward is promised the Jews in *this* life, because they do not recognize the immortality of the soul. "There is no demand for the soul; the slave [demands] only the temporal, only temporal advantages," Hegel's notes read.[25] Punishments too are only terrestrial, expressed in the terrible curses in the Torah: "this people has become an artist in the field of curses."[26]

Judaism unpolitical?

Much of this criticism recalls the biased voice of the young Hegel. So does his renewed discussion, in Berlin, of Judaism and politics. Hegel now accuses Judaism of being both theocratic and nonpolitical at the same time. The argument goes as follows. Judaism is a tribal religion based on the family, not on a truly universal union; therefore it lacks a genuine political character. On the other hand, the Jews were ruled by "theonomical" laws, meaning that God is also the terrestrial ruler; yet this is an inauthentic political form. As a result, Judaism has no genuine, but only a distorted political character. Moses, we hear again, differs from Solon and Lycurgus in that the Greek statesmen were human legislators, whereas Moses merely announced Yahve's laws to the people.[27]

This reiterates almost verbatim what the young Hegel had written a quarter of a century earlier. Jewish "legalism" is returned to center stage and is whipped like an old scarecrow. Almost no mention is made of the fact that Hegel has meanwhile recognized an inner feeling and an exalted poetry in Judaism. Job is quoted here, but only to stress the end of the story, where God overwhelms the individual's consciousness without really satisfying it. In a semblance of systematization, Hegel now "deduces" Jewish legalism as the necessary consequence of sublimity and links it with the other negative features described in his early essays.

This again raises the query: How could Hegel despise the developed legal system of the Jews while admiring the Greek *polis* precisely for its system of laws and customs?

Hegel's personal bias provides only part of the answer. Objectively, there is in his philosophy a basis for distinguishing between mere legality and genuine right (*Recht*). The latter term designates a rightful law, which implies recognition of citizens' status and applies to them universally; it is also supposed to express the people's own spirit and will (even if unconsciously, as in the Greek *polis*), rather than an alien will or that of an arbitrary ruler. Without those features there is no genuine right, only an oppressive law ("legalism") which becomes more despotic the more densely it covers the different areas of life.[28]

The distinction between legality and right, and between *Recht* and mere *Gesetz*, thus has a real anchor in Hegel's system. Yet, the exaggerated way it is applied to Judaism, and Hegel's steadfast image of the law of Moses as the paradigm of an oppressive legalism, goes beyond what the system warrants and echoes a long Protestant anti-Jewish tradition which stretches from Luther to Kant to the young Hegel himself in his Enlightenment/Kantian years.

Anti-Jewish bias in systematic cloak?

Many Jews were offended by Hegel's position and saw it as anti-Semitic; and many anti-Semites believed that they could turn to Hegel for support. Yet Jews, because of their historical experience, are often over-sensitive to criticism; and anti-Semites, because of their blinding passion, are over-anxious to find allies where they do not exist. Hegel's views were not unequivocal, and have undergone several shifts. What can we say of his position as seen in the first Berlin lectures (which are, as I have mentioned, the most complete and representative text on Judaism by the mature Hegel)?

Generally speaking, Hegel has overcome the principal bias of his youth. Judaism now stands at a revolutionary point in history and plays a decisive role in the genesis of Spirit and absolute truth. Although many anti-Jewish demons still cast their shadows over the Hegelian text, on the *cardinal* issue – in what counts most – the Berlin lectures recognize Judaism's essential contribution and, thereby, do dialectical justice to it.[29]

On the other hand, Judaism appears immediately as falsifying its own principle. There is not even a process of decline involved here; Judaism is the alienation of its own message *from the very start*. Does this not prove that, perhaps unwittingly, Hegel is still attached to his former bias and the anti-Jewish feelings of his youth?

Not necessarily, an advocate might answer; for this is the case with *any* inquiry in Hegel. In every partial historical position, the dialectic *requires* that we discover not only the positive elements but the negative too, the defects which undermine that position from within. Also, as long as the historical climax has not been reached, every new idea, every revolutionary principle, will appear as the opposition between its content and its form, and therefore, in a sense, as its own distortion. Judaism is no exception.

Still, a counter-argument will claim, Judaism receives a *particularly* negative treatment, both in the tone of writing and in many relevant details. Otto Pöggeler, an expert on Hegel's text and tonality, testifies to that. Though he tends to stress the places where Hegel seems to favor the Jews, Pöggeler says of the Berlin lectures: "The new and broader ideas on Judaism which Hegel arrived at during the Berlin period did not involve any surrender of the crudely critical positions which he had worked out while at Frankfurt."[30] Liebeschütz and Rotenstreich, too, though with different emphases, point to the continuity between the young and the older Hegel on these issues.[31] A more extreme view is stated by Joachim Schöps: Hegel's mature position is no different from his youthful comparison of the Jews with Macbeth.[32]

This last is a gross exaggeration. Yet Pöggeler's words must be taken seriously, and his illustrations can be complemented by others. For example, we have seen that the fear which characterizes Judaism is not primarily metaphysical dread but a material concern. The Jew is afraid for his life and his property; he prefers life over values and thereby becomes the slavish servant of God and his proxies. Moreover, the Jews suffer from the defects of both the slave and the master. Like the slave, they prefer material existence to higher values and live in fear and servitude; and like the master, they are severed from nature and face a historical dead end. While the slave has a direct interaction with nature (through work), which eventually allows him to overcome his state and redeem himself (and his master too), the Jews are both slavish of mind *and* alienated from nature, without the perspective of redemption which the *Phenomenology* attributes the slave.

In this respect Hegel, even in Berlin, continues to see the Jews as facing a blocked horizon – as cast outside history and condemned to everlasting alienation – just as he had seen them in the passing remark I quoted from the *Phenomenology*, which now turns out to express an enduring, deep-seated pattern in Hegel's thinking about the Jews. If Judaism has a unique peculiarity, it is precisely this *non-*historical existence to which it condemned itself (in antiquity), after Jesus and the destruction of the Temple – when it became a historical miscarriage, merely persisting, and stuck without issue before the gates of salvation.

What is significant in these examples is not the sheer endurance of anti-Jewish bias in Hegel's mind, but *which* prejudices have persisted in particular. Here we observe a remarkable fact. Almost all the negative features of Judaism are said to originate in fear and servitude, the two classic factors upon which the Enlightenment critique of religion is based, and which go far back in time to Epicurus. This is a telling fact. Although Hegel had long ago rejected the Enlightenment critique of religion, he continues to use it himself, perhaps unwittingly, with respect to one particular religion – Judaism. It looks as though he clusters into Judaism all the basic ills and defects which rationalist critics have imputed to the religious phenomenon *in general* – fear, alienation, domination, irrationality, heteronomy, and the rest. Judaism is singled out as the self-alienated religion *par excellence*. Singular among the historical religions, Judaism is made the target of the same blows which religion *as such* has been dealt throughout the ages by its rationalist opponents. Thus, despite the dialectical context of the Berlin lectures, Judaism is made to bear the ills which religion in general used to have in the eyes of the radical Enlightenment, including the younger Hegel himself. While Hegel no longer holds these views of religion in general, he reserves them for the *particular* case of Judaism.

This is the *specific* way in which Hegel's old prejudices are assimilated into the deep structure of his mature system – assimilated, but not eliminated. To the contrary, they reemerge from it with unmistakable clarity.

CHAPTER SIX

Hegel and the Jews:
A Never-Ending Story

The 1827 lectures

The next stage in our story begins in 1827 and continues through
Hegel's death in 1831. In both these years Hegel lectured again on
the philosophy of religion, and his view of Judaism became more
moderate. Most of the hostile tone disappeared, and the criticism was
voiced in a restrained manner. The 1827 lectures resemble the *Lectures on the Philosophy of History* in their tone and the *Lectures on Aesthetics* in their content. A noteworthy change is that Judaism is now
higher than Greek religion. Actually, this should have been the order
from the start, since Jewish monotheism is higher than Greek paganism from Hegel's own, Christian standpoint; but only now has Hegel
drawn the necessary conclusion.[1]

The 1827 lectures focus on the Jewish God's image as creator. The
Aesthetics has taught us what this means. The finite world is cast outside the deity, loses its divinity and becomes contingent (or as Hegel
says now "prosaic" and "profane"), an aggregate of mere finite
things.[2] Hegel warns against confusing the Jewish idea of creation
with emanation or the continuous derivation of the world from God,
in which the deity itself flows into the world; creation indicates a
break between God and world (p. 360). The world becomes God's
absolute Other; it does not retain the divine substance, but is torn
from it and thrown into a finite, dependent, profane reality.

This break is also the meaning of sublimity. Hegel now distinguishes between "holiness" and "sublimity" (p. 365). Holiness characterizes God as he is in himself, regardless of the world; whereas sublimity characterizes God as creator of a contingent universe devoid of any divinity. Sublimity is *defined* in terms of creation: it is the absolute dependence of the contingent world on the one infinite subject. For this reason Judaism conceives of God not as result but as absolute beginning (p. 361), which means that the Jewish God is not a true subject. A true subject (remembering the *Phenomenology*) exists as the result of its own becoming and its mutual dependence upon its "other"; but the Jewish God is infinite in himself before there is a finite world in separation from him.

Goodness and justice, wisdom and reward

Nature's unilateral dependence on God is now also conceived in terms of goodness and justice. These metaphors call for cautious interpretation. The Jewish God's goodness is nothing but his very creation: namely, his allowing finite things to go their own way, separate themselves from him, and constitute finite nature. And divine justice resides in the nullity or "ideality" of the finite world, the fact that it has no true independence (p. 363). (This seems to entail the idea of providence: God constrains the world even after its creation.) Another of God's aspects is wisdom, but in Judaism this is not internal wisdom guiding things from the inside, but a legalistic system of alien decrees which God has imposed on the world externally (pp. 359–60). Hegel thus reiterates one of the most negative motifs of his 1824 lectures: deducing Jewish legalism from God's very concept. But now he treats the flaws of Judaism in a restrained language, without sting or drama.

Reward and punishment are another Jewish principle stressed here. Judaism demands that the course of the world conform to the laws of morality – for example, that it grants reward to those worthy of it – and sees God as responsible for this happening.[3] The belief in a moral world order is essentially Jewish, says Hegel. Fate in Judaism is not blind, as in Hellenism, but purposeful, guided by the link between power and wisdom, between reward and punishment.

The call for justice turns the human being's eye inward, to examine if the will is good and the soul prepared for the good (p. 370). This leads Hegel to note again (as in the *Aesthetics*) the existence in Judaism of an inner world, revealed in the Psalms and the prophetic preaching. (He may have had in mind such sayings as "For I desired mercy, and not sacrifice," Hos. 6:6.) The book of Job now gets a new reading: no longer in terms of submission to God's overwhelming power, but of faith and confidence in his justice. Confidence in God is "a fundamental feature of the Jewish people" and "indeed constitutes one of their remarkable features" (p. 369)

He then makes an unusual point: The fallacy of appropriating the universal God as their own special god is not only Jewish but Christian too. Christianity perceives itself as one human family ("Christendom") and the one God as their family deity! Hegel's barb is aimed especially at Catholics ("catholic" means universal), but, ironically, suits Hegel himself (see Concluding Remarks).

Absent from the new text are the negative Enlightenment characterizations – fear, servility, alienation, master–slave, and so on. Whether the omission was deliberate, or whether it is just that our text is fragmented, is hard to know.[4] In any case the hostile tone is gone, and the older anti-Jewish feelings are restrained, though not actually overcome. This is also Hegel's last word on the matter – last but not conclusive, for Hegel's life was abruptly cut short at the age of 61, and one cannot interpret the last shift of a pendulum as if it summarized a whole lifetime.[5]

Maimonides as a Jewish answer to Hegel

What did Hegel know of Judaism? Not much is the answer. As a Protestant he drew mostly on the Old Testament, supplemented by Flavius Josephus. He was unfamiliar with talmudic and rabbinical sources, and his knowledge of Hebrew was rudimentary. Of Jewish philosophers he knew well only Mendelssohn and Spinoza; of the other sources he mentions – Philo, Maimonides, and the Cabbalah – he seems to have learned from secondary sources. This adds up to a fragmentary, flawed, and limited knowledge of historical Judaism.

It is therefore surprising that Hegel could find support for his view of Judaism as the religion of sublimity in Moses Maimonides, one of the greatest Jewish thinkers. To Maimonides, true religion must indeed assume an infinite distance between God and man, and view all mediation between them as the work of the imagination. Yet, what Maimonides considers to be the purity of Judaism, its religious advantage, Hegel sees as its defect.

Though Hegel mentions Maimonides on several occasions in his lectures,[6] he does not notice how close they are on two issues: the nature of Judaism and the nature of religious language. Maimonides saw philosophical truth as being transformed into lower forms of discourse – metaphor, allegory, story-telling, and so on – that are suited to different audiences' level of comprehension; Hegel held a similar view, albeit set in a post-Kantian and historicized context. As for Judaism, Hegel and the greatest Jewish rabbi shared its basic phenomenological description but differed on its evaluation.

We may therefore see Maimonides' position as a Jewish response to Hegel.[7] A religion of sublimity, Maimonides would say, is the purest and most authentic way to live a religious life, provided that we strictly deny God all earthly, human-like features and avoid all compromise. From a philosophical standpoint, viewing God as a person is an error of the imagination, and from a religious standpoint it is idolatry.[8]

God is absolutely different from all things human and earthly. Indeed, he is so distant as to be incommensurable with anything in our world. If the human mind – or Christian theology – cannot bear that hiatus, this is no reason for allowing the imagination to abolish it. True religion is a hard experience, which no false consolation should soften. The authentic religious way preserves the purity of the experience of transcendence through the distant and awesome image of God it entails. Even the love of God – which counterbalances the metaphysical awe – preserves the distance between man and God. Christianity tried to bridge that hiatus by presenting God as a suffering, agonizing man; but thereby it transformed a human need into a theological principle and ended with an illusion. More precisely, it ended (in Maimonides' view) in a false consolation, a philosophical error, an impure religious experience, and actually in idolatry.

Maimonides, like Spinoza (and later Nietzsche), demands a complete purgation of the human image from the world. This may be very hard for the ordinary human mind; but true religion, Maimonides would say, is indeed a hard matter; and Spinoza would add that "Every excellent thing is as hard, as it is rare."[9] Hegel wished to reconcile the human and the divine through God's incarnation and actualization in human history; yet this is a compromise, a deference to human frailty raised to the level of a philosophical first principle.

Maimonides doubtless recognizes that his view is normative. It concerns Judaism as it *ought to be*, even though ordinary people and the "rabbinical multitude" (the common religious leaders) do not live up to it. Therefore he must distinguish between pure and popular religion. In pure religion, sublimity (as Hegel aptly called it) is expressed in awe before God; the true purpose of religious commands is that they be performed *for their own sake*. The commands concretize (or "schematize") the metaphysical awe which derives from God's absolutely transcendent nature. Although the commands also have a utilitarian practical value, which Maimonides spells out in detail, that value is secondary. And, even the utilitarian value of the commands works as a *self*-rewarding device (for example, is derived from the commands' own hygienic or educational consequences) rather than being granted as a special act of reward or punishment by a feared master.

Thus Maimonides denies the master–slave relation and the materialistic legalism which Hegel "deduced" from sublimity. Moreover, because Judaism demands the performance of commandments for their own sake, the intention, the inner heart, is as crucial in Judaism as it is in Kantian ethics. The love which the Jew owes his God is a subjective, interior factor, which religious cult exteriorizes. It is certainly hard to love a formless entity which breaks the confines of the imagination, so Jews too pray to a personal, human-like God. In this respect, popular religion has the upper hand in both religions. However, Christianity legitimizes this frailty and elevates it to a religious principle, whereas Judaism denounces it.[10]

In Part II we shall see a surprising resemblance between Maimonides (and Spinoza) and Nietzsche, who also wanted to banish the falsely consoling "shadows of God" from the world. For Nietzsche, the "death of God" is primarily the death of the *Christian* God – the personal, comforting "God of the weak." Similarly the mental power necessary for Nietzsche's *amor fati* is also required by Maimonides and Spinoza in order to cope with a dehumanized universe.

Maimonides' view, probably because it goes against the grain of popular religion, did not become dominant in Judaism. But accepting it as a normative ideal, we notice a profound, unbridgeable opposition between the Hegelian and the Jewish view of religion, an opposition which cannot be attributed to Hegel's mistakes and stereotypes of the Jews. Beyond those mistakes, a true gap separates them.

Philo and the Cabbalah

Hegel discusses two other Jewish sources in *Lectures on the History of Philosophy*. One is "Philo the Jew," to whom Hegel was attracted because he was a contemporary of Jesus (living "a little before and a little after him") and the first to blend together Judaism and Hellenism. Thereby Philo set a paradigm to many subsequent followers, including Hegel.

With Philo, "for the first time we see the application of the universal [religious] consciousness."[11] Philo "finds Plato present in Moses." He uses mystical and allegorical interpretations to extract philosophical ideas from the history of the Jews, even when no empirical support is available. Hegel does not mean this negatively. Philo discovered a profound truth: that philosophy has a subterranean presence in Holy Scripture, even though the authors may not have intended it. Such is the nature of the religious texts, says Hegel, that usually there is a great difference "between that which is present [or contained] therein (*darin liegt*) and that which is expressed" (vol. 2, p. 388, my emphasis). Though technically the interpretation comes from outside, essentially its origin lies within the text itself. Hegel, as we know, also extracts philosophical concepts from religious images, not only from the Bible but from diverse other expressions of the religious phenomenon; in this respect the *Lectures on the Philosophy of Religion* may count as a much-extended realization of Philo's (and also of Maimonides') project.

Philo leads to the Gnostics in Christianity and to the Cabbalists in Judaism. Hegel places the origin of Cabbalah around the time of the destruction of the Second Temple and the Bar-Kokhba revolt.[12] He drew his knowledge of the Cabbalah mainly from Christian sources, but also from the book *The Gates of Heaven* by the ex-Marrano Abraham Cohen Herrera, which various German scholars used as a source.[13] Hegel says that the Cabbalah led to a revolution in post-biblical Judaism, by first introducing into it the notions of Hell, the Fall, the Last Judgment, and the sin inherent in the flesh. Thereby Judaism rose above its original crude earthiness and became more spiritual. It is noteworthy that all these novelties are genuinely Christian – so according to Hegel it is Christianity's impact which made Judaism spiritual! It is only now that "the Jews began to carry their thoughts beyond their [earthly] reality; only now does a world of spirit, or at least of spirits, begin to open up before them; before this the Jews cared only for themselves, being sunk in the filth and self-conceit of their present existence, and in the maintenance of their nation and kin [*Geschlecht*; I changed the translation of this word]" (vol. 2, pp. 395–6).

These words may first have been written in the Jena period, and indeed are reminiscent of Hegel's harsh style of the time.[14] They also contain a characteristic Hegelian dialectic. It is the crudest supernatural element, the Cabbalah's magical preoccupation with spirits, that marks the beginning of Judaism's spiritual refinement. In any case, although the historical basis of Hegel's remarks about the Cabbalah is greatly flawed, his text proves that the next-world aspect of Judaism has been known to him from early on, even though he ignores it in most of his other works.

Hegel and Jewish emancipation

I mentioned above that Hegel had little interest in (and scant knowledge of) post-biblical Judaism. Therefore he, the philosopher of history, was cut off from the real history of the Jews. True, for him it was merely a continuous existence and no history at all; but this theological abstraction only distanced Hegel still further from the actual phenomenon of Judaism. After all, Hegel knew perfectly well that the Jews continued not only to exist but to *change* – they stood in reciprocal relations with their environment, with the changing times – and in *this* respect they certainly had a history, even if Hegel considered it to be contingent and "merely empirical."

Following that history, the Jews entered the modern world of which Hegel saw himself the announcer and interpreter, and claimed their rights within it. Thereby they presented Hegel and his contemporaries with the concrete question of how to respond to the Jewish call for emancipation.

This is a better test of anti-Semitism than any theoretical speculation. Not every critic of ancient Judaism, however fierce, is necessarily anti-Semitic; the crucial question is whether he or she uses this critique as a weapon against contemporary Jews, sees the Jews as enemies, feels threatened by them, works out historical reasons to make them hated, to hurt them, and to negate their rights in the present. None of this is true of Hegel. Nor is his sharp style a credible proof of anti-Semitism. We have seen that eminent philo-Semites expressed aversion to the Jews and wished to "cure" them through emancipation. Hegel wrote from within the Christian tradition, which, with rare exceptions, was harsh on Jews as a matter of course. He too referred to their religion in haughty, negative language, but his position on their emancipation was distinctly positive. Unlike many other German intellectuals, Hegel favoured political equality for the Jews. Moreover, he supported their *social* integration and equal opportunities for them, a significant demand given that in

Hegel's system, the state is sustained by intermediary social factors.

The story of Hegel and Jewish emancipation has two moments – practical and theoretical.

The practical moment

In the second decade of the nineteenth century Hegel was indirectly involved with the new student movement known as the *Burschenschaft*. Prior to that time students used to be organized in groups named after their land of origin – "Prussia," "Schwabia," "Saxonia," and so on. These older groups, known collectively as *Landmannschaften*, were basically unpolitical and served to promote a free, somewhat wild student life. With the rise of German nationalism after the wars against Napoleon, the students started organizing in a new, politicized association meant to express the more earnest spirit required by the patriotic tide of the time. They demanded a constitution and a united Germany. At first they set up student fraternities (*Burschenschaften*) on a local basis and later established an all-German union.

As might be expected in a nationalist movement, the *Burschenschaft* was marked by much xenophobia and anti-Semitism. Many students demanded the abolition of the political rights which the Jews started gaining in Germany (i.e., the Rheinland) after Napoleon's conquests. These were the days in which the new anti-Semitism, of the secular, nationalistic brand, grew in virulence, being evident also among first-rate philosophers like Fichte, who opposed Jewish emancipation, and lesser-known philosophers like Fries, Hegel's enemy. While nationalist students hailed *Deutschtum* ("Germanness"), Hegel, changing two letters, dubbed their zealots *DeutschDUMM* (German idiots, or, literally, Germanly stupid).

While the majority of students were hostile to Jewish membership in the *Burschenschaft*, a minority argued that the fraternity ought to be universal and reflect all social ingredients, including the Jews. The minority view was rejected in all German universities except one, Heidelberg, where a fierce struggle to admit Jews was finally successful. The struggle was going on during Hegel's short stay in Heidelberg and while he was lecturing on the philosophy of right. The student who promoted and pushed the resolution was one Friedrich Wilhelm Carové, a close pupil of Hegel and one of his first devotees.[15]

Having succeeded in Heidelberg, Carové and his friend Kobbe

tried, but failed, to pass a similar resolution in the all-German union. In all these struggles Carové needed the support and legitimization of his revered master, Hegel.

Carové's chief opponent, a student named Asverus, complained that "all of his wisdom is copied from Hegel," adding: "No Hegel will drive *me* crazy with his philosophy."[16] This crude indication of the tight bond between Hegel and Carové is also indicated by the following anecdote (cited by Kuno Fischer[17]). The French philosopher Victor Cousin traveled to Germany to learn of new ideas there. In Heidelberg he met the French-speaking Carové and volunteered to be his guide. The two were seen walking in the castle gardens and along the "philosophers' path" (which still exists today), with Carové carrying Hegel's recently published *Encyclopedia of the Philosophical Sciences*. However (so the story goes), despite their long talks, Cousin felt that he did not understand Hegel's meaning and suspected that Carové did not understand much either; so they went to see the master himself, after which the Frenchman left for Munich to meet Schelling and Jacobi.

This story must be read with caution.[18] Hegel's dense *Encyclopedia* is indeed hard to understand without help, or to expound in a foreign language. But Hegel did not think that Carové did not understand him, for a year later he tried to take him to Berlin as his assistant (but failed). There is no doubt that Carové understood Hegel's position on what concerns *our* topic (since he argued for it in the *Burschenschaft* meetings). Modern times must be governed by universal reason, embodied in diverse historical forms, and the Jews were entitled to political emancipation and social acceptance. As we shall see in the next section, this vein is explicitly stated in Hegel's "remarks" on the *Philosophy of Right* which were made orally.

Hegel knew the difficulties which the Jewish question presented for the students. The *Burschenschaft* was a major symbol of the German nation. Admitting Jews to it meant admitting that Jews were part of the German nation and were worthy to fight for its unity. From a social perspective too, membership in the fraternity signified a certain class and belonging, which could enhance the Jews' acceptance and personal careers. Jews at that time were not admitted to the legal profession and were barred from public offices, including university professorships. A few years later, some of Hegel's Jewish students, like Gans and the poet Heine, had to convert to Christianity in order to "buy an entry ticket to society."[19]

Under these conditions, the Heidelberg resolution, which Carové achieved with Hegel's support, was a significant feat. And given the master's influence on his pupil, we may say that Hegel was not merely giving Carové advice but performing a political act himself. At stake, moreover, were not formal rights only, but the Jews' *social* acceptance, their eligibility to claim German identity and enter *civil society*. This seems to indicate that Hegel favored Jewish emancipation not merely in terms of an abstract theory of rights, but was ready to admit Jews into the domain of *Sittlichkeit* and the concrete community.

The theoretical moment

Jewish rights are mentioned twice in Hegel's *Philosophy of Right*. In section 209, Remark, he says:

> It is part of education . . . that the ego comes to be apprehended as a universal person in which all are identical. A man counts as a man in virtue of his manhood alone, not because he is a Jew, Catholic, Protestant German, Italian, etc. This is an assertion which thinking ratifies and to be conscious of it is of infinite importance. It is defective only when it is crystallized, e.g. as a cosmopolitanism in opposition to the concrete life of the state.[20]

This quote presupposes a "universal subject," which exists only through individual subjects and their equal political status. Thus the Enlightenment view is preserved within the dialectical system. The only qualification is Hegel's rejection of "cosmopolitanism" and his demand that each state have some special character. A person must be universalized through the *specific* character of his or her actual state. Yet a person's rights do not derive from that special character, but from the universality embodied in his or her humanity.

  Later on, in a long addition to paragraph 270, Hegel discusses *toleration* of outstanding religious minorities. He recommends absolving Quakers and Anabaptists (who refuse participation in the political unity) from military service and oaths of allegiance, provided the state enjoys enough allegiance from others to be able to afford showing consideration to such "anomalous" groups. To Hegel this is toleration "in the strict sense": that is, patronizing toleration, an act of *grace*. As for the Jews, who do not shun the body politic, Hegel goes on to demand equal *rights*: in the modern world, now that consciousness has reached the level of education discussed in paragraph 209, discrimination against Jews is out of order.

Technically it may have been right [in the past] to refuse a grant of even civil rights to the Jews on the ground that they should be regarded as belonging not merely to a religious sect but to a foreign race. But the fierce outcry raised against Jews, from that point of view and others, ignores the fact that they are, above all, *men*; and manhood, so far from being a mere superficial, abstract quality (see Remark to paragraph 209), is on the contrary itself the basis of the feeling of selfhood.[21] (Ibid., p. 169)

Persons enjoying civil rights have a sense of self – they feel they are somebody, that they have worth – and this is the basis of their normative resemblance and cooperation upon which a stable society depends.[22] Thus, the status of humanity requires rights and at the same time makes them possible. Civil rights realize a person's abstract humanity, making it concrete and self-conscious.

Hegel continues: "To exclude the Jews from civil rights on the other hand, would rather be to confirm the isolation with which they have been reproached – a result for which the state refusing them rights would be blamable and reproachable, because by so refusing, it would have misunderstood its own basic principle, its nature as an objective powerful institution."[23] Hegel then adds a pragmatic consideration which may be designed for public persuasion: Excluding the Jews from civil rights has been shown by experience to be "the silliest folly," whereas "the way in which governments now treat [the Jews] has proved itself to be both prudent and dignified."

The pragmatic argument echoes perhaps the debates in Hegel's vicinity, for example, around the *Burschenschaft*. More noteworthy is the theoretical argument, which calls for several observations. First, Hegel accepts the Enlightenment principle that a human being *qua* human is the bearer of rights. This principle, although abstract, was not rejected but *absorbed* by the dialectical system. Yes, says Hegel, a self-conscious human being is the subject of rights, which translate his or her being a self-conscious "I" into social and institutional terms. Secondly, however (this qualifies the former view), a principle that is true in the abstract does not gain meaning and actual validity unless it is realized historically in some actual consciousness and civilization, specifically at the level of ethical practice and education (its *Bildung* and *Sittlichkeit*). From this perspective, the time for Jewish emancipation "has arrived" in the *serious* sense, because modern consciousness has ripened to this universal principle and recognizes it as the essence of a new era.

Third, Hegel draws a line between the patronizing toleration he recommends for the Quakers and the outright equality he demands for the Jews. Toleration for him is an act of grace which depends on the good will and strength of the state suffering the "anomaly." When these conditions cease to exist, toleration has no place. But the Jews must be more than tolerated; they should be given equal rights *on principle*, regardless of the circumstances.

Hegel's defense of the Jews lacks warmth; it discloses no emotional sympathy, only political and philosophical objectivity. But remembering that the Iberian Inquisitors had burnt Jewish converts at the stake in the name of love, in order to save their souls, we would doubtless consider Hegel's objective cool to be the better political principle.

The Jews' place in the modern world

So much for Hegel's political treatment of modern Jews. By contrast, his interpretation of ancient Judaism is part of a *non*political, quasi-theological study that reconstructs the history of the world Spirit. The evaluation of ancient Jews has little bearing, for him, on their surviving modern offspring, who must be treated as they are *now*, and judged according to the new ethical consciousness of the era they are entering, rather than by the religious phenomenon from which they came. Hence the gulf between Hegel's critique of historical Judaism and his support of Jewish emancipation in the present.

But what beyond that? Pöggeler argues that Hegel tried to find a place for the Jews within the modern world, whose foundations he was conceptualizing. What place was that to be? I can see no clear answer to this question either in Pöggeler or in Hegel. Let us examine a few possibilities.

Assimilation

Kant had suggested that Jews should convert to a nominal Christianity, not as an inner change of religion but as a mode of social assimilation. This solution was ineffectual to Hegel, who saw the Jews' uniqueness as lying in their fidelity to their separate identity (which he insisted on calling "hard-necked fanaticism"). Hegel recognized there was no Jewish identity *apart* from this fidelity; it was partly *constitutive of being Jewish*. Therefore one could expect the Jews to assimilate in the partial sense of absorbing modern culture, but not in the sense of erasing their different identity.

This conclusion had a systematic ground. Hegel's dialectic qualifies the Enlightenment view of humans as "universal rational beings." Reason exists only as embodied in actual individuals within a concrete historical culture. At bottom, therefore, obliterating the Jews' identity was incompatible with Hegel's way of thinking – be his *personal* inclinations what they may.

Pluralism: retaining a unique identity within a pluralistic society

This prospect is better suited to Hegelian thinking, according to which a human person *qua* human is always specific and particular – a Russian, a Swab, a countryman, a Jew, an artist, etc. – and it is *as such* that he or she must be recognized as a universal person. Today this extension of liberalism (and toleration) is sometimes dubbed "postmodern," although it has a ground in the thinking of one of the founders of modernity. Pluralism is a Hegelian possibility – it is latent in the logic of his system – because the Hegelian state presupposes a social base of diverse groups and forces, which the state not only *transcends* but also *maintains* within its higher domain and more objective unity. Though Hegel did not mean a "multi-cultural society" in today's sense, he may be interpreted, with qualifications, in that sense too.[24]

However, this solution clashes with Hegel's prejudicial view of the Jews as having been thrust outside history. Since he sees them as an archival relic of their own past, what real, vital element could he expect the Jews to contribute to a living, vibrant pluralistic society?

Reviving the Jewish identity

The answer, one might think, is to *revive* Jewish identity and *return* it to actual history. This has become the program of post-Hegelian Jewish nationalism, especially Zionism. Yet Hegel's interest in the Jewish question does not reach so far. Hegel reflects on the Jews not for their own sake, but from the standpoint of European history, in which the Jews' role has long been consummated and submerged. Had they preserved a *living* historical identity, it would have to be included in a pluralistic modern world – but revive it specially for that purpose? The attempt would have seemed artificial to Hegel, no less anachronistic than Jewish existence itself.

Nationalism and Zionism

What, more broadly, would Hegel's attitude have been toward Jewish nationalism and Zionism, the two main modern attempts to revive Jewish identity? Jewish nationalism views the Jews as a people, a separate nation, prior to their being a religion; it is therefore in conflict with the universal claims of the host nation-state, which demands that the Jews belong to the British, German, or American nation and be Jewish *only in their religion*. This may lead to the conclusion that the Jews, in order to restore their identity by way of nationalism, need to take a further step and create their own nation-state. This is the Zionist solution (which, coincidentally or not, was first suggested by a left-Hegelian thinker, Moses Hess). Zionism maintains that Jews must earn their place in the modern world by returning to history and creating a separate political entity in which to develop their cultural identity, be it a religious or a secular version. Hegel did not foresee Zionism, but the texts we have been examining suggest that he would have dissented from it because of his view that the Jews are irremediably stuck "before the gates of salvation" and can no longer have a history.

Let us observe that neither Zionism nor cultural pluralism oppose Hegel's *systematic* philosophy. They clash only with his particular prejudice concerning Jewish history, a prejudice which echoes a Christian polemical claim and reframes it in dialectical terms. If so, what prevents Hegel from assigning the Jews a place in modernity *as Jews* (apart from recognizing their individual rights) is his refusal to grant the Jews a deeper kind of equality: recognition of their equal spiritual and historical status as a nation and a community.

However, Hegel's position is not so much complex as it is unfinished. One might also conceive him as favoring, without contradiction, a kind of paternalistic pluralism which says that the Jews deserve recognition not only as individuals but as a human group which carries its past with it, regardless of whether this past is now a mere relic retained only by its bearers' stubborn will; their will must be respected even if it no longer has any broader historical value. According to this presumed Hegelian position, once the Jewish individual has crossed the frontier of modernity, he or she has both rights *and a future*, even if *Judaism* as nation or religion has no historical value or future. The individual has the right to adhere to anything with which he or she feels identified, be it something antiquarian or spiritless. Therefore the Jew has the right to adhere to his or her religion and demand that his or her humanity be recognized not in separation from his or her ancestral identity but *through and within it*. Herein lies the relative progress in the liberal principle which Hegel's *system* makes possible, relative to those of Lessing, Kant, and the Enlightenment, though it is hard to know whether Hegel personally would have chosen this possibility.

In any case, modern Jews left Hegel pretty cold. He supported their rights without pathos or passion; he was ready to accept them, but with no special feeling. And unlike Nietzsche, he did not see their acceptance as a special interest of Europe, but only as a consequence of modern times which must be applied also to this "anomalous," marginal group.

Critical remarks: Hegel's Christocentrism

Hegel has come a long way since his early writings and has clearly tried to overcome them. Was his overcoming successful? Yes and no. The early writings expressed a sharply negative attitude: Judaism had made no worthwhile contribution to European history and the world Spirit but had only falsified and distorted them.

The first turning point occurred in the *Phenomenology*, though furtively, in the subtext only. The reversal took place only years later in Berlin, especially in the *Lectures on the Philosophy of History* and the *Aesthetics*. Hegel had meanwhile overcome both the anti-Jewish venom of his youth and his inhibitions at the time of the *Phenomenology*. In Berlin he concerned himself with Judaism with considerable ease, sometimes with empathy, and as the pendulum shifted, he came to recognize an inner, poetic depth in Judaism. Above all, he saw Judaism's historical contribution not only as positive, but also as crucial.

Yet Judaism presented its novelty – the subjectivation of the Absolute – in a way that was initially false, and thereby missed its own principle and its realization. This is the view of the Berlin lectures on the philosophy of religion, the most important text on Judaism by the mature Hegel. Although essentially overcoming his youthful position, Hegel's tone wavers between opposing poles and, under the surface, we rediscovered the Enlightenment critique of religion in general – the charges of fear, servitude, and alienation – now aimed specifically at the Jewish religion.

However, Hegel never settled on a final, well-formed position, as witnessed by the new shift of the pendulum in 1827; his tone again mellowed considerably, but he did not budge from his substantive criticism of Judaism.

We may therefore speak of a partial self-overcoming in Hegel – a slow process which saw several regressions, lagged behind the changes in his overall system, and was never consummated. Hegel died before his position could take a final form, so we might say that the end of the story is that it has no end.[25]

We thereby take leave of Hegel's system. He did not solve the aporia of Jewish existence, and certainly not that of its place in modernity. But did any other thinker, Jew or Gentile, solve it? The mature Hegel was not free of stereotypes and ambivalent feelings toward Judaism. But in all important respects he was not anti-Semitic. He did not seek to hurt the Jews, did not feel threatened by them, did not view them as enemies of German society, and did not deny their rights, but on the contrary, supported the Jews' political emancipation and social acceptance in Germany. Also, Hegel's dialectics provided, at least implicitly, the beginning of a more pluralistic version of tolerance, which goes a significant way beyond that of the Enlightenment, even though it does not avoid a patronizing, Christocentric sense of superiority.

Christocentric and absolute vantage point

Any debate with Hegel must start from the assumption that he has a right to maintain his critical view of Judaism without being denounced as an anti-Semite. Patronizing he certainly was, and very Christocentric, but not, on that account, necessarily an anti-Semite. Jews who resent expressions of superiority by others often confuse their sense of hurt pride with another's anti-Semitism. However, one does not necessarily do violence to another's humanity by thinking that one's own beliefs or customs are better: toleration, I believe, is compatible with competition about values, identity, opinions, and so on.[26] Just as a socialist may think that his or her doctrine is superior to liberalism, or a Harvard freshman may be sure that his college tops any college in Oxford, so a Muslim may believe that her religion is better than Buddhism, and a Catholic may think his Church's teaching surpasses that of Judaism, without the first being immediately branded an imperialist and the last an anti-Semite.

Yet Christianity (and following it, Hegel) was not satisfied with saying that it was superior to Judaism; it saw itself as draining Judaism of meaning and spiritual assets and leaving it an empty shell – and this, indeed only this, is an act of spiritual violence. Christianity gave itself the title of the "true Israel," and thereby took away not only the Jews' election (a doubtful concept) but their history as well. The ancient history of the Jews became the Church's own "sacred history," and Jewish history after Jesus was thrust outside the realm of religious and spiritual meaning. The history of an ancient people with an identity of its own – above all, with a distinct identity of its own – was sunk into the history of the Church, which Christians believe to be the Savior's body (*Corpus Christi*) – the same Savior whom the Jews consider their absolute Other and reject with all their strength. Moreover, although Diaspora Jews have built their ongoing identity in part on that rejection, here they are forced into the Savior's Body as a "moment" which preceded and was sunk into their absolute Other, while their own life, existence, and self-perception do not count.

This, strongly put, is the Christocentric significance of Hegel's critique of Judaism and of the concept of *Aufhebung* around which it revolves. True, in overcoming his venomous youthful bias, Hegel, as I said above, did Judaism "dialectical justice" – justice in terms of his own dialectical system. But the dialectic itself expresses a fundamental *in*justice toward Judaism, because it sublates it into Christianity while dismissing its post-Jesus history as meaningless. In this respect, Hegel's dialectic does to Judaism what the medieval church (*ecclesia*) has done to the synagogue (*synagoga*).

These remarks no longer explicate Hegel's immanent viewpoint but criticize it from the outside, as, *pace* Hegel, I believe any genuine thinking must do. What I take to be outdated and dangerous in Hegel's system is the absolute, totalizing vantage point from which it pretends to evaluate all of Spirit's manifestations. Hegel thereby retreats from the most important critical achievement of modernity – Kant's idea of human finitude – and becomes, in this specific but crucial respect, a very *un*modern philosopher.

Where, one might ask, does Hegel's immense confidence originate, which allows him to speak of "absolute knowing"? I think it derives not from ontological considerations only, but, more fundamentally, from a powerful theological/religious drive at the base of his system.[27] Without the belief that God himself is being actualized and becoming known to himself through human history (a heterodox reading of a Christian idea), Hegel would not have been able to break the barrier of Kantian criticism on his way to absolute knowledge. His confidence is strengthened by the view, inspired by medieval thought, that philosophy is the conceptualization of religious truth – which makes of philosophy a form of God-worship and of God's self-knowledge. Of course, the theological ingredient is secularized in Hegel's system, and embodied in this-worldly areas like society, history, work, ethical life, empirical persons, actual thinking, and so on; but thereby it endows *them* with a quasi-sacral dimension. Secularization works both ways; it is also a form of sacralization: the profane and the sacred are dialectically reunited.[28]

An independent feature of Hegel's thought is that Spirit's religious dimension is consummated in Christianity – more specifically, in the Lutheran (or post-Lutheran) phase of Christianity, which tops the ladder of historical religions and paves the way to absolute knowing. This is a second Hegelian contention – a Christocentric and even Germano-centric claim – which rides on the claim of absolute knowing and serves as a major channel for its realization.

All this, even to a sympathetic critic (like myself), entails a surprisingly closed horizon. For all his broad historical outlook, Hegel remains attached to his village. The Euro-Christian region is the quintessence of world history for him. Historical progress, the formation of Spirit, even actuality itself depend on Euro-Christian culture, in relation to which Asia and other regions serve as a primitive substrate whose contribution has been exhausted, while Judaism serves as a dialectical vehicle bridging between the two worlds, a function that has also become obsolete.

Hegel's deep, yet unorthodox, Christianity also explains how, after Kant, Newton, Laplace, and the acute awareness of the "open universe" created by modern astronomy and expressed by poets like Haller (whom Hegel liked to quote), Hegel could hold that, out of all the vast galaxies in the universe, it is on our own planet, in our human history and culture, and especially among the Christian and European inhabitants of our planet, that the infinite God becomes finite spirit and evolves toward concrete infinity – a phase which God himself needs in order to become actual. To the critical, non-Christian eyes of Kant (and other modern critics), this may appear to be a form of cosmic provincialism; but that criticism will leave Hegel unmoved, because, at bottom, this is the core idea of Christianity: namely, the Incarnation. In both Christian teaching and Hegelian dialectic, the infinite God is empirically embodied (and, Hegel adds, evolves and develops) in some specific place, though for Hegel, this place is not Bethlehem or Galilee, but the planet Earth and the (Euro-centered) history of its inhabitants.

In this respect Hegel's metaphysics accepts the central issue separating Christianity from Judaism in its very foundations. Equally, Hegel's metaphysics secularizes the idea of election, which Christianity inherited from Judaism and claimed to have universalized. In a cosmic perspective, the residents of our planet play the role of a Hegelian "chosen people," through whom the divine history itself takes place.

Hegel's implicit Christocentric standpoint is thus at work at both the beginning and the end of his philosophy. Having presupposed a secularized version of the Incarnation, he takes it to its climax in "absolute knowing" by which the beginning is validated. Clearly, within such a self-sustaining teleological circle, Judaism can occupy no other place than that which it is assigned by Hegel's dialectic. There is something pathetic, therefore, in the attempt of Hegelian-leaning Jews (like Nachman Krochmal) to "correct" their master's doctrine by placing Judaism higher than Christianity in *Hegelian* terms.[29] As long as Hegel's system entails the secular conceptualization of a Christian truth, any such move is doomed to fail. Emil Fackenheim calls Hegel's view of Judaism "a flaw in the Hegelian system";[30] yet this is no accidental flaw which can be amended locally. The flaws and limitations of Hegelianism cannot be remedied by offering particular, eclectic local corrections (as in the case of the Jewish issue), but only, I think, through a bolder and more comprehensive move – by renouncing the claim to absolute knowledge in one critical stroke. This will open up a treasure of fertile, often profound, Hegelian ideas and thought patterns by which one can philosophize in a dialectical and historically conscious manner, free from the illusions of much of contemporary analytic philosophy (the illusion of a timeless, univocal truth ruled by some formal canon), and free also of Hegel's illusion of a religious Absolute wearing a conceptual apparel (which Nietzsche, our next subject, rightly saw as the "shadow" of the dead God). Only when this radical move is taken can Hegel's Christocentric position also be overcome.

PART II

Nietzsche and the People of Israel

CHAPTER SEVEN

Nietzsche and the Shadows of the Dead God

To everyone his Nietzsche. Who has not relied on this philosophical revolutionary, perhaps the most exciting and *in*citing spirit of modern times, and who did not use (or abuse) him? It seems that next to the Bible, only Nietzsche's works have given rise to so many contradictory interpretations and served to justify divergent views in so many cultural battles. Nietzsche himself was aware that he might be abused, and bears some of the responsibility for it. His aphoristic writing, deliberately blending philosophical with personal views, and claiming to abstain from systematic rigor, provides ample scope for quotation-hunters and lovers of paradox and contradiction. In particular, Nietzsche loved masks. He believed that noble spirits must conceal their intentions, their struggles and suffering, their coping with the temptations of the abyss, behind the veil of a sophisticated style, many-sided irony, and deliberate equivocation. While cheerfully shooting his venomous arrows at the heavy, verbose philosophers who mistake their murkiness for depth, he also mocked the Cartesian (and British) ideal of clarity, and viewed all direct, univocal writing as a sign of superficiality and, worse (to him), plebeian mentality and a lack of taste.

In addition, Nietzsche wrote for a minority, the happy few who might understand him because they have in part undergone the same psychological transformations as him. Nietzsche did not expect to create a "school" and would have considered a simple "yes" given to his views as yet another sign of superficiality. His few true readers were expected to oppose him, precisely because the basic affinity which unites means, among other things, that each person is an individual unto him- or herself and that truth cannot be captured by some dogmatic "thesis" (see later) but must rather be undermined in order to be of value. When such individuals are emancipated from the established truths of universal reason and the (spurious) images of conventional morality, each is supposed to develop his or her life as a free experiment beyond good and evil; and this experiment has no rules, neither in Nietzsche's theory nor in that of another.

Nevertheless, it is a mistake to see Nietzsche's writings as an anarchic, or merely "poetic," body of work. His ideas on most important issues are linked together in a fairly intelligible and explicable way. True, there may be some further dimension of understanding involved here, an experiential *Verstehen*,[1] which only someone living in a world different from the ordinary can perform – Nietzsche's essential message may require that deeper level (which also explains his strong attachment to rhetoric). But we are not dealing with a prophet, a poet, or an esoteric mystic. In the background there is in Nietzsche a set of explicable concepts which a philosophical reader can interpret rather distinctly by relating them to each other, uncovering the structure of the underlying thought or argument, and identifying classic philosophical flaws in them. This makes it possible to offer, eventually, a reasonably fair, distinct explication of Nietzschean thought, which, characteristically, is not merely a set of pure concepts but also – mainly – attitudes and evaluations.

Philosophy and life

Methodologically, Nietzsche's basic view is that philosophy – or rather, philosophizing – is not aimed at some scientific ideal or objective but at taking an evaluative stance toward existence and life. Philosophy, as science, has been a dominant ideal since the beginning of philosophy, from Thales and Plato to Descartes, Kant, Hegel, and, after Nietzsche, Frege, Husserl, Russell, and analytic philosophy. To Nietzsche this ideal is a corruption of philosophy and of life itself, the rationalistic poison poured into Western culture by Socrates and his followers. Nietzsche follows Schopenhauer in stating that philosophy's essential business is to cope with the meaning or value of life; and since life is always some individual's life, philosophy is necessarily an activity with a personal focus and goal. Philosophizing means that some individual takes a position regarding life, gives it meaning, negates or affirms it, and thereby shapes it. This is supposed to occur not through mere intellectual consciousness but through one's life as a whole, with all the instincts, passions, and will to power that it embodies. Therefore life is both the subject and the object of that activity. It is both that which judges and shapes, and that being judged and shaped. In other words, the philosopher's relating to his or her own life is itself a form of life, which should invest meaning in mere, given life and thus overcome it by shaping, forming, and enhancing its power.

This activity – the formative, meaning-giving self-overcoming of life – is what Nietzsche understands by spirit (although he tries avoiding the term, he does have the idea). Spirit is not some lofty, abstract factor added to a person's life from without, allegedly through pure consciousness. Spirit is life itself, with its full power of instinct and interest, insofar as it overcomes itself by shaping and producing meaning, without thereby losing its vitality, but rather enhancing it and providing creative avenues for it. This creativity cannot be limited by the constraints of reason, morality, religion, and universal values of any kind, which tradition has mistakenly taken to constitute the concept of spirit, but which on the contrary, inhibit and prevent the emergence of spirit. They are but vacuous metaphysical idols,[2] products of a decadent imagination moved by existential fear which produces and projects them upon the structure of world in order to feel more comfortable in it metaphysically – an illusory solace in a domain of sheer mystification.

A net of metaphysical idols

Such metaphysical fictions are involved in the central concepts and values of Western culture, which dominate and distort every individual's life. Nietzsche first attacks the conceptual scheme/world of classical philosophy, which is based on the search of truth for its own sake and also on the concept of universal reason, notions of identity, permanence, and causality, the laws of logic, and the all-human moral values. All these constitute a net of unreal metaphysical figures which enables the weak, decadent person to find calm and consolation in the belief that the universe is governed by reason, that one can orient oneself in it by dint of reason and the *logos*, and that rational – even teleological – meanings are embodied in it. Such a universe is no longer a frightening chaos that endangers and threatens the weak person's vitality – the person who is unable to stand before a world devoid of an objective, logical meaning. The whole network of epistemological and moral concepts in which we live expresses, in this respect, a psychology of escape and repression. In Nietzsche's terms it is a fear of facing truth,[3] the cowardice of the person retreating before the abyss. Further, the system of rational fictions we project on the world enables us, the weak, to dominate the world in an imaginary way and thus express our will to power in a rather devious manner. In subjecting, as it were, the world to a network of rules and laws of our own invention, we establish our alleged superiority over it and subject the universe itself to our metaphysical illusions.

The Christian religion, even more than rationalistic science and morality, produces and offers a veil of mystification which serves human weakness, meekness, and the negation of life. Images of a transcendent God and a next world make real, earthly life appear null and worthless; and by means of moral images of punishment and reward, divine Providence, a moral world order, conscience, repentance, and guilt feelings, men and women interiorize their hatred of life and become self-oppressed. Though Nietzsche was called a nihilist, he himself regarded nihilism as his number one enemy. Genuine nihilism, he claims, resides in *Christianity*, whose essence is to deny life's value, to oppress life, and to fight against it. This battle against life is conducted not only from without but from within, through the subtler means of education and training, by which the origin of the oppression is transposed into the person's inner forum through feelings of piety and faith, and especially through the manipulation of conscience and guilt. The ascetic ideal – the summit of spirituality in Christian eyes (and also in the eyes of the atheist Schopenhauer) – is to Nietzsche the greatest distortion of the spirit which Christianity propagates.

The hammer and the scalpel

Nietzsche's critique of rationalistic philosophy and Christian theology ends in an onerous picture. All of us in the West are living in a world of corrupting idols and images, of artificial fictions tightly woven into one another, whose *raison d'être* is to oppress life and to prevent it from developing its true power. Basically, therefore, that world is also anti-spiritual, although it appears to be built upon a notion of spirituality (which has also been corrupted by it). Nietzsche's labor of removing the web of decadent images is therefore a monumental task, one which cannot leave a single stone unturned in the present culture. It was not for nothing that he felt himself alone in his discoveries, lonely to the point of agony and madness, and that he had, as he says, to "philosophize with a hammer."

No less than a hammer, however, Nietzsche had recourse also to a scalpel. His attack on the basic concepts of philosophy and religion is based on a rather exacting analysis, whose model derives from the skepticism of the Greeks and also, in large measure, David Hume.[4] Just as Hume attacks the use of the concept of cause and effect, arguing that it has no logical but only a psychological basis, and that it is habit and the needs of life which make us project a subjective image upon the world, so Nietzsche attacks all important concepts – in science, metaphysics, and morality. And in each of these areas he is not satisfied with a generalized critique, but goes down to the foundations of each concept, its ingredients, and especially the psychology of its production and usage. This he names genealogy.[5] In this respect his writings contain minute discussions and analyses in the style of conventional philosophy; and this is the connecting link (which necessarily exists in him) between philosophy as life, which he favors, and philosophy as science, which he rejects.

More precisely, Nietzsche does not deny the analytic component of philosophy as a set of arguments and analyses of concepts like cause, identity, truth, knowledge, value, etc. He continually needs and uses this method and these concepts himself. His view of philosophy as life does not exclude, but rather requires, the analytic dimension of philosophy; since it is our very life, for us Westerners, which is shaped (and in Nietzsche's view, distorted) by the dominion of the web of traditional philosophical concepts, the act of philosophical cure, whose aim is to remedy life, must pass through a critical analysis of these concepts.[6] It cannot take place immediately, by some direct exhortation, persuasion, or poetic inducement. True, the analytic argument itself is intended in the last analysis to coax, induce, and entice, but that does not make it any the less necessary.

A philosophical reversal: genealogy

We see that the goals of changing life and shaping a new human person require the philosopher of life to reoccupy him- or herself with traditional philosophy so as to upset (or revolutionize) its conceptual world; or, using a Kantian phrase, in order to subject it to a

comprehensive critique. Yet, in opposition to Kant (and again following Hume and greatly extending his approach), Nietzsche's critique relies on a basically psychological method. Traditional
philosophy used to ask: "What is the ground for our cognitive,
ontological, and moral principles?" Its main concern was with the
foundations of knowledge and morality. Nietzsche engages in a
methodological reversal. Renouncing the search for (and the question of) foundations, he asks two different questions, linked to each
other. First he asks: What is the worth of those traditional values
whose grounding we used to seek, like "truth" or "the moral good"?
He thereby presents them, and their grounding, not as absolute,
inherent values but as dependent upon something else – namely,
life. This reversal – which is methodological, but also deeply philosophical – can also be reformulated in Nietzsche's words as follows.
Kant and all the rationalists asked: What is the *grounding* of synthetic
a priori judgments in knowledge and morality? Whereas Nietzsche
asks: Why do we need the belief in such judgments? What kind,
what form, of life does this belief serve and make possible? This is
not only an "anti-foundationalist" turn, as one might call it today,
but also a turn to existential ethics – asking questions of worth and
value (though beyond the traditional terms of "morally good" and
"morally evil") as the most decisive philosophical issues. Hence the
second part of his methodology: to search for the covert psychological apparatus, which resides not in consciousness but in life's
instinctual and desiring setup (of which consciousness is but the
upward-peering tip of the iceberg) by which we form or adopt certain philosophical, moral, and religious beliefs as a nonintentional
means for sustaining the kind of life and culture in which we are
profoundly – though almost always unconsciously – interested.

Nietzsche thereby becomes the *genealogist* of philosophical and religious concepts – the person who unearths their occult origin and the
process by which they are born[7] from certain kinds of life instincts
and interests, which are hidden from our consciousness and have
driven us to form the illusion of independently valid concepts and
values (hence Freud's complex affinity with Nietzsche, which he
both admitted and tried to conceal).[8] By discovering the genealogical
origin of concepts we shall also be able to undercut their claim to
purity and permanent validity, and be cured of our servile dependence upon them. This is a critical and therapeutic work not unlike
Kant's critique, though opposed to most of Kant's positive results.
Kant's critique set out to ground and renew the current culture's
universe of values and scientific beliefs while ridding it of the meta-

physical (and theological) illusions to which it has been enslaved, whereas Nietzsche's critique shows that whole universe of scientific and moral beliefs (including Kant's critical foundation of it) to be the product of a vast metaphysical illusion whose web has spread over all areas of life and thought in the West.

God's shadows

This attempt at a radical critique, both in its roots and in its scope, is dramatically expressed in Nietzsche's dictum about the death of God, and even more in his less well-known but more accurate exclamation in *The Gay Science*: "When will all these shadows of God cease to darken our minds? When will we complete our de-deification of nature [*entgöttlicht*, literally 'freed of God']?"[9] The madman with a lantern running through the markets shouting "God is dead . . . and we have killed Him" (*GS*, §125) is of course Nietzsche himself, who knows that this awesome act, the most terrible in human history, has already been done, and that the human gain from this deicide is a life of freedom and solitude in a meaningless universe. This price is not unbearable, but rather a sublime recompense; for only through this new recognition can the human person endow his or her life with genuine meaning (which Nietzsche calls "Dionysian") and become the creator of his own life, world, and values.

However, even after God's death, his shadows still dominate the world. Hence the true role of philosophical criticism is to purge the world of the shadows of the dead God (*GS*, §108).

These shadows are the vestiges of belief in a rational world, a cosmos ruled by a *logos*, the validity of the natural sciences, of the "pure" laws of logic, the dominion of causality, and the cogency of the concepts of substance and identity. Modern natural science pretended to have banned God from the picture of nature, but has reinstated God's shadows through the back door. Philosophical rationalism and the belief in science are disguised versions of the old religious notion of a moral world order, and are likewise based on anthropomorphism – the projection of man's wishes, needs, customs, and aspirations on the structure of the universe. Anthropomorphism must be rejected so radically that not only must wisdom, beauty, order, form, and purpose not be attributed to the world, but we must also "beware of believing that the universe is a machine" (*GS*, §109). That is, even mechanical causality, which constitutes the basis of modern, allegedly nonmetaphysical science, is a form of the same illusion. In contrast to Spinoza, for whom the world was saturated (because identical) with God, for Nietzsche the demand to grasp nature as "clear of God" is the precondition for man to "become nature again": that is, to be cured of decadence. This means that he must, without illusion, face a universe having no rational meaning – no purposes, no eternal laws, not even causes, nor any other inner order responding to the intellectual aspirations of weak persons. The universe in its purity, as only the strong, "Dionysian" person can perceive, is "eternal chaos," pictured as a blind, purposeless flow of energy whose forms repeat themselves in perpetual monotony. It is (in Platonic terms) a world of Becoming without Being, or the world of Heraclitus without the *logos*. Even describing cosmic power as "will," in Schopenhauer's way, is a form of anthropomorphism – the shadow of God in an atheist's heart.

In this ever-flowing world, without any permanence, there is no room for identity either. Everything differs from everything (and from itself). The laws of logical thought are themselves grounded in an absurdity, for they presuppose the existence of identical cases and that every thing and state can be identified with itself. This belief stems from the basic needs of life; for without being able to re-identify something as "the same" and to ascribe permanent features to entities like food and natural phenomena, we would perish. In this way a covert apparatus has produced a series of useful fictions which have been passed from one generation to the next. We believe that "there are enduring things; that there are equal things, that there are things [at all], substances, bodies; that a thing is what it appears to be" (*GS*, §110). These and other "fundamental errors" have become invested in our very organism, and their dominion has become so powerful we have made them the norms for logic and for all "truth" and "untruth" in knowledge, thus making them immune to criticism.

Such fictions, at a more sophisticated level, also serve science and are produced for the sake of life in a different sense. Science creates a further series of fictions which are required by its own operation – like "causality and substance," or imaginary entities like "lines, planes, bodies, atoms, divisible time spans, divisible spaces," etc. (*GS*, §112), all of which are forms of anthropomorphism – "pictures, our pictures." These fictions operate within the primary principles which make science possible, thereby enabling the rationalist world view and the decadent way of life which sustains it. Here Nietzsche is clearly speaking of life in a different sense – no longer its basic biological substrate but its psychological quality and cultural features and properties. Rationalistic fictions serve a life built upon illusion; they provide a person with bogus metaphysical consolations and enable him or her to avoid looking into the abyss of existence. Nietzsche's critique of science and wish to uproot its world view do not therefore stem from a scientific interest or the drive for truth for its own sake (which he considers one of the most decadent fictions); rather, his interest in metaphysical issues is driven by the same interest he has in a new kind of life – the Dionysian kind he holds preferable to others.

The problem of truth

Nietzsche's notion of truth, however, is one of the most difficult issues in his writings. Given the lack of objective truth and a disinterested "will to truth," all modes of knowledge are only perspectives, which are subject to certain kinds of life-preferences. Yet, like any sweeping skeptical claim, this one too refers back to itself. What, then, is the status of Nietzsche's own view? Apparently he takes it to be another perspective on the world which is linked (as its necessary condition) to the Dionysian way of living. But there are many contexts in his works where Nietzsche uses the term "truth" in a non-perspectival – indeed, an absolute – way, accompanied by all the value marks and the emotive connotations which usually come with "truth" in its ordinary (daily and philosophical) sense. The Nietzsche who refuses to accept dogmatically the value of truth, demanding first to know "its worth," nevertheless set out in a dozen places to scold those who run away from the hard metaphysical truth, preferring fictions and false consolations. More than once he states that his Dionysian person is measured by "how much [hard] truth he can bear." Does this entail a contradiction? Perhaps the admonition to those running away from truth means that Nietzsche has implicitly already responded to the question of the value of truth – to the effect that while truth has no value in itself, it is valuable insofar as it makes Dionysian life possible, which means that it is no longer truth in the old cognitive sense but a kind of "true life," a new concept of truth referring not to the status of statements but to the status or quality of a life – something close to "authenticity." It seems that, for all its inner problems, Nietzsche's view of truth tends toward some version of the notion of "authenticity" – a congruence not between a statement and an object (or between several statements) but between subjective life and itself, by which it acquires a new inner quality. To simplify a little, the problem is no longer how to reach true *knowledge* but how to *live* truly – that is, in a "true" (authentic) way. And this means not to live by some external, universal, and objective norm, but to bring life into a dynamic agreement with *itself* – dynamic, because life's meaning is not something ready-made, by its mere existence, but is shaped through a process of self-overcoming.

A precondition for this is the recognition that there are no objective meanings and values out there in the world, that the world is disrobed of God and his shadows. Therefore the test of the noble person – the "overman" which Nietzsche pretends to announce – lies in the question: "How much truth can he bear?" Tearing away as many of his protective masks as he or she can, the Dionysian person is supposed to face a universe stripped of rational meaning and of all support by permanent values, and to be capable of converting this terrifying recognition into a new source of life's power and even a new kind of joy. ("Joyous knowing" is, I think, a better rendering of Nietzsche's famous subtitle "La Gaya Scienza" expressing the very same idea.) But what kind of knowing is this? It is certainly not merely a cognitive disposition; it is equally a self-commitment, a passion, and a form of willing. It is a mode of *recognition* and *realization*, two words which imply taking a stand, performing an act, placing oneself in some firm position. The Dionysian person's "knowing" is not the affirmation of a statement, nor even a simple disillusionment, but an act of the whole person which affirms a whole existential "fate" and accepts a certain way of living, which others would consider miserable, as a basis for joy and creativity. The psychology of ordinary people is different. When facing hard truths, such people are liable to react by negating life, plunging into despair and nihilism, or running back to the consoling lap of illusion. Weak persons opt for optimism because they cannot overcome pessimism, whereas for the kind of person Nietzsche foresees, a "pessimist" view of existence is merely a starting point to be overcome, an introduction to the affirmation of life and the acceptance of difficulty and suffering, by which to gain new sources of power and joy. This dialectical overcoming of the temptation of nihilism (and also of superficial optimism) is Nietzsche's main message; it is the crux of his "Dionysian" stance, the essence of tragedy and the tragic way of life. The Dionysian person neither shuns suffering (mental and physical) and the recognition of chaos, nor lets them drag him into the abyss of despair. Rather, by saying "Yes" to life with all its contingent, absurd, and horrible aspects, he converts this recognition into a source of existential power.

The first revaluation

On many occasions Nietzsche spoke of a "revaluation" of all values (or their reappraisal), and he prepared several drafts of a work by that name which was never completed. Many commentators have asked what is the new "table of values" which Nietzsche recommends, and whether such a table can exist at all, given Nietzsche's insistence on going "beyond good and evil." The answer is that Nietzsche is primarily an ethical philosopher, not in the sense of being concerned with moral commands, but in preferring a certain way of life. He rejects normative, commanding good and evil but accepts as significant the distinction between "good" and "bad" as indicating the values (or worth) residing within a person or a form of life. The (mental) aristocrat is better than the plebeian (or the masses), and the Dionysian way of life is better than the Christian one. The lesser thing, in both cases, is not morally evil but qualitatively bad: that is, low or inferior. It points to the concept of a bad person (in his or her quality) rather than to that of a sinner (Nietzsche distinguishes between *schlecht* ("bad") and *böse* ("evil")). In this respect his philosophy is full of evaluations and in many cases is oriented toward them.

Yet values and evaluations do not belong only to the narrow ethical domain. The primary revaluation around which everything revolves is rather (I think) *ontological* in Nietzsche. It concerns the questions: What is the value of life without certainty, solidity, and permanence? What is the value of a purely immanent existence which flows on and passes away without being irradiated by some transcendent light, be it from a divine origin or from a Platonic kingdom of ideas? Nietzsche, as we have seen, demands that one affirm this immanent existence, and endow it with value through one's *own* will and life, making it a source of power and joy rather than of nihilistic (= life-negating) despair. Thus the very first value in Nietzsche's new table is the affirmation of life without a mask, a life of pure, transient, ever-flowing immanence.

In asking, What is the value of truth?, Nietzsche means: What is the value of believing there is truth? Most people assume that there is an eternal, fixed truth even if they do not (or cannot) reach it. To Nietzsche, we all live in *this* world – an ever-flowing, transient world in which nothing is permanent and everything is grasped and evaluated from a plurality of perspectives – yet we tend not to accept (that is, to reject, not to agree with) this picture of reality and therefore conceal it from ourselves by assuming an objective, scientific, rational truth. This, then, is the value of truth: to disguise and conceal from us the anxieties – the horror even – of an existence which lacks permanence and has no transcendent dimension, but is purely this-worldly, an everlasting flux. Thus, truth's value is to delude us, to serve as untruth in some deeper sense.[10] This is a form of running away – the flight of the weak person who is afraid of existence and life and can exist only under the veil of some illusion. To Nietzsche, the first act of revaluation is to view as valuable precisely the kind of life which rejects the illusion of truth and accepts immanent existence – transient and flowing, lacking inner permanence, not to say eternity – and to discover sense in the kind of life which creates meaning rather than seeking it externally by deluding oneself into believing that it can be deduced or copied from the objective structure of the world. Whoever grasps this as the first value and succeeds in interiorizing it no longer lives in fright and despair in a world which lacks permanent truth, but rather lives in it with joy, a life marked by *amor fati* and "joyous knowing."

What could be – and what was – such a thinker's position on anti-Semitism and the Jews? This is our concern in part II of this book.

Methodological remarks

Imagine a Jewish thinker saying the following:

> I raise against Judaism the most terrible of all accusations that any accuser ever uttered. It is to me the highest of all conceivable corruption. It has had the will to the last corruption that is even possible. Judaism has left nothing untouched by its corruption; it has turned every value into an un-value, every truth into a lie, every integrity into a vileness of the soul [...] This eternal indictment I will write on all walls [...] I call Judaism the one great curse, the one great innermost corruption, the one great instinct of revenge, for which no means is poisonous, stealthy, subterranean, small enough – I call it the one immortal blemish of mankind.[11]

Such words have often been heard in Europe, ever since Jewish emancipation, coming from the poisonous mouths of anti-Semites. But did a Jew ever say anything similar? In all the piercing criticism, self-torturing, painful hatred that Jews have often felt for themselves and their people, one may doubt if such words have ever been pronounced, or will be in the future. The quote is from Nietzsche's book *The Antichrist*, except that I substituted "Judaism" for "Christianity" in the original text. Nietzsche has framed here his indictment of the culture and religion from which he sprang. The text should therefore read: Christianity is for me the highest kind of corruption, etc.

This is the rhetorical context in which one should read – and also listen to, for sounds and tones are no less important in Nietzsche than linguistic contents – his words about Judaism too. But before taking on this subject, a methodological reminder: First my interest is with Nietzsche's own thought and philosophical project not with its various uses, abuses, vulgarizations (although these are of great interest and importance when studying empirical history), nor with what is called "Nietzscheanism." Second I am concerned with Nietzsche as a philosopher; that is, I consider his view of the Jews in its link with the rest of his thinking, rather than as a fleeting or occasional reflection that any intellectual, artist, writer, or scientist might have framed about the Jews. Third while examining Nietzsche's words in their philosophical context, I also try to listen to their *rhetorical context* and to how they sound among the other voices issuing from Nietzsche and others. Fourth, and above all, I am not satisfied with repeating the commonplace that Nietzsche's relation to the Jews was "ambivalent," but try to clearly explicate the structure and ingredients of that ambivalence.

To do this, I shall have to make certain distinctions: first, between Nietzsche's attitudes to anti-Semitism and to historical Judaism; second, within historical Judaism, three stages are to be distinguished: Old Testament Judaism, whose "grandeur" Nietzsche adored; the "priestly" Judaism of the Second Temple, which he profoundly despised and condemned as the parent of Christian culture; and the post-Christian Judaism of Jews in the Diaspora and in modern times, whom he defended, admired, and saw as a healing ingredient in his "new Europe."

To understand this complex relation – a seeming paradox – we must recognize a major methodological point. When Nietzsche attacks anti-Semites or defends the Jews, he has in mind concrete entities: the contemporary Jewish communities living in Europe and the actual anti-Semitic movement acting against them. By contrast, when criticizing ancient Judaism, Nietzsche approaches it as a psycho-cultural (or "genealogical") *category*; it is for him a qualitative feature deeply ingrained in Western culture, whose psychological structure Nietzsche – as "genealogist" of that culture – is out to analyze and expose. Hence the characteristic gap between his critique of Second Temple Judaism and his defense of contemporary Jews. Unlike anti-Semitic theorists, both vulgar and subtle – and also unlike many Jewish apologists – Nietzsche avoids carrying over his negative analysis of ancient Judaism into his attitude toward contemporary Jews. This methodological *epoché*, a self-disciplinary move (and a hallmark of his uncommon psychology), allows Nietzsche to be – at the same time, and with the same passionate ardor – both an anti-anti-Semite and a critic of ancient Judaism as the cradle of Christianity.

CHAPTER EIGHT

The Anti-*Anti*-Semite

> I have not met a German yet who was well disposed toward the
> Jews; and however unconditionally all the cautious and politi-
> cally-minded repudiated real anti-Semitism, even this caution
> and policy are not directed against the species of this feeling
> itself but only against its dangerous immoderation, especially
> against the insipid and shameful expression of this immoderate
> feeling – about this, one should not deceive oneself.
> *Beyond Good and Evil*, §251

As in the case of other such testimonies (another example is Sartre), I
think we may accept Nietzsche's words. He himself as a young man
was affected by the same "disease," as he calls it (see below). It is,
indeed, plausible to expect virtually any child exposed to a Christian
upbringing to have absorbed some anti-Jewish sentiment. The question is what one does with this sentiment in maturity. Does one make
a theory of it? Contend against it? Allow it to persist but, for "political"
reasons of the kind Nietzsche mentions, restrain its more brutal manifestations, yet let some "soft" or "subtle" anti-Semitism permeate
one's life?

Speaking for himself, Nietzsche writes that "during a brief daring
sojourn in very infected territory I, too, did not altogether escape this
disease."[1] Nietzsche is referring to his student years and, especially,
the brief but intense period of his association with Richard Wagner, a
rabid anti-Semite, and his wife Cosima. As a young professor in

Basel, he came under the influence of Jacob Burckhardt, the famous historian of the Renaissance whom Nietzsche had reasons for perceiving as anti-Semitic, and whose master-figure hovered problematically over Nietzsche to his last lucid days. And, of course, Nietzsche had the "infected territory" much closer to home in the form of his sister Elizabeth and her future husband, Foerster. However, as I shall suggest, the intimacy of Nietzsche's complex relations with these figures eventually served as a lever for a powerful self-overcoming and for inner reinforcement of his stand as an *anti*-anti-Semite.

Nietzsche in the zone of the disease

Documentary evidence of the "disease" exists in sporadic anti-Jewish remarks which Nietzsche made in several letters dating especially from 1866 to 1872.[2] These were the years around the unification of Germany and Bismarck's wars, when political anti-Semitism became a major theme and passion in Germany. Nietzsche was then under the influence of Wagner and Cosima; earlier, as a freshman in Leipzig, he had anti-Semitic companions like Carl von Gersdorff, whom Nietzsche liked personally and spent many hours with in bars and restaurants, and with whom he kept up a friendly correspondence in later years.

Thus Nietzsche complained to his mother and sister (22 April 1866; *BW*, 1/2, no. 502) that the food in Leipzig restaurants was terrible and that the town swarmed with "appalling spiritless monkeys and other merchants"; in the end, he and Gersdorff discovered a *Kneipe* ("pub") where they could be alone and didn't have "to enjoy melted butter and watch Jewish faces" [*Judenfratzen*]. (Nietzsche may be repeating Gersdorff's table remarks.) Five days later he complained again (in a letter to H. Mushacke, 27 April 1866; *BW*, 1/2, no. 504) that the food is bad and expensive, and that "in the theater there is some permanent African woman, and wherever you look you see Jews and their kin [*Judengenossen*]." He adds: "I spend a lot of time in Gersdorff's company."

Nietzsche was then a German patriot for a while, and twice tried to enlist in Bismarck's army (and was eventually rejected because of myopia). The letter which speaks of "melted butter and Jewish faces" is signed: "The one ready for war." When he was admitted to the artillery, he wrote proudly to Gersdorff (who meanwhile had become an officer) and signed the letter "Your friend Friedrich Nietzsche, gunner" (1 December 1867; *BW*, 1/2 no. 554). Philosophically he was under the influence of Schopenhauer and German romanticism, and after becoming friendly with Wagner, saw him as Europe's designated redeemer. The concept "Jews" signified to him everything that opposed the spirit of Wagner and Schopenhauer. In a letter to Wagner and Cosima (whose anti-Jewish obsession Nietzsche knew well) he wrote that "Jewish greed" was one of the causes of Germany's decline (22 May 1869; *BW*, 2/1, no. 4). And in a letter to Gersdorff he praised Schopenhauer's doctrine of the denial of the will (which he denounced in maturity), adding: "our 'Jews' – and you know how broad this concept is – hate Wagner's idealistic manner which links him tightly to Schiller and his kin" (11 March 1870; *BW*, 2/1, no. 65). Everything here is the opposite of the mature Nietzsche's position.

The young Nietzsche's admiration for Wagner reached a climax in *The Birth of Tragedy from the Spirit of Music* (1870). That year, Gersdorff came across Wagner's anti-Semitic tract, "Jewishness in Music", and was so enchanted that he wrote to Nietzsche that thus far he had been misled about Wagner by the "Judaized press," but now he is convinced that "your friend Wagner is a genius. That essay completely opened my eyes. . . . I am still at the beginning . . . but am already thrilled by the truth of his thoughts and admire the rich content and the splendid form" (11 March 1870; *BW*, 2/1, no. 65).

In that essay Wagner attacked especially the Jewish composers Meyerbeer and Mendelssohn, so Gersdorff must have been titillated by Nietzsche's letter, over a year later (4 February 1872; *BW*, 2/1, no. 197), telling of the following episode: "For the Easter holiday I am being strongly urged to travel to Athens, Naxos and Crete with a professor from neighboring Freiburg (Baden) – what do you say to this! Especially when you hear who this is – the son of Felix Mendelsohn-Bartholdi [sic] – well, I shall say No." Perhaps Nietzsche was in any case unwilling to go to Greece, but his letter to Gersdorff hints that he declined not because Professor Mendelssohn was Jewish (actually he was a second-generation Christian), but because he was the son of the man who more than anyone else represented everything that Wagner rejected. As Hayman points out,[3] Nietzsche could not have accepted without severely offending Wagner and Cosima.

In another small incident, Nietzsche avoided speaking to an acquaintance, one Dr Volkmann, "because he was dressed with an appalling lack of taste, like some theatrical Jew" (letter to Oscar Oehler, 13 February 1870; *BW*, 2/1, no. 63). And before taking a hike, he noticed that one of the company in the hotel was "unfortunately a Jew" (letter to his mother, 1 October 1872; *BW*, 2/1).

Nietzsche at that time had no reason to oppose his anti-Semitic friends and reappraise the prejudice against Jews he had received from his upbringing. Yet his anti-Jewish prejudice was more casual, more dispersed, and very far from the eager – sometimes agitated – anti-Semitism of Wagner, Gersdorff, and later Elizabeth. The sporadic anti-Semitic remarks in his letters from the period of the "infection" express a more conventional aversion to Jews, somewhat enhanced by Nietzsche's milieu at the time (and perhaps also catering to it: most of the recipients of his anti-Jewish remarks were known by him to be anti-Semitic); but it never reached the ideological intensity of the others. It was an "infection" which Nietzsche discovered was curable.

And he indeed overcame it – powerfully, with an inner storm – though this was not achieved fully until after he had broken completely with Wagner. As already pointed out, his anti-Wagnerian feeling served the mature Nietzsche as one of the levers for this overcoming, which occurred well before he wrote most of his major mature works.

His mood during the transition period – after his liberation from Wagner – is illustrated by his attitude toward Siegfried Lipiner, a Jewish admirer who wrote a book entitled *Prometheus Unbound*. As Hayman reports,[4] Nietzsche's friends spoke ill of Lipiner. Paul Rée (himself a self-hating Jew) said that Lipiner was "an un-appetizing creature," and Erwin Rhode wrote that he was "the most bow-legged of Jews" (29 June 1877; *BW*, 2/6, no. 425). Yet Nietzsche was unaffected; he wrote to Rhode that Lipiner was a "genius" and wrote on the same day to Lipiner: "Tell me frankly whether in respect of origin you have any connection with the Jews. The fact is that I have recently had many experiences which have aroused in me the highest expectations of young men of this origin" (24 August 1877; *BW*, 2/6, no. 652). The last sentence is very significant, for it anticipates what the mature Nietzsche was to say a few years later in *Daybreak* and elsewhere about the high expectations he had for the Jews in the new Europe (see ch. 10).

Henceforth we shall discuss the mature Nietzsche.

Self-overcoming

Self-overcoming is the key concept here. Not only is it central in Nietzsche's philosophy in general, but it also describes what Nietzsche seems to have realized in his own personal case concerning

the Jews. The "new philosopher's" self-overcoming entails sur-
mounting the decadent culture in which he has been bred – and that
includes not only rationalistic metaphysics and Christian morality
but also lesser deformations such as nationalism and anti-Semitism,
which equally derive from a deviant will to power and *ressentiment*.
Nietzsche had to – and to a great extent did – overcome *both* the
"Jewish" (Judeo-Christian) element in his upbringing *and* anti-
Semitism.

The Jew is embedded in Christian consciousness as an archetypal
negative figure, his image so deeply incised as to be almost ineradicable. There is a sense of the death of God for which the Jew is held
responsible. He is God's murderer, who by rejecting the savior had
justifiably been deprived of his election and historical mission; his
due is to be outcast and downtrodden. Yet the Jew stubbornly per-
sists in his error, protests his outcast status, and, full of hatred, seeks
revenge against the Gentiles.

The primal Jewish consciousness, on the other hand, perceives the
Gentile Christian as alien and hostile – an unreachable "other" representing the world of negation, who vainly pretends to supplant the
Jew and usurp his divine history and election. On top of this, of
course, are the bitter memories of persecution and torture.

Given such powerful primary images, self-overcoming is the only
way. Nietzsche, of course, does not mean by this liberal civility or
simple political restraint; nor is he talking about good will and tolerance as universal values. These are fragile shields which the first vol-
canic outburst will destroy. Self-overcoming, as Nietzsche conceives
it, is an act – or, rather, a process – which penetrates and reshapes a
person's inner drives and urges, rather than merely imposing external rational restraints or censorship upon them. This process requires
personal strength, and a kind of hard honesty toward oneself that
ordinary psychology does not provide, and which cannot, therefore,
be expected from the wider public. Nietzsche's solution, here too,
seems suitable only for a minority.

Furthermore, in order to mobilize the power required for an inner
transformation of one's drives, an energy boost is needed, which (as
Freud, a semi-Nietzschean, suggested in his theory of transference) a
person's privileged relationship to another may generate. In
Nietzsche's case, his intimate relations and intense grappling with his
sister and others mentioned above could have provided some of the
energy needed to overcome the temptation of anti-Semitism.

The *anti*-anti-Semite: *Quid facti*

To first establish the textual case – a kind of *quid facti* – I shall cite a sample of Nietzsche's comments on anti-Semitism. I have drawn these comments from four different types of texts: (1) Nietzsche's publications; (2) his intimate letters – to his sister, mother, and close friends; (3) an ironic correspondence with Theodor Fritsch, a renowned anti-Semite propagandist; and (4) Nietzsche's last letters written in mental twilight.

The published works

A strong statement against anti-Semitism appears, not surprisingly, in the *Genealogy of Morals*, the same work in which ancient Judaism is also condemned – and for the same genealogical reason. "They [the anti-Semites] are all men of *ressentiment*, physiologically unfortunate and worm-eaten, a whole tremulous realm of subterranean revenge, inexhaustible and insatiable in outbursts against the fortunate and happy."[5] In *Beyond Good and Evil* Nietzsche chides the anti-Semites who seek to curb Jewish immigration into Germany:

> "Admit no more new Jews! And especially close the doors to the east (also to Austria)!" thus commands the instinct of a people whose type is still weak and indefinite, so it could easily be blurred or extinguished by a stronger race. The Jews, however, are beyond any doubt the strongest, toughest, and purest race now living in Europe; they know how to prevail even under the worst conditions (even better than under favorable conditions), by means of virtues that today one would like to mark as vices – thanks above all to a resolute faith that need not be ashamed before "modern ideas"; they change, *when* they change, always only as the Russian Empire makes its conquests – being an empire that has time and is not of yesterday – namely, according to the principle, "as slowly as possible." (*BGE*, §251)

In contrast to the young and artificial nations now arising in Europe, Nietzsche adds, the Jews are a stable and ancient race, of the sort that exists forever. Then he makes a significant observation, which I cite here for its tone and timbre (expressing clear empathy for the Jews) no less than for its content.

> That the Jews, if they wanted it – or if they were forced into it, which seems to be what the anti-Semites want – *could* even now have preponderance, indeed quite literally mastery over Europe,

that is certain; that they are *not* working and planning for that is equally certain.

Meanwhile they want and wish rather, even with some importunity, to be absorbed and assimilated by Europe; they long to be fixed, permitted, respected somewhere at long last, putting an end to the nomads' life, to the "Wandering Jew"; and this bent and impulse (which may even express an attenuation of the Jewish instincts) should be noted well and *accommodated*: to that end it might be useful and fair to expel the anti-Semitic screamers from the country. (*BGE*, §251)

This passage, which clearly defends the Jews, should be read in conjunction with another high-sounding passage on the Jews, from *Daybreak*, which says among other things:

[T]he psychological and spiritual resources of the Jews today are extraordinary [. . .]. Every Jew possesses in the history of his fathers and grandfathers a great fund of examples of the coldest self-possession and endurance in fearful situations, of the subtlest outwitting and exploitation of chance and misfortune; their courage beneath the cloak of miserable submission, their heroism [. . .] surpasses the virtues of all the saints. [. . .] They themselves have never ceased to believe themselves called to the highest things, and the virtues which pertain to all who suffer have likewise never ceased to adorn them. [. . .] They themselves know best that a conquest of Europe, or any kind of act of violence, on their part is not to be thought of: but they also know that at some future time Europe may fall into their hands like a ripe fruit if they would only just extend them. To bring that about, they need, in the meantime, to distinguish themselves in every domain of European distinction and to stand everywhere in the first rank [. . .]. And whither shall this assembled abundance of grand impressions which for every Jewish family constitutes Jewish history, this abundance of passions, virtues, decisions, renunciations, struggles, victories of every kind – whither shall it stream out if not at last into great men and great works![6]

With his proposal to expel not the Jews, but the "anti-Semitic screamers," Nietzsche gives pointed expression to his view of anti-Semitism itself. In *Nietzsche contra Wagner* he cites Wagner's offense as one of the worst signs of decay: "Since Wagner had moved to Germany, he had condescended step by step to everything I despise – even to anti-Semitism."[7] And in *The Antichrist*, another late work, speaking of the anti-Semites' "inner conviction," he says:

Long ago I posed the problem whether convictions are not more dangerous than lies as enemies of truth. . . . "Respect for all who have convictions!" I have heard that sort of thing even out of the mouths of anti-Semites. On the contrary gentlemen! An anti-Semite certainly is not any more decent because he lies as a matter of principle. (*A*, §55)

The published texts speak for themselves. Of even greater significance are Nietzsche's intimate letters – especially those written to members of his family, in which he cannot be suspected of "political" caution. These letters reveal the pain Nietzsche suffered from the infection of his own family by anti-Semitism.

Personal letters to his sister, mother, and Overbeck

To Overbeck, he wrote:

This accursed anti-Semitism ... is the reason for the great rift between myself and my sister. (2 April 1884; *BW*, 3/1, no. 503)

To his mother:

Because of people of these species [anti-Semites], I couldn't go to Paraguay [where members of Foerster's anti-Semitic circle had set up an experimental colony]. I am so happy that they voluntarily exile themselves from Europe. For even if I should be a bad German – I am in any event a *very good European*. (17 August 1886; *BW*, 3/3, no. 736)

He wrote to his sister, who married the virulent anti-Semite Foerster:

You have committed one of the greatest stupidities – for yourself and for me! Your association with an anti-Semitic chief expresses a foreignness to *my* whole way of life which fills me ever again and again with ire or melancholy ... It is a matter of honor to me to be absolutely clean and unequivocal in relation to anti-Semitism, namely *opposed*, as I am in my writings. I have been persecuted in recent times with letters and *Anti-Semitic Correspondence* sheets; my disgust with this party (which would like all too well the advantage of my name!) is as *outspoken* as possible ... and that I am unable to do anything against it, that in every *Anti-Semitic Correspondence* sheet the name of Zarathustra is used, has already made me almost sick several times. (Christmas 1887; *BW*, 3/5, no. 968)

The Fritsch affair

One of the anti-Semites whom Nietzsche had in mind in the previous letter – who "persecuted" him in the hope of winning his favor – was Theodor Fritsch, editor of a journal called *Der Hammer* and author of virulent, best-selling anti-Semitic tracts. In complaining about Nietzsche's "perverted judgment" of the Jews, Fritsch suggested that it was due to personal relations with Jewish friends (such as Paul Rée). The anti-Semitic material he sent Nietzsche contained a pamphlet by Foerster, Nietzsche's brother-in-law, which praised other well-known preachers of anti-Semitism as follows: "Those who deal with the Jewish question from the most exalted moral point of view are ... Richard Wagner, Paul de Lagarde, Eugen Dühring, and Adolphe Drumont. Their writings must serve every anti-Semite as indispensable weapons, just as the Talmud serves the rabbis."

The dull-witted Fritsch could not have been more off target. The "authorities" he cited only aroused Nietzsche's ridicule and contempt or, in Wagner's case, aversion. In his first reply (dated 23 March 1887) Nietzsche was still ironic, even relatively polite:

> Very Dear Sir,
>
> Your letter, which I have just received, accords me such great honor that I cannot but direct your attention to yet another place in my writings which deals with the Jews, be it only in order to give you a redoubled right to speak about my "perverted judgments." Please read *Daybreak*, page 94 (*BW*, 3/5, no. 819)

Nietzsche here refers Fritsch to the famous section 205 in *Daybreak* cited above (which Nietzsche clearly understands as pro-Jewish and irritating to an anti-Semite). Then he goes on:

> Objectively, the Jews are more interesting for me than the Germans: Their history raises many fundamental questions. And in such serious matters I am used to ignore sentiments of sympathy or antipathy, as is required by the scientific spirit and its ethics, its training – and in the final analysis, its *sense of taste*. In addition I must confess that the "German spirit" of our times is so alien to me that only with great impatience can I observe its [idiosyncratic] mannerisms, among which I especially include anti-Semi-

tism. To the "classic literature" of that movement, which your pamphlet lauds on page 6, I owe several entertaining moments: if only you knew how much I laughed last spring when reading the works of that crooked-minded sentimentalist known as Paul de Lagarde! I evidently lack that "most exalted moral point of view" referred to on that page. All that remains for me now is to thank you for having courteously supposed that "it is not out of some consideration for society" that I have arrived at my "perverted judgments" [concerning Jews]; and perhaps it will help assuage your mind if I say, finally, that there are no Jews among my friends, but neither are there anti-Semites.

> Your most devoted servant,
> Prof. Dr. F. Nietzsche

A request: Please publish a list of German scholars, artists, poets, writers, actors, and virtuosi of Jewish extraction or intraction! That will be a valuable contribution to the history (and criticism!) of German culture.

The final witticism, "there are no Jews among my friends, but neither are there any anti-Semites," clearly mocks the well-known protest of the anti-Semites: "Many of my best friends are Jewish." In saying that he, on the contrary, "does *not* have Jewish friends," Nietzsche is ironically dissociating himself from the anti-Semites, just as he does in the second phrase ("but neither are there any anti-Semites"), now spoken seriously.

It seems that, meanwhile, the mail delivered to Nietzsche more anti-Semitic material from Fritsch. Six days later (29 March 1887) Nietzsche wrote Fritsch another letter, more caustic this time and with cruder irony:

> I hereby return your three *Correspondence Sheets* with gratitude for the trust that enabled me to get a glimpse of the concoction and confusion of principles upon which this strange movement of yours is founded. That being the case, I request you no longer continue to privilege me with these mailings: I do fear finally for my patience. Believe me, that nauseating desire of naive dilettantes to have their say about the value of peoples and races; and submission to "authorities" whom any intelligent mind would reject with abhorrence (such as A. Dühring, R. Wagner,

Drumont, de Lagarde ...), those constant and absurd distortions of vague concepts: "Germanic," "Semitic," "Aryan," "Christian," "German" – all that is liable to rouse my ire seriously and for long and to extirpate from my heart the generous irony with which I have so far observed the gyrations of hypocrisy of the Germans of our time.

Finally, what do you think I feel when Zarathustra's name is borne in the mouths of anti-Semites?

Yours submissively,
Dr. F. Nietzsche   (*BW*, 3/5, no. 823)

Nietzsche's twilight letters

Early in January 1889 Nietzsche collapsed on a street in Turin. He was taken to his lodgings, and after regaining consciousness, he wrote many letters in a few days – to his close friends (Franz Overbeck, Peter Gast [Heinrich Köselitz], Erwin Rhode), to Jacob Burckhardt, August Strindberg, Malwida von Meysenburg, and others. Most of the letters are signed "The Crucified" or "Dionysus," which recalls to mind the conclusion of Nietzsche's last book, *The Antichrist*, where he says: "Did you understand me? Dionysus against The Crucified." There is no contradiction here: Dionysus has come to oust the Crucified but is himself a new Crucified of sorts. Similarly, in his twilight letters, Nietzsche sees himself in the role of God's son, a demi-God who recreates the world and culture and shapes totally new values. Even his suffering, perseverance, and power are Christ's. He is the Antichrist *as* a new Christ; or he is Dionysus come to unsettle Christianity, but thereby fills a role like that of the founder of Christianity himself. A characteristic example of 4 January 1889:

> *To my maestro Pietro* [Peter Gast, a musician]:
> Sing to me a new song: The world is transfigured and all the heavens rejoice.
>   The Crucified One
>
>   (*BW*, 3/5, no. 1247)

To friend Overbeck and his wife:

> Although so far you have demonstrated little faith in my ability to pay, I yet hope to demonstrate that I yet am

somebody who pays his debts – for example, to you . . . I
am just having all anti-Semites shot.
                    Dionysus   (*BW*, 3/5, no. 1249)

Perhaps the longest letter was addressed to Jacob Burckhardt, the old
cultural historian who had influenced the young Nietzsche in Basel,
and with whom he had sustained a complicated relationship. Burckhardt, a pessimistic humanist and student of the Renaissance, was
then at the end of his career and lived in fear of a great cultural
eruption that would shake Europe. Although, compared to his contemporaries, he was relatively free of bigotry, Burckhardt did persist
in one prejudice – against the Jews, who would, he thought, be the
only beneficiaries of the looming European catastrophe (a cruel
irony in retrospect). There is no doubt that Nietzsche, like many
others, regarded him as an anti-Semite.[8] In the dim last hours of his
active life, Nietzsche wrote to Burckhardt (6 January 1889):

> Dear Professor,
> In the end I would much rather be a Basel professor than
> God; but I did not dare push my private egoism so far as to
> give up the creation of the world on its account. You see,
> one has to make sacrifices. . . .
>   (*BW*, 3/5, no. 1256)

Nietzsche goes on to describe his life in Turin in concrete detail: how
he does his shopping, the room he has rented, how he suffers from
torn shoes – as if alluding to Jesus as an earthly God. He also identifies himself with various figures in the news, and through them
again projects his image as an inverted son of God, or a Dionysus
functioning as the Antichrist. His signature – or farewell – is unusu-
ally warm: "Cordially and lovingly, Your Nietzsche." However, in a
postscript, he adds: "I had Caiaphas put in chains . . . , Wilhelm Bismarck and all anti-Semites deposed."
    Here Burckhardt too gets his due as an anti-Semite – and from the
hand of the Crucified himself, who at the same time takes his revenge
against Caiaphas, the high priest who recommended his crucifixion.
This is confused, but not without sense. In his waning hours, Nietzsche
lashed out especially against nationalist, anti-Semitic Germans and
against the ideology of the new Germany. In his frenzied state he put
forward a plan for the unification of Europe under his scepter, and
sent letters ordering the king of Italy, Umberto I, and Cardinal Mariani
in Rome to organize the necessary congress on 4 January.

Thus his final remarks before he sank into darkness bring into the open – in distorted but instructive relief – some of the deepest motifs in Nietzsche's mind: the inversion of the existing world, the creation of a new culture, his role as Dionysian prophet and Antichrist, and also the political unification of Europe, as a means to renewing its decadent culture. All these drives and ideas are now thrust outside and illumined by a high beam of madness. His mental twilight thus has considerable hermeneutic importance in providing clues to Nietzsche's inner mind as it was when he was sane. It shows that his opposition to anti-Semitism, and the German nationalism with which it was connected, were among the most powerful negations agitating his mind.

We may find it significant that Nietzsche castigates Caiaphas in the same breath as the anti-Semites. The Jewish priest not only sent Christ to his cross but, in a deeper sense, begot him. Thus Christianity stems from the same distortion that later made anti-Semitism possible. So Caiaphas, the Jewish priest; Bismarck, the German nationalist and state-worshipper; and modern anti-Semites, all have the same genealogical ancestor, *ressentiment*. In the next section we shall see how Nietzsche makes this clear in saner and more systematic texts, especially the *Genealogy*.

"I am just having all anti-Semites shot," "Wilhelm Bismarck and all anti-Semites deposed" – this is not an incidental cry issued by Nietzsche in his struggle "against those [he] holds responsible for the corruption of German culture, and thereby for the corruption of the culture of Europe as a whole."

The intimate texts and, especially, the twilight letters carry special hermeneutical weight, because they prove that Nietzsche's opposition to anti-Semitism was not merely external and "political" (or "politically correct"), as with many liberals, but penetrated into the deep recesses of his being. This may have been reinforced by Nietzsche's intense relations with anti-Semites: his sister, Wagner, Cosima, and perhaps also Jacob Burckhardt. These relations could have served to provide the heightened energy for overcoming his early anti-Semitism in the intense way he did: that is, not as liberal rationalist but with all the passion of his being – the "Nietzschean" way.

The four types of texts I have cited also show that, far from being marginal, this issue was central to Nietzsche both theoretically and psychologically. No less univocal is his defense of, and admiration for, *contemporary* Jews. But what are his theoretical grounds? Having answered the question *quid facti*, we must, so to speak, now ask: *Quid juris?* What is it in Nietzsche's *philosophy* that makes anti-Semitism both so central and so antipodal?

The sources of Nietzsche's *anti*-anti-Semitism: *Quid juris*

When dealing with an existential thinker like Nietzsche, it is, of course, difficult to depart completely from the theoretical. As I have suggested, his overcoming of anti-Semitism must have been assisted by his struggle with such figures as Elizabeth, Wagner, and Burckhardt and by refashioning his love–hate relationships and overt and covert conflicts with them. However, even outside the psychological arena, there is sufficient philosophical anchorage in Nietzsche for his active anti-anti-Semitism. I shall enumerate the main points and illustrate each one with a quotation or two.

A new slave revolt

Anti-Semitism is a mass movement, ideological and vulgar. As such, it is a popular neurosis that affects weak, insecure people, who are deficient in self-confidence (in contrast to Nietzsche's Übermensch or Dionysian individual); it represents a new kind of "slave revolt." A mass movement generally derives its strength from the coalescence of weak individuals held together by an object of common hatred. Moreover, despite his sense to the contrary, the weak individual sinks even lower in the crowd, because he draws a semblance of strength from *outside* – from the faceless mass within which he has let the remnant of his personality be submerged. His originally petty insecurity is not redeemed within the crowd, but rather compounded. Through the veil of self-deception, he acquires a sense of counterfeit power (political, nonexistential) which he cannot sustain other than by projecting it negatively against his "other."

Furthermore, the anti-Semitic movement as Nietzsche understood it was not even the decline of a strong, creative position. Already from the start, and in the mouths of its originators, it expressed mass psychology in its direct and most primary form. If the image of a "herd" has meaning in Nietzsche, its derogatory connotations apply most distinctly to the anti-Semitic movement, as a modern embodiment of a "herd" and "slave" mentality, though without its original creative power.

The nationalist neurosis

Especially in Germany, anti-Semitism was the other Janus face of nationalism, which Nietzsche also opposed as madness and neurosis. Nietzsche attacked both nationalism in general and the new German nationalism of his time, then reaching an exalted climax through the unification of Germany under a Prussian Kaiser and Bismarck's *Reich*, in particular. In exposing nationalism as another, modern form of "herd mentality," he also identified the context within which German anti-Semitism functioned and from which it drew much of its motivation and negative energies.

In place of nationalism in its various guises, Nietzsche favored *Europeanism* as an ideal – not in today's basically economic form but as the product of "a grand politics" that would overcome all petty, aggressive nationalisms and set forth a supranational culture fused with a "Dionysian" quality and a "revalued" sense of life. The Jews were to have a constitutive role in the new Europe, which would set the normative tone for the rest of the world. (In this respect, Nietzsche remained parochial and Eurocentrist.) This can be seen in the following textual illustration.

> A little fresh air! This absurd condition of Europe shall not go on much longer! Is there any idea at all behind this bovine national-ism? What value can there be now, when everything points to wider and more common interests, in encouraging their boorish self-conceit? And this in a state of affairs in which spiritual depen-dency and disnationalization meet the eye and in which the value and meaning of contemporary culture lie in mutual blending and fertilization![9]

> Owing to the pathological estrangement which the insanity of nationality has induced, and still induces, among the peoples of Europe, owing also to the shortsighted and quick-handed politicians who are at the top today with the help of this insanity [. . .] the most unequivocal portents are now being overlooked, or arbitrarily and mendaciously reinterpreted – that Europe wants to become one. (*BEG*, §256)

It should be noted that in conventional terms, Nietzsche's attack on nationalism would be classified as coming "from the Right" (though in a cultural sense, rather than a political one). Today nationalism is linked with right-wing politics; but in the early nineteenth century, especially under the repressive "Holy Alliance," it drew much of its

vigor from the liberal "Left," which demanded the liberation of ethnic peoples as the condition for liberating the individual, too, within
his or her genuine identity. Nationalism was later transformed into a
chauvinistic, right-wing movement; and Nietzsche, living under Bismarck, was witness to that transformation. But he was aware of its
earlier career and continued to see it as among the "modern ideas"
originating in the Enlightenment (liberalism, democracy, socialism,
equality, utility, and the like), all of which he opposed as the offspring of Christianity, enhanced by the modern culture of the
masses, and thereby belonging to the same genealogical family.

The cult of the state – the new idol

Anti-Semitism is also objectionable because it reinforces the German
Reich and the cult of politics and the state – especially the modern
nation-state, which Nietzsche denounces as a "new idol."[10] He is
entirely opposed to the apotheosis of politics and to letting it dominate all other dimensions of life. The modern nation-state, and the
German *Reich* in particular, is venerated for doing precisely that and
thus has become the object of idolatry and fetishism. Observing this,
Nietzsche calls himself the "last nonpolitical German."[11] For him politics is the enemy of culture, and its lowest form. The polarization of
Germany has led to the destruction of German spirit and the decline
of its culture.

> I wish to be just to the Germans [. . .] One pays heavily for coming
> to power: power *makes stupid*. The Germans – once they were called
> the people of thinkers: do they think at all today? [. . .] the Germans
> now mistrust the spirit; politics swallows up all serious concern for
> really spiritual matters. *Deutschland, Deutschland über alles* – I fear
> that was the end of German philosophy.[12]

> Even a rapid estimate shows that it is not only obvious that German
> culture is declining but that there is sufficient reason for that [. . .]
> Culture and the state – one should not deceive oneself about this –
> are antagonists [. . .] All great ages of culture are ages of political
> decline: what is great culturally has always been unpolitical, even
> *anti-political*.
>
> (*TI* VIII, §4)

To this, in stylized wrath, Zarathustra too joins his voice:

> State is the name of the coldest of all cold monsters. Coldly it tells

lies too; and this lie crawls out of its mouth: "I, the state, am the people."

Every people speaks its tongue of good and evil [...]. But the state tells lies in all the tongues of good and evil [...]. Everything about it is false; it bites with stolen teeth, and bites easily. Even its entrails are false . . .

Where the state *ends* – look there, my brothers! Do you not see it, the rainbow and the bridges of the overman?

(Z I, "On the New Idol," §14)

This too is part of the context in which we should understand Nietzsche's opposition to anti-Semitism: namely, as a component of the cult of the German *Reich*. The adoration of the German nation projects itself into the idolatry of the German *Reich* and depends on anti-Semitism for its mass hysteria and fire.

Racism and the new Europe

Anti-Semitism also depends on racism – meaning the defense of racial "purity." Nietzsche's theory admits the *concept* of race, but rejects value differences linked to biology alone and calls for an amalgamation of the races in a new European synthesis. This means that, while adhering to a dubious scientific theory about races as a factual issue, Nietzsche rejects racism as a normative doctrine and ideology. Admitting races as a fact, he does not clearly distinguish between them and "peoples." Moreover, he seems to believe that a race's historical experiences can be embedded in its biological inheritance. According to this semi-Lamarckian position, races have the capacity to interiorize their past experiences, imprint them in their "blood," and thus pass them on to new generations (cf. *WP*, §942).

However, Nietzsche did not see race distinction as having value import, and with a single (though quite outstanding) exception did not demand the preservation of racial purity; on the contrary, his repeated demand was for a *blend* of many European races rather than segregating them. The Jews in particular have trained themselves for centuries in self-overcoming and discipline. Now they carry in their "blood" a long, profound history of faithfulness to their identity, which makes them a most desirable candidate and invigorating ingredient in the new European mix. Thus, while Nietzsche's stand on *races* is questionable and confused, his stand on *racism* is clear and rather unequivocal.

On more than one occasion, mental forms are found to be more fundamental than racial differences. For example, the "priestly" mental form is more fundamental than "Semitism" in endangering Christianity:

> A lot is said today about the *Semitic* spirit of the New Testament: but what is called Semitic is simply priestly – and in the racially purest Aryan law-book in Manu, this kind of "Semitism," i.e., the *spirit of the priest*, is worse than anywhere else. The development of the Jewish priestly state is *not* original: they learned the pattern in Babylon: the pattern is Aryan. (*WP*, §143)

The link between Nietzsche's negation of racism, nationalism, and the nation-state as three factors of his anti-anti-Semitism, is well expressed in a section of *Human, all too Human* entitled "European Man and the Abolition of Nations." Nietzsche explains his choice to be a "good European" rather than a nationalist, and continues:

> Incidentally: the entire problem of the *Jews* exists only within national states, inasmuch as it is here that their energy and higher intelligence, their capital in will and spirit accumulated from generation to generation in a long school of suffering, must come to preponderate to a degree calculated to arouse envy and hatred, so that in almost every nation – and the more so the more nationalist a posture the nation is again adopting – there is gaining ground the literary indecency of leading the Jews to the sacrificial slaughter as scapegoats for every possible public or private misfortune. As soon as it is no longer a question of the conserving of nations but of the production of the strongest possible European mixed race, the Jew will be just as usable and desirable as an ingredient of it as any other national residue.[13]

This passage covers a good part of the intellectual ground on which Nietzsche's objection to anti-Semitism and the cult of politics and the nation-state are interrelated and reinforce one another.

The underlying pattern: *ressentiment*

Underlying all the above points is a common psychological pattern: fear, insecurity, existential weakness, a "slave" mentality, and, above all, *ressentiment* – that vengeful animosity and rancor toward the mentally powerful and self-affirming, and hatred of the other, as a person of higher worth, which mediates the inferior person's sense of selfhood and makes it possible. The anti-Semite's ardor conceals his or her profound lack of self-confidence. His primary position is not the celebratory affirmation of his own being and worth, but the negation of the Jew, conceived as his absolute other – and, under the shroud of his inferiority, sensed as a feeling of himself as (and probably being) superior. Only through such negation is the anti-Semite able to recognize himself and affirm himself too – which he or she does in an overblown, empty manner, relying on counterfeit power of the masses and substituting the arrogance of petty moralizing for existential self-confidence.

No wonder, then, that it is precisely in the *Genealogy* that we read the following passage linking anti-Semitism and *ressentiment*. This linkage is the genealogical basis for all the rest. No less noteworthy, Nietzsche attacks the anti-Semites as the modern "Pharisees" (whom he confounds with the "Jewish priests"). I have already cited part of this passage earlier in the chapter; here it is in full:

> This hoarse, indignant barking of sick dogs, this rabid mendaciousness and rage of "noble" Pharisees, penetrates even the hallowed halls of science (I again remind readers who have ears for such things of that Berlin apostle of revenge, Eugen Dühring, who employs moral mumbo-jumbo more indecently and repulsively than anyone else in Germany today: Dühring, the foremost moral bigmouth today – unexcelled even among his own ilk, the anti-Semites). They are all men of *ressentiment*, physiologically unfortunate and worm-eaten, a whole tremulous realm of subterranean revenge, inexhaustible and insatiable in outbursts against the unfortunate and happy. (*GM* III, §14)

Thus, in an ironic turn of events, the anti-Semite becomes the legitimate heir of the ancient Jewish priest, from whom he took over as a modern paradigm of the psychology of *ressentiment*. In the meantime Judaism, fortified by its long trials and self-overcoming in exile, has become a storehouse of positive power which modern Europe badly needs – and which Nietzsche hopes will fuel the creation of a higher cultural synthesis in Europe.

What distinguishes the anti-Semite as a *modern* phenomenon is not only *ressentiment*, but its fusion with the psychology of the masses. The modern mass society compounds the power of *ressentiment* and provides a new terrain for its expression. The ancient Jewish priests, in performing their revolution in values, worked in relative privacy. Their subtle vengeance against pagan Rome was profound but tacit, almost underground; and its bearers, the early Christians, were a repressed minority with no public voice. In

Nietzschean terms, they should therefore be deemed stronger spirits than their genealogical cousins, the modern anti-Semites, who must project their *ressentiment* into a vulgar mass movement as a further (second) precondition for their ability to affirm themselves. Modern anti-Semitism *depends* on the imaginary power emanating from a crowd united in hatred against an "other." This also means that it must eventually become externally repressive: pogrom and holocaust are its natural expressions.

Combined, Nietzsche's four negations – of nationalism, racism, anti-Semitism, and the cult of the state – also explain why his philosophy is inherently opposed to fascism and Nazism, although these ideologies have used and abused Nietzsche for their own purposes. Nietzsche's enmity for anti-Semitism does not necessarily make him a philo-Semite. Characteristically, the *Genealogy* also contains some of Nietzsche's most critical attacks against Judaism – more precisely, against the Second Temple "priestly" phase, from which Christianity was born. This will be discussed in the next chapter.

CHAPTER NINE

Nietzsche and Ancient Judaism: The Antichrist

The previous chapter discussed anti-Semitism and found Nietzsche unequivocally opposed to it. This chapter will turn to ancient Judaism, and see that Nietzsche's attitude toward it was complex and ambivalent. Our task will be to analyze the components of this ambivalence and also to distinguish between the relevant periods.

First let us listen to Nietzsche:

> The Jews – a people "born for slavery" as Tacitus and the whole ancient world say; "the chosen people among the peoples," as they themselves say and believe – the Jews have brought off that miraculous feat of an inversion of values, thanks to which life on earth has acquired a novel and dangerous attraction for a couple of millennia: their prophets have fused "rich," "godless," "evil," "violent," and "sensual" into one and were the first to use the word "world" as an opprobrium. This inversion of values (which includes using the word "poor" as synonymous with "holy" and "friend") constitutes the significance of the Jewish people: they mark the beginning of the slave rebellion in morals. (*BGE*, §195)

"Slaves" are a psychological, not a political, concept to Nietzsche. They are "the meek of spirit" to whom the kingdom of heaven was promised by the Jew Jesus, an offspring of the priestly culture of his time. The early prophets who proclaimed a universal morality have sown only the *seeds* of the Jewish revolution. They have only *begun* it (and thereby proved to be more powerful than their followers). It was only later, through the priests and the Pharisees of the Second Temple that the culture of weakness gained control over Israel and, in the form of priestly morality (which Nietzsche dubs "slave morality"), burst out and gradually dominated the rest of the world. The Jewish people bequeathed Christianity to the world as an act of spiritual revenge against the Gentiles.

Nietzsche's attack on ancient ("priestly") Judaism is as fierce and uncompromising as his assault on anti-Semitism. The Jewish priests have spread the spurious ideas of a "moral world order," sin, guilt, punishment, repentance, pity, and the love of the neighbor. Thereby they have falsified all natural values. The meek and the weak are the good who deserve salvation; all men are equal in their duties toward a transcendent God and the values of love and mercy he demands. (Nietzsche thus attributes to the Jewish priests a direct Christian message, and often describes them as Christian *from the start*). Yet, underneath his doctrine of mercy, the priest's soul was full of malice and *ressentiment*, the rancor of the mentally weak whose will to power turns into hostility and revenge against the other, which is his only way of affirming himself. This, genealogically speaking, is how the Jewish priests – pictured as early Christians – created the "slave morality" which official Christianity then propagated throughout the world. Whereas anti-Semites accuse the Jews of having killed Jesus, Nietzsche accuses them of having *begotten* Jesus. Priestly morality is the morality of the existentially impotent, in whom *ressentiment* against the powerful and the self-assured has become a value-creating force. The existential "slaves" take vengeance on their "masters" on an ideal plane, in that they succeed in imposing their own values upon the masters, and even cause them to interiorize those new values, thereby subjugating them. Henceforth the powerful person sees him- or herself as a sinner not only in the other's eyes but in his or her self-perception as well, which is the ultimate form of subordination and corruption.

Nietzsche thereby places the critique of ancient Judaism at a crucial juncture of his philosophy. It is grounded in ressentiment, *a key Nietzschean category, and is responsible for the corruption of Europe through Christianity.* However, Nietzsche uses this critique to fight not against contemporary Jews, but rather against contemporary Christianity and the "modern ideas" he sees as its secular offshoots (liberalism, nationalism, socialism, etc.)

Dionysus against the Crucified

Nietzsche thus criticizes ancient Judaism not as an anti-Judaeus but in the role of the Antichrist. His repeated complaint is that Judaism has begotten Christianity, a far greater evil. "Was I understood? Dionysus against the Crucified" – this outcry signs off *The Antichrist*, a late book which, not accidentally, is one of the two main sources for his critique of Judaism (the other is the *Genealogy of Morals*). If we reexamine this startling statement, we shall see that Nietzsche is not only Dionysus *against* the Crucified but (as in his twilight letter) the Crucified himself, now in a new, Dionysian apparel, setting out to eradicate the *old* Crucified. Within the confrontational union of the two, it is Dionysus rather than Jesus who determines the joint message, and the union is called the "Antichrist." A new Christ whose real significance is Dionysian, Nietzsche is thereby declared the Antichrist. He too, like that mythological creature (wrongly vilified), rises to destroy Christ and his Church and to purge the world of their decadent morality.

This is how Nietzsche depicts himself also in the provocative, antinomistic self-portrait he draws in *Ecce Homo*. The book's title refers to Nietzsche in words that usually point to Jesus. Nietzsche is a counter-Jesus who threatens Christian culture. In the text he exclaims again: "Have I been understood? What defines me, what sets me apart from the whole rest of humanity is that I uncovered Christian morality."[1] This uncovering presupposes an analysis of ancient Judaism, which thereby becomes essential in Nietzsche's thought.

This analysis has its own rhetorical presuppositions. Unlike his discussion of contemporary Jews and anti-Semites, which aimed at real, flesh-and-blood people, Nietzsche's attack on ancient Judaism – or its "priestly" phase – treats it as a psycho-cultural category embedded in Western culture, which the philosopher must expose as part of this culture's meaning and as a basis for its critique. No wonder the second major text in which he criticizes Judaism is called a *Genealogy*: Nietzsche, as "genealogist," looks for the psychological origins of Christianity from which its modern, secularized forms also arose; and these he finds in a psycho-historical construct he calls "Priestly" Judaism – just as he had found scientific rationalism, the other source of Western decadence, to derive from the "Socratic" phase of Hellenism. *The Birth of Tragedy* (which actually discussed its death, too) was his earliest exploration of genealogy.

Note on the genealogical method

A professional historian may find this method crass and imprudent, but Nietzsche does not pretend to offer a factual picture of the past. He uses historical materials to construct hermeneutic paradigms that illuminate the covert drives and attitudes toward life which stand at the source of various cultural shapes – like the Olympic, tragic, and Socratic phases of Hellenism, or the biblical, "Priestly," and Diaspora phases of Judaism. Whatever else one may think of these triads, it is clear that Nietzsche does not treat either Judaism or Hellenism (or any other historical form) as having a fixed essence; and his critique of ancient Judaism is intended not as a theoretical basis for anti-Semitism, but as a genealogical basis for rejecting Christianity.

Nietzsche's genealogical method was intended neither as empirical history nor as a direct causal account. It frames a number of deep psychological patterns and categories by which the covert inclinations and life-preferences of different kinds of people can be described; these patterns are said to dominate larger cultural forms – in science, morality, religion, etc. – where they become concealed (even from their own originators) under contrary self-perceptions and professed goals. Nietzsche's task as genealogist is to uncover the true origins of these cultural forms and the people who promote them, thus determining their *psychological* lineage and whether it is base or aristocratic.

Such an approach is clearly no less speculative than Hegel's *Phenomenology of Spirit*. Indeed, it is more speculative: Nietzsche has no dialectical logic to rely upon, and he does not offer intermediary stages by which to make the transitions more intelligible. Also, the moving force in Nietzsche is not the desire for freedom and self-awareness, as in Hegel, but the darker desire for "power" (meaning primarily existential power, the power to transcend one's being and "be more"). Above all, there isn't in Nietzsche that complex but ultimately optimistic Hegelian *Aufhebung* which endows the whole process with an ascending, progressive line. To Hegel, the shift from Judaism to Christianity signifies progress, whereas to Nietzsche it is a sign of degeneration. Even within Judaism, the transition from biblical times to Second Temple Judaism was a dramatic setback.[2]

Of course, Hegel criticizes the Enlightenment and, against the simpler optimism of Kant, recognizes the force of irrational factors – passion, contingency, violence – working in history; yet ultimately these factors contribute dialectically to historical progress. History has a rational purpose in Hegel, which works through its opposites – violence, ambition, domination, etc. – and therefore is usually hidden from view; also, the rational goal is modified by the contingency on which it depends. This makes Hegel a sober, non-utopian, nonmoralizing philosopher of progress – yet a philosopher of progress all the same (and thus a target for some of Nietzsche's fiercest criticisms).

For Nietzsche, historical change is not necessarily progress. The march of history is devoid of purpose and rationality. It is a play of forces, each expressing the immanent "will to power" which is the stuff of all being and life. Whatever the outcome, there is no transcendent pattern – no providence, purpose, value, inner rationality, etc. – hovering over history or embodied in it.

This negation of transcendence, the view of being as all-embracing immanence, free of metaphysical illusions, lacking eternal truths, purposes, values and other (falsely consoling) human-like features, and attached to the ever-passing moment, Nietzsche dubs "the eternal recurrence of the same." Despite its ring as another metaphysical doctrine, eternal recurrence is but a fable, a myth, a narrative by which the strong Dionysian person represents his immanent world experience and tests his resolve to uphold it. By contrast, all theories of progress, from Jewish messianism and Christian eschatology to modern, Hegelian-issued philosophies of history – and all belief in a kingdom of God, either sacred or secular, to be realized in this world or the next – derive from the psychology of weakness and life-weariness, from the "slave" mentality which Nietzsche places at the origin of Western culture. Through Christianity, this Jewish-begotten slave psychology reversed the moral values of the West. The will to power which penetrates all being turned against itself and took an imaginary, degenerate path which made Western man (and woman) sick of life and alien to it.

I mentioned earlier that the "will to power" is an existential, not a political, concept for Nietzsche – certainly in its primary meaning. Will to power is the thrust "to be more," to affirm and transcend one's being by enhancing the energy and activity of one's life. It also involves the effort to surpass one's limits, to overcome the fears and burdens of existence, the threats of the environment, and the obstacles presented by others. A primary expression of will to power is *self*-overcoming, in which the instincts are not simply restrained (and thereby neutralized or enfeebled), as in rationalism, but *reshaped* – that is, made to take a different course while preserving and even enhancing their life energies. This may sometimes take the form of a physical expansion or of political dominion, though as an occasional, but not an essential, consequence. It may also involve causing harm to others, not because of ill feeling toward them, but as a natural consequence of the act that affirms and expresses power. The same "Dionysian" person will, under different circumstances, show generosity to other people, support and encourage them, not because of altruism, pity, or remorse (which are life-suppressing emotions and therefore as bad as grudges and resentment), and not because of calculated interest or a sense of moral duty, but again, as the expression of the same self-affirming power (and its overflowing excess). This is clearly an aristocratic outlook, though in the mental, not the political or hereditary, sense of aristocracy. Actually, those who are most likely to hold political power (and religious and ideological power, too) are the psychologically "weak." Nietzsche's aristocratic goal attests to his belief in a kind of human perfectibility which precedes morality and is basically independent of politics.

Who, then, has "Dionysian" power according to Nietzsche? Primarily a person whose sense of existence and self-confidence do not depend upon external reinforcements drawn from the hostile negation of other people (as is the case of exigent moralists, for example), or from comforting metaphysical illusions about the universe. The Dionysian person, says Nietzsche, affirms his or her life *out of itself*, rather than by negating (or affirming) the life of others. Also, free of guilt or remorse, he or she need not instill those feelings in others as a means of controlling or subtly punishing them. Dionysian aristocracy is singular, self-sufficient, and rather lonely. No relation to others (whether social, political, moral, or emotional) is a precondition for the Dionysian character's self-feeling and self-affirmation. Whether he or she harms or helps another person, this is not a prerequisite for his or her own sense of personality and self-worth, but the natural expression and affirmation of a powerful personality that *already* exists. The Dionysian person's action is thereby beyond good and evil (in the sense of moral obligation): it expresses the person's very being.[3]

Another sign of Dionysian power is the lack of metaphysical illusion, accompanied by the rejection of nihilism. The Nietzschean view of being as Godless and immanent throughout must not produce nihilistic despair but, rather, joy and creative energies. If centuries of Christian usage had not trained us to see the "spiritual" as exclusive of the "material" (or "earthly"), we might have said that in Nietzsche Dionysian power replaces the traditional concept of spirit. But in order to give this idea its true meaning, we must set it in Nietzsche's own context, which rejects the matter/spirit dichotomy.

Though will to power is active everywhere, it can have both genuine and devious expressions. The latter is typically illustrated by the self-deceptive "will to truth," which derives from the weak person's imaginary wish to subjugate the universe to a network of laws, causes, reasons, and a moral world order, thus overcoming its chaos by the force of an illusion. To this drive corresponds another: the drive toward social conformity, "herd morality," which is another deviant form of will to power.

All our world images, says Nietzsche, originate in moral and existential interests. Everything depends on the kind of life we (unconsciously) desire to live and on how much unsettling truth we can endure consciously. Nietzsche's genealogy sees moral drives at work behind the so-called will to truth and all rational science; then, scrutinizing morality itself, it finds – or alleges – that our lofty moral claims also have their source in a deviant will to power, which can affirm itself only through the aggressive, rancorous negation of other people – usually those whose personality is more powerful, more self-contained, and more self-content than ours. This is *ressentiment*, a key concept in Nietzsche's critique of morality.

Ressentiment, the Jewish priests, and slave morality

Historically, *ressentiment* became a revolutionary force in ancient priestly Judaism, which created new values and projected them into Christianity, whereby the morality of the "weak" became a universal, all-powerful system.

At this point all the asperity and scathing abuse of which Nietzsche is capable are mercilessly cast against the ancient Jews. No ambivalence exists at this point; Nietzsche is as categorical here as he has been in rejecting anti-Semitism – or Christianity. His rhetorical flair, too, is enlisted in service of his wrath, as in the expression "slave morality" and other inventive phrases. He decries priestly Judaism with the same intensity as he had decried anti-Semitism and Christianity – because he sees the three as genealogical cousins.

Here is a selection of quotations:

> The slave revolt in morality begins when *ressentiment* itself becomes creative and gives birth to values: the *ressentiment* of natures that are denied the true reaction, that of deeds, and compensate themselves with an imaginary revenge. While every noble morality develops

from a triumphant affirmation of itself, slave morality from the outset says No to what is "outside" what is "different," what is "not
itself"; and *this* No is its creative deed. (*GM* I, §10)

Ressentiment, Nietzsche adds, consists in this reversal: The source of
value no longer resides in the noble person's looking inwardly into
what he is, but in the petty, rancorous gaze which the slave takes
outwardly, at what he is not.

In order to exist, slave morality always first needs a hostile external
world; [. . .] its action is fundamentally reaction. The reverse is the
case with the noble mode of valuation: it acts and grows spontaneously, it seeks its opposite only so as to affirm itself more gratefully and triumphantly – its negative concept "low," "common,"
"bad" is only the subsequently-invented pale, contrasting image in
relation to its positive basic concept – filled with life and passion
through and through – "we noble ones, we good, beautiful, happy
ones!" (Ibid.)

While the noble man lives in trust and openness with himself (*gen-
naios* "of noble descent" underlines the nuance "upright" and probably also "naive"), the man of *ressentiment* is neither upright nor
naive nor honest and straightforward with himself. His soul squints;
his spirit loves hiding places, secret paths and back doors. (Ibid.)

In a word,

[The person of *ressentiment*] is quite the contrary of what the noble
man does, who conceives the basic concept "good" in advance and
spontaneously out of himself and only then creates for himself an
idea of "bad". (*GM* I, §11)

The person of *ressentiment* affirms his existence through the petty
negation of another. Therefore his concept of evil is primary and is
more powerful than his concept of good. The "good" which originally was supposed to designate him and affirm his power and worth
now has a more important task: to serve the concept of evil and the
aggressiveness it entails towards others, by providing a norm by
which one can blame and negate the other as a means of affirming
oneself. This is the perverse good, whose twin (equally devious and
perverse) is "evil." In the noble person, however, good is the primary force: the feeling of plenitude and self-worth which needs no
outward negation to reassure itself. Even when regarding the other
as "bad" [*schlecht*] in the sense of "lower quality" rather than

morally evil, its value framework is a paler reflection of its own self-affirmation. No rancor is involved here, no blame, venom, or hatred; there is a natural sense of superiority, at times an aristocratic contempt not lacking in humor and generous indulgence. In this respect, the noble person's mental economy is alleged to be cleaner and saner, because it does not bear the burden of vengefulness and hatred which poison the mind of the person of *ressentiment*.

In the distant past, Nietzsche thinks, when the rulers spontaneously identified themselves as good and created the "good/bad" division, as distinct from "good/evil," there was a partial overlap between mental and political aristocracy; but this is no longer true. So Nietzsche proposes a *different* model of human excellence, one in which true aristocracy is existential rather than political or hereditary. Also, contrary to a common view, we must point out that Nietzsche's Dionysian person, although standing outside the Christian morality of love, does not step outside the domain of value (the ethical domain) altogether. On the contrary, such a person embodies value (the "good") within him or herself, whereas his opposite, the self-righteous moralist acting under the mask or guise of charity and love, is the lower human figure who embodies the "bad" in his very fight against "evil." This makes of Nietzsche a moralist, not in the sense of making demands or prescribing obligations, but in the sense of aspiring to human perfectibility – to attaining what he takes to be a higher quality of existence. "My last book: *Beyond Good and Evil* [. . .] does *not* mean 'Beyond Good and Bad' ", he states explicitly (*GM* I, §17). As Nietzsche realizes (and as befits his theory), there are moral drives and interests behind his own philosophy too.

We stand, then, within the world of value and ethics, which the ancient Jewish revolution has taken over. For Nietzsche, to "rule" is not primarily to hold political or physical power, but to control the cultural values, to shape the norms and basic evaluations which dominate people's lives. (We shall meet this view in the next chapter, when dealing with the Jews of the present.) In this respect the ancient Jews took control over Europe while working in the service of decadence. Exploiting the apparatus of *ressentiment*, they enabled the "weak" person to perform an imaginary vengeance against the powerful ones and dominate them. Thereby the Jews took vengeance on the Gentile world. The morality of *ressentiment* provided new avenues for aggressive venom to hit the opponent, because now it became possible to make demands on him, reproach him for his moral offenses, blame and decry him, and so on.

Moreover, to crown the process, the opponent interiorized the aggressivity against him and transformed it into an aggressiveness toward himself, expressed as remorse, bad conscience, repentance, and other forms of self-denial.

> *Who* is "evil" in the sense of the morality of *ressentiment*. The answer, in all strictness, is: *precisely* the "good man" of the other morality, precisely the noble, powerful man, the ruler, but dyed in another color, interpreted in another fashion, seen in another way by the venomous eye of *ressentiment*. (*GM* I, §11)

Though Nietzsche does not say so explicitly, Christianity by itself was unable to carry out its revolution, which required more than a simple aggregate of soft, vengeful *ressentiment*. For the Christian revolution to take place, "*ressentiment* itself should [have] become *a creative, value-generating power*" (ibid., my emphasis); and this creative power was supplied by Judaism, especially by the "Jewish hatred," which is of the kind that is capable of creating ideals."

> *That*, however, is what has happened: from the trunk of that tree of vengefulness and hatred, Jewish hatred – the profoundest and sublimest kind of hatred, capable of creating ideals and reversing values, the like of which has never existed on earth before – there grew something equally incomparable, a *new love*, the profoundest and sublimest kind of hatred [...]. One should not imagine it grew up as denial of that thirst for revenge, as the opposite of Jewish hatred! No, the reverse is true! That love grew out of it as its crown, as its triumphant crown spreading itself farther and farther into the purest brightness and sunlight, driven as it were into the domain of light and the heights in pursuit of the goals of that hatred. (*GM* I, §8)

This is an exercise in genealogical analysis. Christian love is the same as its parent, Jewish hatred. Thereby it embodies Israel's subtle and bitter vengeance against the Gentiles. The Jews effected this vengeance in the Second Temple period, when they themselves became subjugated by the clergy and turned into a "priestly people" – an expression which immediately evokes the Christian priest for Nietzsche, and repels him even as he coins it.

> As is well known, the priests are the *most evil enemies* – but why? Because they are the most impotent. [...] The truly great haters in world history have always been priests; likewise the most ingenious haters: [...] let us take at once the most notable example. All that has been done on earth against "the noble," "the powerful," "the

masters," "the rulers," fades into nothing compared with what the *Jews* have done against them; the Jews, that priestly people, who in opposing their enemies and conquerors were ultimately satisfied with nothing less than a radical revaluation of their enemies' values, that is to say, an act of the *most spiritual revenge*. For this alone was appropriate to a priestly people, the people embodying the most deeply repressed priestly vengefulness. It was the Jews who with awe-inspiring consistency, dared to invert the aristocratic value equation (good = noble = powerful = beautiful = happy = beloved of God) and to hang on this inversion with their teeth. (*GM* I, §7)

And with what did Jews replace this noble equation? Nietzsche's text is both interesting and significant. They replaced it forthwith with the message of Jesus Christ: "The wretched alone are the good; the poor, impotent, lowly alone are the good; the suffering, deprived, sick, ugly alone are pious, alone are blessed by God, blessedness is for them alone" (ibid.).

One need not have a specially trained ear to hear the genuine Christian tones and ideas in this text. This is the voice of the New Testament. Placing the kingdom of heaven and the issue of salvation at the center of religious concerns, and promising them to the meek and the modest – these are essential themes of Christianity, not Judaism, which derive from Jesus' challenge to the aristocratic priestly establishment of his time. Here is an interesting feature that occurs in other texts as well: Nietzsche identifies Judaism and Christianity from the outset. He does not start with two distinct doctrines between which he later sets a causal or genealogical link, but interprets Judaism itself (at least its "priestly" phase) as having forthwith a Christian content. In this respect the Jewish message is not Christianity's parent only, but Christianity itself.

No wonder that, later, when characterizing the war between Rome and Judea as a conflict between two universes of value, Nietzsche cites canonical Christian texts to illustrate Judaism: "In Rome the Jew stood *'convicted* of hatred for the whole human race'; [. . .] How on the other hand, did the Jews feel about Rome? A thousand signs tell us; but it suffices to recall the Apocalypse of John, the most wanton of all literary outbursts" (*GM* I, §16). Nietzsche is alluding to the book of Revelation, in which Rome is treated as "the great whore of Babylon." But here we stand wondering again: How can the Apocalypse, a most Christian book, be taken to illustrate a *Jewish* text? Is the New Testament the most evident testimony of the Jews' attitude to Rome? Clearly, Nietzsche tacitly identifies Christianity with Judaism. If so, the "Jews" whom he makes the object of his attack are the early Christians, and not only the Second Temple priests. The early Christians were indeed Jews in every important respect: in their origin and language, in other people's image, and even, for a long time, in their *own* image. Nietzsche shrewdly uses this fact as a rhetorical weapon with which to deal the Christians of his day an awkward "blow beneath the belt."

> Consider to whom one bows down in Rome itself today, as if they were the epitome of all the highest values – and not only in Rome but over almost half the earth [. . .] : *three Jews*, as is known, and *one Jewess* (Jesus of Nazareth, the fisherman Peter, the rug weaver Paul, and the mother of the aforementioned Jesus named Mary). (Ibid.)

These quotes illustrate how Nietzsche sometimes exploits an anti-Semitic image in order to derogate his opponents by attributing a "Jewish" quality to them. In the present case, the despicable image of the Jews which resides in the Christian mind is used as a device against Christianity. If the anti-Semites blame the Jews for having killed Christ, Nietzsche blames them for having begotten him; either way, the Jews are guilty. This guilt is their depth image which Nietzsche too has absorbed from childhood and which he uses here in an untraditional way – no longer as a weapon against the Jews who rejected Christ or against their offspring today, but against the Jews who *engendered* Christ; and, no less, against the Jew who was Christ himself and the Jews who were his first disciples and apostles.

Thereby the difference between the Christians and the ancient Jews is blurred. Jesus is the emissary of the Jewish priests, who caused him to be crucified so as to produce a shocking (and profound) religious symbol by which to conquer the world with their ideas:

> This Jesus of Nazareth, the incarnate gospel of love, this "Redeemer" who brought blessedness and victory to the poor, the sick, and the sinners – was he not [. . .] a seduction and bypath to precisely those *Jewish* values and new ideals? Did Israel not attain the ultimate goal of its sublime vengefulness precisely through the bypath of this "Redeemer," this ostensible opponent and disintegrator of Israel? (*GM* I, §8)

Nietzsche's fascination with his own idea is so great that he really takes off. The Jews performed an act of truly great revenge, an act of "farseeing" vengeful design. By crucifying the man who served as the instrument of their revenge, they tended a bait for the world to swallow. And what a bait! – Nietzsche's excitement grows. What could resemble the explosive, overbearing image of "God on the cross" which Jewish genius invented to serve its purpose? It was an intoxicating and awesome image that stirred up the depth of people's minds, "that mystery of an unimaginable ultimate cruelty and self-crucifixion of God *for the salvation of man.*" (Ibid.)

Does Nietzsche attribute a conscious Machiavellian intention to the Jews? Probably not. The process whose inner logic he describes was, rather, unconscious, flowing intuitively from the depths of a creative vengeful genius. In any event, Nietzsche's flamboyant rhetoric seems to veil a serious genealogical thesis: that Christianity continues "priestly" Judaism not in its overt ideological content but in its underlying, covert psychological structure. At the root of the religion of love, Nietzsche's genealogy has uncovered hatred.

A typical aspect of Nietzsche's ambivalence manifests itself here: his admiration for the Jews' power and genius and his no less great aversion for the psycho-cultural content of their revolution. This ambivalence takes, at times, a dangerous rhetorical form, when Nietzsche tries to subvert Christianity by using anti-Jewish stereotypes. These stereotypes are active in his intended audience's mind; we might conjecture that they also reside passively in his own mind, as traces of a past he had overcome but could not erase from memory.

Indeed, four negative images of Judaism seem, on further examination, to continue to reside in Nietzsche's mind, though he radically reverses their course and subjects them to his own rhetorical needs. The first three are content stereotypes, but the fourth is basically an emotive-evaluative image:

1 Jews are commonly represented as the people of hatred (Tacitus: *odium humani generis* – they hate the human race and are hated in return). Nietzsche translates this image into the psychology of *ressentiment.*

2 Jews are guilty of Europe's misfortunes (whatever they may be at the time), which they have perpetrated out of revenge. Nietzsche shifts this to what he sees as Europe's greatest misfortune, Christianity.

3 The Jews have killed Jesus. Nietzsche reverses their blame: they have begotten him.

4 Words like *Jew* and *Jewish* connote something despicable and evoke aversion. Nietzsche diverts this reaction to Christianity by presenting its ideals as "Jewish" and its founders as "three Jews and a Jewess." Thereby he exploits anti-Semitic images (compounded by anti-female prejudice) to hurt Christianity and embarrass its believers.

There is little doubt that Nietzsche's rhetoric draws on the negative image of the Jews as it had existed in his own mind in the past. Though, meanwhile, he has overcome his youthful anti-Semitic "disease," he has not erased its traces from memory, but uses them in the war he now wages against Christianity (and, as we shall see, also against the anti-Semites themselves). Possibly his self-overcoming enabled Nietzsche to use the traces of his conquered anti-Semitism without allowing them to re-poison his mind. Yet this is a dangerous game. Nietzsche is playing with fire here, both with himself and with his audience. (A temptation is never fully resisted, and Nietzsche's German and European audience was especially liable to miss his dialectical irony and take his image at face value.)

The three phases of Judaism

Nietzsche, however, is no essentialist, and Judaism does not have a single shape for him. Nor does he attribute an unchanging essence (or "fate") to any people or historical culture (this too distinguishes him from racism in its fundamental metaphysical sense). Just as Hellenism did not have a fixed essence but knew several transformations (as described in the *Birth of Tragedy* and elsewhere), so too there is no single Judaism, but a people assuming several radically different forms of existence, while at the same time gathering experience and historical "depth" in the course of their peregrinations.

Thus, Nietzsche finds an early, pure phase in Judaism which has not yet taken a proto-Christian turn and is worthy of admiration – partly because, in certain respects, it comes close to the Nietzschean ideal. This is expressed in the radical distinction he draws between the Jewish Bible (the Old Testament) and the New Testament.

Contrary to the claims of Christian theology, the move from Judaism to Christianity is not progress but a regression. Compared with the grandeur and sublimity of the Jewish Bible, Second Temple ("priestly") Judaism marks an era of decline and degeneration.

How can anyone today still submit to the simplicity of Christian theologians to the point of insisting with them that the development of the conception of God from the "God of Israel," the god of the people, to the Christian God, the quintessence of everything good, represents *progress*? [...] After all, the opposite stares you in the face. (*A*, §17)

This difference is reflected in the gap between the Old Testament and the New:

In the Jewish "Old Testament," the book of divine justice, there are human beings, things, and speeches in so grand a style that Greek and Indian literature have nothing to compare with it. With terror and reverence one stands before these tremendous remnants of what man once was [...]. To have glued [the] New Testament, a kind of rococo of taste in every respect, to the Old Testament to make *one* book, as the "Bible," as the "book par excellence" – that is perhaps the greatest audacity and "sin against the spirit" that literary Europe has on its conscience. (*BGE*, §52)

I do not like the "New Testament," that should be plain; [...] The *Old* Testament – that is something else again: all honor to the Old Testament! I find in it great human beings, a heroic landscape, and something of the very rarest quality in the world, the incomparable naiveté of the *strong heart*; what is more, I find people. In the New one, on the other hand, I find nothing but petty sectarianism, mere rococo of the soul, mere involutions, nooks, queer things, the air of the conventicle, not to forget an occasional whiff of bucolic mawkishness that belongs to the epoch (*and* to the Roman province) and is not so much Jewish as Hellenistic. Humility and self-importance cheek-by-jowl; a garrulousness of feeling that almost stupefies; impassioned vehemence, not passion; embarrassing gesticulation. (*GM* III, §22)

If we compare covert mental structures rather than explicit arguments, we shall see how Nietzsche's characterization of the New Testament as a petty web of "mere involution, nooks," and so on echoes the way in which the *Genealogy* portrays the person of *ressentiment*: "his soul *squints*, his spirit loves hiding places, secret paths and back doors" (*GM* I, §10). We might also compare the noble person's sincerity and the aristocratic innocence of someone living in openness and self-confidence (ibid.) with the human landscape of the Old Testament, where Nietzsche finds "the innocence of strong hearts" and "great men" operating in a "heroic landscape." The comparison reveals that Nietzsche recognizes the noble features of his Dionysian person manifested in the Jewish Bible, whereas the New Testament expresses those of the person of *ressentiment*. While both are Jewish books, Judaism itself divides into several periods and life-forms. The original Jewish spirit is embodied in the Old Testament, whereas the "Judaism" which Nietzsche rejects is the spirit of the New Testament.

The gap between the two books expresses a wider distinction in ancient Judaism which Nietzsche draws – between the biblical era and that of the Second Temple. All the grandeur and sublimity of ancient Judaism reside in biblical times; whereas the New Testament – also a Jewish text for Nietzsche – manifests the "priestly" Judaism of the Second Temple. As for the third and longest period in Jewish history – the exile and Diaspora which followed the destruction of the Second Temple and the loss of the Jewish state – it too arouses admiration in Nietzsche, however qualified (see next chapter). Biblical Judaism was marked by inner grandeur and an unbroken harmony with nature, whereas Diaspora Judaism displayed a power of will, endurance, long-suffering, and much self-discipline.

By breaking ancient Judaism in two, Nietzsche suggests that its "legalistic" feature had not existed from the start but emerged only during the Second Temple era. Biblical Judaism was a totally different religion – natural, vital, and sublime. Of course, its sublimity should not be understood in Hegel's sense but in its opposite. Hegel's "religion of sublimity," as we saw in Part I, wasn't at all sublime; its laws expressed man's self-effacement before a sublime God and thus was slavish in character. For Nietzsche, biblical religion is the religion of a free, natural people, flowing with vitality and positive power, and thereby sublime in itself.

Nietzsche's division between biblical and priestly Judaism is influenced by the well-known (and controversial) biblical scholar, Wellhausen, though Nietzsche invests Wellhausen's distinction with his own thoughts and feelings. Here is his voice again:

> At the time of the kings, Israel also stood in the right, that is, the natural, relationship to all things. Its Yahweh was the expression of a consciousness of power, of joy in oneself, of hope for oneself: through him victory and welfare were expected; through him nature was trusted to give what the people needed – above all, rain. Yahweh is the god of Israel and therefore the god of justice: the logic of every people that is in power and has a good conscience. In the festival cult these two sides of the self-affirmation of a people find expression: they are grateful for the great destinies which raised them to the top; they are grateful in relation to the annual cycle of the seasons and to all good fortune in stock farming and

agriculture. This state of affairs long remained the ideal, even after it had been done away with in melancholy fashion [. . .] above all, that typical prophet (that is, critic and satirist of the moment), Isaiah. (*A*, §25)

Nietzsche is clearly injecting his own value terms into this idealization. In biblical Judaism the feeling of gratitude flows from the source of self-confidence, not from a sense of duty and obligation which exist beforehand. The God of Israel is not a terrorizing despot imposing external moral laws but the expression of the people's own self-affirmation and flowing power; the self-confident gratitude of the people assumes a most natural form in holidays and celebrations; and justice is the outcome not of *ressentiment* (as it is later in the "religion of the law"; see again *GM*, "On the Origin of Justice") but of self-affirmative power. The God of Israel is just (and the people of Israel, we might add in this text's spirit, is good) as a primary natural fact rooted in spontaneous power, and neither because it had subjected itself to external moral norms, laid down by those who resent its power, nor because it had conformed to the image of a "moral world order" which governs the universe.

This ideal was destroyed by the priestly culture, which set an example of the "denaturation" of natural values:

The concept of God becomes a tool in the hands of priestly agitators, who now interpret all happiness as a reward, all unhappiness as punishment for disobeying God, as "sin": that most mendacious device of interpretation, the alleged "moral world order," with which the natural concepts of cause and effect are turned upside down once and for all. (*A*, §25)

Thus, by their principle of reward and punishment, the "priests" replaced natural causes with supernatural ones and performed the denaturation which characterizes their work. Henceforth God is an exigent God rather than an assisting God. He no longer inspires confidence and daring encouragement but becomes onerous and demanding. Moral commands are "no longer the expression of the conditions for the life and growth of a people, no longer its most basic instinct of life but [. . .] the antithesis of life" (ibid.).

The concept of God falsified, the concept of morality falsified: the Jewish priesthood did not stop there. The whole of the *history* of Israel could not be used: away with it! These priests accomplished a miracle of falsification, and a good part of the Bible now lies before us as documentary proof. With matchless scorn for every tradition, for every historical reality, they translated the past of their own people into religious terms, that is, they turned it into a stupid salvation mechanism of guilt before Yahweh, and punishment [...] they made either wretchedly meek [...] or "godless cries" out of powerful, often very bold, figures in the history of Israel; they simplified the psychology of every great event by reducing it to the idiotic formula, "obedience *or* disobedience to God."

One step further: the "will of God" (that is, the conditions for the preservation of priestly power) must be *known*: to this end a "revelation" is required. In plain language: a great literary forgery becomes necessary, a "holy scripture" is discovered; it is made public with full hieratic pomp, with days of repentance and cries of lamentation over the long "sin." The "will of God" had long been fixed: all misfortune rests on one's having become estranged from the "holy scripture." (*A*, §26)

From now on all things in life are so ordered that the priest is indispensable everywhere; at all natural occurrences in life, at birth, marriage, sickness, death, not to speak of "sacrifices" (meals), the holy parasite appears in order to denature them – in his language: to "consecrate."

For one must understand this: every natural custom, every natural institution (state, judicial order, marriage, care of the sick and the poor), every demand inspired by the instinct of life – in short, everything that contains its value *in itself* is made altogether valueless, *anti*-valuable by the parasitism of the priest (or the "moral world order"): now it requires a sanction after the event – a *value-conferring power* is needed to negate what is natural in it and to *create* a value by so doing. The priest devalues, *desecrates* nature: this is the price of his existence. (Ibid.)

To this analysis of sacrality as the negation and alienation of nature, Nietzsche adds a second, more traditional motif: exposition of the priesthood as an interest group and a power establishment.

Disobedience of God, that is, of the priest, of "the Law," is now called "sin"; the means for "reconciliation with God" are, as is meet, means that merely guarantee still more thorough submission to the priest: the priest alone "redeems." Psychologically considered, "sins" become indispensable in any society organized by priests: they are the real handles of power. The priest *lives* on sins, it is essential for him that people "sin." Supreme principle: "God forgives those who repent" – in plain language: those who submit to the priest. (Ibid.)

And again, as in the *Genealogy*, this "breed of priests" generated an

even greater evil: "On such utterly *false* soil, where everything natural, every natural value, every *reality* was opposed by the most profound instincts of the ruling class, *Christianity* grew up – a form of
mortal enmity against reality that has never yet been surpassed" (*A*,
§27). These are clear, poignant words. Nietzsche in this text takes off
his mask, or many of its layers. But he forgets that the contrast
between the natural and the sacral is not specifically Jewish. Jews
certainly tend to sacralize many daily activities, tearing them away
from the spontaneous flow of nature by way of a special benediction,
prayer, or ritual. Thus in every part of the day, the Jew injects a
wedge between the natural and the sacral. Yet, to a lesser degree,
other religions do so too. Also, the phenomenon of priests as consti-
tuting a power structure which uses the sacral to promote its interests is equally a quasi-universal phenomenon. It seems that
Nietzsche, somewhat like Hegel, projects on Judaism (in its Second
Temple variety) all the negative features he finds in religion in general (perhaps excepting pantheism).

The critique of Judaism in the *Antichrist* differs in certain important respects from the earlier *Genealogy*. The *Genealogy* stressed the
psychology of *ressentiment* (manifested in pity, guilt, self-negation,
and offering the other cheek) as the origin of the Jewish reversal of
values; whereas the *Antichrist* places that origin in what he calls
"denaturation," meaning the negation of life, disgust for reality, and
artificial imposition of a "moral world order" upon nature. The main
distortion now arises from pitting the sacred against the profane –
that is, against the natural. The Jewish priests treat natural existence
as devoid of all value. Being can gain value only when stamped with
the mark of the sacred, which abolishes its natural character and
transforms it into something different and imaginary.

These two changes are linked. If natural existence is experienced
as meaningless and devoid of value, then it must draw its value from
some "moral world order" governing it; likewise, the ritual which,
through the imagination, transforms the natural into the sacral is
supposed to impart value and significance to a being that lacks them
in itself. In both ways, nature is drained and depleted, and man's
self-experience as a natural being is undermined. No longer can
there be a sense of plenitude, of self-sufficient life which requires no
external justification (but feels, on the contrary, that the very search
for such justification alienates natural existence and vacates its
immanent significance). This dilutes nature and destroys man's original confidence and self-experience as an immanent being, at one
with nature.

The reader, at this point, may hear strong echoes of Hegel's analysis of Judaism. The Jews divested the natural world of its spirituality and immanent meaning and made it "prosaic." For Hegel this was major progress: overcoming the idolatry inherent in "natural religion," the Jews transferred all spirituality to God and placed spirit above nature; but because they did so in the defective mode of "sublimity," they remained alienated from the principle they had themselves established. To Nietzsche, the Jews became alienated *because of that very principle*, which "denaturalized" their existence. Their revolution was regressive; it drained nature of immanent worth while creating an imaginary domain of value over and above nature, perceived as a "moral world order."

Another apparent difference from the *Genealogy* is that the *Antichrist* no longer stresses the Jewish "slave morality" revolution, with its ideas of guilt, conscience, self-denial, and so on, but complains mainly that the original Jewish spirit has petrified into a rigid "priestly code." Superficially, this sounds close to Kant's charge of "legalism" – the rigidity of the law as opposed to inner morality; but, of course, this cannot be what Nietzsche means, since Kant's argument itself is, in Nietzsche's terms, an anti-Dionysian moralistic claim inherited from the same priestly Judaism. The actual complaint of the *Antichrist* continues that of the *Genealogy*: Jewish moralism in both its inner spirit and its legal manifestations expresses a decaying will and form of life.

Historical imprecision

Nietzsche's historical account is imprecise; among other things, he confuses the priests and the Pharisees. Jesus was certainly not a spokesman for the priestly elite, but rather its opponent; his reform was a popular one, arising probably from a radical wing which separated itself from the Pharisean movement – the popular, anticlerical scholars and spiritual leaders of the common folk, even of the poor of the land; whereas the ruling priests mainly belonged to the aristocratic class and the Sadducee party, which denied the ideas of the next world and the kingdom of heaven. Christian tradition presents Jesus as the enemy of the Pharisees, but he was probably a radical member of the Pharisees who opposed the ruling Sadducee priests. Nietzsche's mistake is to drive Jesus directly into the priestly camp – perhaps because, according to the New Testament, both Jesus and the priests opposed the Pharisees. Yet Jesus opposed the Pharisees "from within," so to speak, because they weren't pure enough and radical enough; and like them, he fought against the priestly establishment, which eventually fought back by arresting him and extraditing him to the Romans as a rebel. It may be that Nietzsche's dialectical, ambivalent identification with Jesus made him confuse Jesus' milieu with that of his opponents.

Another philosophical change introduced in the *Antichrist* is Nietzsche's reliance on "nature" as a positive model for life and action. This may suit the popular image according to which Nietzsche glorifies the "natural" and the "vital," but actually it is a problematic approach which Nietzsche takes only occasionally. More fundamental in his work is the opposite approach, which refrains from any normative use of the concept of nature (or the "natural") and avoids picturing nature as a given, finished entity. For example, Nietzsche rejects the "natural law" approach to ethics and politics, as well as the romantic movement of a "return to nature" which, following Rousseau, sees civilization as a necessarily corrupting force. The crucial factor for Nietzsche is not nature but culture, which always entails the shaping and overcoming of nature. What has deformed European life is not culture as such, but a specific culture – Christian and rationalistic culture – which ought to be replaced not by crude nature, but by a new, Dionysian culture. The Dionysian vitality which Nietzsche seeks is not "natural" but culturally reshaped; there is nothing primal in it, nor is it merely instinctual. When Nietzsche praises actions driven by "instincts," he means *culturally shaped* instincts, instincts that have not lost their vitality by having been molded by culture, or, putting it differently, cultural factors that have so penetrated one's vital being as to become instinctual. They are not "mere" instincts, nor do they express or impose some pre-cultural "natural" model.

The concepts of life and power which occupy center stage of Nietzsche's ethical vocabulary entail a challenge to nature and the overcoming of nature. Nietzsche loathed "barbarian Dionysianism" – the raw, self-abandoning natural drive which lets itself go without shape or discipline. The Dionysianism he defended was a synthesis of raw power with formal and aesthetic shaping, which disciplines it and gives it shape.

It is therefore inapt for Nietzsche to accept mere nature, nature as such, as a desirable or even required model, yet he *seems* to be doing just that in the text before us (and occasionally elsewhere). Is this yet another case in which Nietzsche contradicts himself, or oscillates without reaching a conclusion? I do not think so. There is a way out of the problem, as follows. Raw nature is *never* a normative model for Nietzsche. Value always depends on the shaping power that overcomes raw nature. Yet this power too is "nature" (or "natural") in the sense that it is inner-worldly and immanent. In other words, the creative, overcoming power which transcends given nature is itself "natural," since it springs from the real world and expresses it, rather than being imposed on it by another world. The affinity which Nietzsche discovered between himself and Spinoza may help us here. If "naturalness" is understood in a semi-Spinozistic sense – as immanence and as the power of being and action which affirms itself without guilt or self-effacement – then breaking from this natural attitude must indeed be considered bad in Nietzschean terms. The first value which Nietzsche wishes to restore is the life-experience of immanence – the sense that the stream and modulations of this-worldly life are all there is, that they comprise the total horizon of being and that no eternal value ought to be pursued beyond this life which will make the latter appear valueless. So understood – if we recognize that the first step in Nietzsche's revaluation of values is to restore immanent life-experience and affirm it with acceptance, even joy, without seeking consolations and justifications beyond this life – it is clear what Nietzsche means by the "denaturation" caused by the ancient Jewish priests, and why he so fiercely denounced it.

Nietzsche and Wellhausen

When Nietzsche accuses the Second Temple priests of having falsified the Bible, he is referring to an actual textual forgery. Nietzsche is influenced by the well-known biblical scholar Wellhausen, whose *Prolegomena to the History of Israel* in the second, 1883 edition Nietzsche owned and studied thoroughly (as his many marginal annotations testify). Nietzsche's allegation of forgery seems to refer to (a) the book of Deuteronomy, which, according to Wellhausen, was actually written (not merely "discovered") under the reign of King Josiah; and (b) what Wellhausen called the *Priesterkodex* (the "priestly code") – new scriptural material composed in the Second Temple period and expressing its petrified religious outlook. The term *Priesterkodex* does not designate a specific *book* but an ingredient of the Pentateuch written much later and inserted apocryphally into the text. Here, then, was scholarly support for Nietzsche's fierce claim that the priests have falsified not only the *spirit* of biblical

Judaism but the ancient books as well, into which they have fraudulently introduced both new material and a foreign spirit.

A major falsification consisted in subjecting all great biblical events to an external scheme of punishment and reward. Everything came to depend on whether the Israelites "would do the good – or the evil in Yahwe's eyes." This is characteristic of a "priestly" religion engendering a "priestly code."

The term "priestly code" was current among Protestant scholars, who used to view Judaism as "the Religion of the Law." Nietzsche is not interested in the law as such, but in the psychology of the person who creates this law and lives by it. Hence his emphasis on the priest as the kind of person who makes this religious form possible and uses it to make *himself* – the vindictive mentality and petty life-quality he represents – possible. This contrasts with the overflow and self-confident greatness (bordering on innocence) which Nietzsche sees everywhere in the Old Testament.

The basic psychological form underlying "the religion of the law" (and the cult of angry "justice" in general – see *GM*, "On the Origin of Justice"), is again *ressentiment*, whose work is equally found in the religion of love and brotherly morality; so Nietzsche as before ascribed the features of Christianity directly to "priestly" Judaism, as if no difference existed between them and no passage was necessary.

Wellhausen was more than a biblical philologist; he was also a theologian with strong ideas. Nietzsche could read in Wellhausen a sentence like: "Religious worship was a natural thing in Hebrew antiquity; it was the blossom of life, the heights and depths which it was its business to transfigure and glorify."[4] He could also find the following difference between the biblical religion and the later "priestly code": "A sacrifice was a meal, a fact showing how remote was the idea of antithesis between spiritual earnestness and secular joyousness ... It is earthly relationships that receive their consecration thereby, and in correspondence are the natural festal occasions presented by the vicissitudes of life."[5] And elsewhere: "The festivals rest upon agriculture, the basis at once of life and of religion. The soil, the fruitful soil, is the object of religion; it takes the place alike of heaven and hell."[6]

By contrast, the "priestly code" (Second Temple Judaism) represents the corruption of life and of religion.

The Creator of heaven and earth becomes the manager of a petty scheme of salvation; the living God descends from His throne to make way for the law. The law thrusts itself in everywhere; it commands and blocks up the access to heaven.[7]

See what Chronicles has made out of David! The founder of the Kingdom has become the founder of the temple and the public worship, the king and hero at the head of his companions in arms has become the singer and master of ceremonies at the head of a swarm of priestesses and Levites; his clearly cut figure has become a feeble holy picture, seen through a cloud of incense.[8]

Although Nietzsche draws heavily on Wellhausen, the resemblance is superficial. As in many such cases, Wellhausen merely supplied the material which Nietzsche adapted to his own terms and needs. At bottom, Wellhausen recognized an ascent in the history of religion; not so Nietzsche. He molded Wellhausen's findings into his own theory about grand and petty power and the difference between overflow and *ressentiment*. The ancient Hebrew's superiority is portrayed in terms of Nietzsche's special theory of Dionysian power (which the people's relation to its god is said to incarnate). Through his God, the ancient Hebrew affirms and expresses the flow of his own being; he does not efface himself, nor is he filled with guilt and remorse before a foreign, commanding deity. *This is a (rare) case of Dionysian power operating within religion itself.* Nietzsche seems to believe that this was possible in the archaic world only, but is no longer in a reflective period like ours, when God is already dead. Therefore, God in biblical times could symbolize man's Dionysian identification with nature, whereas in modern times the Dionysian position requires, on the contrary, that we free ourselves of God's image (and declare it obsolete).

Let us listen again to the feverish finale of the *Antichrist*, to which the whole book leads:

I raise against the Christian church the most terrible of all accusations that any accuser ever uttered. It is to me the highest of all conceivable corruption. It has had the will to the last corruption that is even possible. The Christian church has left nothing untouched by its corruption; it has turned every value into an unvalue, every truth into a lie, every integrity into a vileness of the soul. [. . .] This eternal indictment I will write on all walls [...]. I call Christianity the one great curse, the one great innermost corruption, the one great instinct of revenge, for which no means is poisonous, stealthy, subterranean, small enough – I call it the one immortal blemish of mankind. (*A*, §62)

Such agitated words were never uttered by Nietzsche against Judaism, or against any other religion or life-form. If we listen to these feverish words within their rhetorical context – which requires distinguishing between tonalities no less than between ideas – then Nietzsche's critique of Judaism takes on different dimensions. The real evil, the actual villain, is Christianity, and Judaism, in one of its phases, leads to it. Yet even in perversity, Judaism is superior to Christianity because it retains part of its ancient power, whereas Christianity is only feeble – it is priestly Judaism in the pure state, without these vestiges.

Is this an anti-Jewish stand? The generalization as such has no sense. Precisely because Nietzsche has freed himself of anti-Semitism, he can let himself distinguish within Judaism between a period of grandeur and one of decadence (both in terms of his philosophy of power). His scorn for one period of Judaism and admiration for another testify to a certain maturity and/or freedom of mind gained in dealing with the Jews. A person who has not overcome anti-Semitism will often hesitate to express even fair criticism of the Jews.

Jesus as a paradoxical "pure" instant

There is one paradoxical point at which the continuity between priestly Judaism and Christianity is broken. According to the *Antichrist*, Jesus was not the father of Christian decadence but a "holy anarchist" who transcended the culture of his time and, as the head of a "little rebellious movement," opposed the ruling priestly establishment (*A*, §27). Of course Jesus was Jewish too, but what he announced was "true Christianity," something very different from the doctrine which Europe later accepted, and especially distinct from what became institutionalized in the Church. In his ambivalent admiration for Jesus, and perhaps in his unconscious attempt to resemble his crucified opponent in human depth, Nietzsche draws Jesus' portrait with a sympathetic psychological brush. Still, his Jesus is not at all a Dionysian person – especially because Jesus' most powerful instinct turned against reality. Jesus is no Nietzschean figure, yet he displays certain features that resemble the Nietzschean ideal. From a structural standpoint he resembles Spinoza, and also the collective figure of Diaspora Jews. That all three cases involve Jews is certainly no accident.

Thus Nietzsche, the self-proclaimed Antichrist, sets out to separate and defend Jesus against the figure of Christ (that is, the "Messiah") as created by Paul and the Church. In the continuous decline from priestly Judaism to Christianity, Jesus is not only a link, but equally a break. He constitutes a pure "instant" which transcends decadence, even though others have used him to amplify that decadence.[9] Nietzsche says all this of the *man* Jesus, the mortal person, for he does not recognize his divinity. Nietzsche is interested in the savior's psychology, not in his history. He remonstrates against the quasi-historical literature about Jesus, like the Lives of D. F. Strauss (a Hegelian) and Ernest Renan. We have no access to the history of saints, Nietzsche claims, and "to apply scientific methods to them, in the absence of any other documents, strikes me as doomed to failure from the start" (*A*, §28). However, the scriptural text, despite some ambiguities, enables us to reconstruct the savior's psychological type, even though, because of the Gospel, our portrait may be tinged with a few "alien features" (*A*, §29). As a rule, canonical texts are better suited to the purposes of the psychologist and genealogist of culture than the historian.

Nietzsche's Jesus has features that put him in opposition to Christianity. Jesus did not actively negate the world; he used signs to go beyond reality in a symbolic way only (*A*, §32). Also, Jesus did not oppose other doctrines, because he himself did not propagate any doctrine, in the sense of a "truth" that can be set against other truths. "His proofs are inner 'lights', inner feelings of pleasure and self-affirmations, all of them 'proofs of strength' " (ibid.). Jesus does not polemicize against people who think differently, because he does not understand them to be possible; he cannot conceive of someone being blind to the source from which he himself draws light. Therefore Jesus knows no envy, no hatred of other people; his life streams forth from its own sources in an overflow of self-affirmation – a semi-Nietzschean Jesus, to be sure! Unlike Christianity, Jesus did not negate the world, for the concept of "the world" was unknown to him. He was a mystic living in a universe of symbols above reality, above science and politics. This was Jesus' *special* mode of withdrawing from the world; but there is nothing ascetic in his withdrawal, no negation directed toward the outside, only the self-enclosed affirmation of what Jesus himself is and symbolizes.

Jesus is a special case for Nietzsche, enjoying the benefit of exception. His rejection of the world is of a laudable kind, very different from the monk's ascetic ideal (castigated in the *Genealogy*) and unrelated to negative petty feelings like hatred, envy, and so forth. Morally too, Nietzsche's Jesus stands beyond the world of sin, reward, and punishment (*A*, §33). Blessedness for him is not a reward which one receives for obeying God, but the first and only reality. The rest is a sign with which to speak of it. And when projecting his attitude outward as a model for a way of life – for this is all that Jesus preached – the outcome is peculiar and very interesting: a new kind of Christianity, purified and based no longer on *ressentiment* but on a quasi-Nietzschean spirit.

> It is not a "faith" that distinguishes the Christian: the Christian *acts*, he is distinguished by acting *differently*: by not resisting, either in word or in his heart, those who treat him ill; by making no distinction between foreigner and native, between Jew and not-Jew [. . .] ; by not growing angry with anybody, by not despising anybody; by not permitting himself to be seen or involved at courts of law; [. . .] The life of the Redeemer was nothing other than *this* practice – nor was his death anything *else*. (*A*, §33)

> This practice is his legacy to mankind: his behavior before the [. . .] accusers and all kinds of slander and scorn – his behavior on the *cross*. He does not resist, he does not defend his right, he takes no step which might ward off the worst; on the contrary, he *provokes* it. And he begs, he suffers, he loves *with* those, *in* those, who do him evil. *Not* to resist, *not* to be angry, *not* to hold responsible – but to resist not even the evil one – to *love* him. (*A*, §35)

These are not the features of a Nietzschean noble person – but of a *non*-Nietzschean nobility, perhaps of the only nobility Nietzsche considers possible. This combines what Nietzsche attributes to Jesus with what he ascribes to Socrates and Spinoza, two other objects of his profound ambivalence. While all three are very different from the Dionysian "overman," they also resemble him in several major respects which provoke Nietzsche's admiration.

In this respect Jesus transcends both Judaism and Christianity and constitutes a unique "instant," a break in the decadent continuum linking the two religions. This is true regardless of Jesus' historical role as the cornerstone of Christianity and in spite of the fact that the Church has falsified his image and made him, as Christ, a primary agent in the process of decadence against which Nietzsche now rises as the modern "Antichrist" (though not as anti-*Jesus*).

The indulgence with which Nietzsche treats Jesus is puzzling. Unconsciously, as I mentioned above, Nietzsche wants to resemble his "crucified" opponent in psychology and human depth, and this leads him to an empathic, if paradoxical, identification with the man Jesus – though not with the figure of Christ. The ideal way in which Nietzsche portrays Jesus could almost make him a model for

Dionysian self-containment and affirmation – and a layer in Nietzsche's own self-ascribed role. For it is the semi-Dionysian "crucified" in Nietzsche that is now preaching in the name of Zarathustra. Though the content of Jesus' message is untenable for Nietzsche, his person and psychology, if rightly understood, are compatible with the new Dionysian culture.[10] This is not the case with Christ, the Messiah, the figure constructed by the Church to suit its own distinct aims.

It is ironic to see Nietzsche come so close to the strategy of Protestant reformers who also raise Jesus above whatever degenerate practices were later adopted in his name. This is another instance of Nietzsche's revolution being both informed and constrained by the religion he rejects. The arch-enemy of Christianity is a very Christian (and even Protestant) heretic.[11] Yet this does not change my conclusion that his attack on priestly Judaism is an inner genealogical moment of his assault on Christianity, and draws its significance (and ferocity) from it.

CHAPTER TEN

The Diaspora and Contemporary Jews

Let us now examine Nietzsche's attitude toward Diaspora Judaism, the longest period of Jewish history, leading to the Jews of the present. Here Nietzsche's admiration takes over again and, in the process, prevails over the negative stereotypes which still inhabit his mind.

Praise through paradox

The image of the shabby, hustling, money-loving Diaspora Jews repelled Nietzsche, as it did most philo-Semitic Christians and, no less, many Jewish modernizers too, who spoke of the ghetto and *Stetl* Jews – or the bankers and stock-exchange speculators – with the same ferocity as can be found in anti-Semitic pamphlets. Nietzsche, however, makes himself the advocate of Diaspora Jews, even with their shoddy qualities. He does so first before the court of his own feelings, and then before the outer world.

> Every nation, every man, possesses unpleasant, indeed dangerous qualities: it is cruel to demand that the Jew should constitute an exception. In him these qualities may even be dangerous and repellent to an exceptional degree; and perhaps the youthful stock-exchange Jew is the most repulsive invention of the entire human race. Nonetheless I should like to know how much must, in a total

accounting, be forgiven a people who, not without us all being to blame, have had the most grief-laden history of any people and whom we have to thank for the noblest human being (Christ), the purest sage (Spinoza), the mightiest book and the most efficacious moral code in the world. Moreover: in the darkest periods of the Middle Ages, when the cloudbanks of Asia had settled low over Europe, it was the Jewish freethinkers, scholars and physicians who, under the harshest personal constraint, held firmly to the banner of enlightenment and intellectual independence and defended Europe against Asia; it is thanks not least to their efforts that a more natural, rational and in any event unmythical elucidation of the world could at last again obtain victory and the ring of culture that now unites us with the enlightenment of Graeco-Roman antiquity remain unbroken. If Christianity has done everything to orientalize the occident, Judaism has always played an essential part in occidentalizing it again: which in a certain sense means making of Europe's mission and history a *continuation of the Greek.* (*HH*, §475)

Like most things Nietzsche says, this text is not free of paradox. It is odd to hear Nietzsche praise so warmly the rationalist Enlightenment and its conquest over myth;[1] nor is it any less strange to read that Jewish scholars were the bearers of Greco-Roman rationalism, while Christianity expressed "orientalism." The paradox is dissolved if we consider that by Greek rationalism Nietzsche means its skeptical, critical side (not its dogmatic teaching), and that the Jewish scholars he has in mind are the small group of heterodox thinkers (like Spinoza, whom he cites by name and possibly sees as paradigmatic). Thus in Nietzsche's image, Diaspora Jews assume a *preparatory* role, compensating Europe for what they did to it in antiquity. It was they, through their dissident scholars rather than their religion, who preserved the flame of critical thinking during the many centuries when Europe was dominated by superstition and religious illusion. Nietzsche's overstatement – for he clearly exaggerates[2] – significantly points to the role he reserves for post-Christian Jews *in general*, especially those of the present. In his time Spinoza was still an isolated case; but two centuries later, Nietzsche could already cite many other names, contemporary Jews who had also left behind their religion without accepting Christianity, and whose peculiar, uprooted state enabled them to perform less arduously the task that Nietzsche felt he had to do the hard way, through suffering and self-overcoming: namely, recognize the death of the ancient God (the Jewish as well as the Christian one) and find new ways to make this worldly life meaningful without metaphysical illusion. Heinrich Heine, the poet and philosopher with whom Nietzsche had many affinities, was a celebrated example; another was Freud, whom Nietzsche could also have cited had he known him; but there were a great many others, not as famous but, cumulatively, even more influential.

Nietzsche's praise of the Bible, Jesus, and Spinoza – another seeming paradox – is in fact compatible with his philosophy, because he admires not the *content* of their doctrines[3] but the psychological structure they embody. More problematic are his words about Jewish morality, which have a false laudatory ring.[4] Actually they express the following duality. On the one hand, Nietzsche is resolute in rejecting Jewish theism and the moral values propagated by Judaism; but on the other hand, he (1) is impressed by the ancient Jews' ability to "create values" – however bad – and make the rest of the world accept them; and especially (2) he admires the Jewish power of existence in the Diaspora, which involves hard discipline and the relentless negation of Christianity. When the Jews rejected Jesus, they became Christianity's genuine Other (or "antipode," to use a Nietzschean idiom), which Nietzsche considers a great merit. What is more, the persecutions they suffered for this rejection helped the Jews to amplify their affirmation of life in a semi-tragic attitude and draw renewed power from their suffering, all the while gaining historical depth and multi-faceted experience.

Power and the schooling of suffering

Nietzsche's admiration for Diaspora Jews overcomes his negative evaluation of priestly Judaism. His praise in this text (*HH*, §475) of "their accumulated capital of spirit and will which they have gained through a long schooling in suffering" is further elaborated in other texts as well, especially *Beyond Good and Evil* and *Daybreak*, which I quoted above in part and now, with the reader's indulgence, shall quote more extensively.[5]

> The Jews, however, are beyond any doubt the strongest, toughest, and purest race now living in Europe; they know how to prevail even under the worst conditions (even better than under favorable conditions), by means of virtues that today one would like to mark as vices – thanks above all to a resolute faith that need not be ashamed before "modern ideas"; they change, *when* they change, always only as the Russian Empire makes its conquests – being an empire that has time and is not of yesterday – namely, according to the principle, "as slowly as possible."

A thinker who has the development of Europe on his conscious will, in all his projects for the future, takes into account the Jews as well as the Russians as the provisionally surest and most probable factors in the great play and fight of forces. What is called a "nation" in Europe today, and is really rather a *res facta* than a *res nata* (and occasionally can hardly be told from a *res ficta et picta*) is in any case something evolving, young, and easily changed, not yet a race, let alone such an *aere perennius* as the Jewish type: these "nations" really should carefully avoid every hot-headed rivalry and hostility! (*BGE*, §251)

And Nietzsche adds a few strong words, which shed more light on the famous passage from *Daybreak* that I shall presently quote:

That the Jews, if they wanted it – or if they were forced into it, which seems to be what the anti-Semites want – *could* even now have preponderance, indeed quite literally mastery over Europe, that is certain; that they are *not* working and planning for that is equally certain. Meanwhile they want and wish rather, even with some importunity, to be absorbed and assimilated by Europe; they long to be fixed, permitted, respected somewhere at long last, putting an end to the nomads' life, to the "Wandering Jew"; and this bent and impulse (which may even express an attenuation of the Jewish instincts) should be noted well and *accommodated*: to that end it might be useful and fair to expel the anti-Semitic screamers from the country. (Ibid.)

The text speaks for itself. The last part reveals Nietzsche's profound empathy with the Jews' longing "to be fixed, permitted, respected somewhere at long last" – to put an end to "wandering" life. It is actually written with warmth – a rare phenomenon in Nietzsche. But the main point is given at the beginning: The Jews, by coping for many centuries with great obstacles, have bred and enhanced their existential power. Nietzsche takes a thesis which Spinoza made current – that Jewish survival is fortified by the hatred of the Gentiles – and implants it within his own conceptual scheme: in the case of strong, nobly inclined people, obstacles are a means of amplifying their power.

Our text also illustrates the fact that Nietzsche's concept of "race" is not merely biological but assumes a commonly inherited *historical* experience (see pp. 135–6 above). The Jews' historical depth as a nation contrasts with the artificial "nations" which are hastily being created in contemporary Europe because of political considerations.[6]

Mastering Europe or losing it

The most striking sentence is the one about the Jews' ability to achieve mastery over Europe. Nietzsche is playing with a familiar anti-Semitic slogan current in his time (which reached a climax in *The Protocols of the Elders of Zion*), and he shapes his text as a response to it. True, Nietzsche tells the anti-Semites, the Jews are certainly capable of becoming Europe's masters – but not because of any base quality in them, or a sordid plan on their part, but rather because of their virtue, the human superiority they have gained through the experience of the Diaspora. However, he "re-assures" the anti-Semite (and starts diverting the stereotype) that the Jews are not at all interested in ruling Europe; their whole aspiration is to be admitted and absorbed in it; and this can only be a blessing for Europe. Thus, using a (rather dangerous) dialectical technique, Nietzsche plays again with an anti-Semitic image while reversing its import.

Daybreak: promise, menace, apotheosis

In the same spirit one should read the famous aphorism in *Daybreak* which I shall now quote in full. Here again the shocking sentence recurs: The Jews face a choice, either to dominate Europe or to lose it. After Hitler and the Nazi genocide, these words have taken on an ominous ring. Readers who project their memories and associations into the text cannot avoid hearing a Nazi-like menace in it. But such a reading is uncritical and misleading.[7] Nietzsche is not threatening the Jews – nor does the possibility of their extermination enter his mind. He is genuinely concerned that the Jews will "lose Europe," by which he means that they may be forced to emigrate or be expelled, not physically exterminated. His analogy is the way the Jews "lost" Egypt in the biblical exodus. Similarly, he fears that because of political anti-Semitism, or the Jews' own seclusion, they will not find their place in modern Europe and may be driven to exile or emigration. Incidentally, the more astute Zionists had a similar vision, but they saw a positive potential in it.[8] Nietzsche, however, opposes Zionism no less than he does anti-Semitism.[9] He wants the Jewish resources of power and breeding to remain in Europe and help reform it. Therefore, the prospect of the Jews "mastering Europe" does not frighten Nietzsche but is, rather, the option he prefers.[10] Nietzsche *wants* the Jews to "dominate Europe" – by which he does not mean to control politics, finance, and the press, but *cultural* mastery: determining new standards and values.

OF THE PEOPLE OF ISRAEL

Among the spectacles to which the coming century invites us is the decision as to the destiny of the Jews of Europe. That their die is cast, that they have crossed their Rubicon, is now palpably obvious: all that is left for them is either to become the masters of Europe or to lose Europe as they once a long time ago lost Egypt, where they had placed themselves before a similar either–or. In Europe, however, they have gone through an eighteenth-century schooling such as no other nation of this continent can boast of – and what they have experienced in this terrible time of schooling has benefited the individual to a greater degree than it has the community as a whole. As a consequence of this, the psychological and spiritual resources of the Jews today are extraordinary; of all those who live in Europe, they are least liable to resort to drink or suicide in order to escape from some profound dilemma – something the less gifted are often apt to do. Every Jew possesses in the history of his fathers and grandfathers a great fund of examples of the coldest self-possession and endurance in fearful situations, of the subtlest outwitting and exploitation of chance and misfortune; their courage beneath the cloak of miserable submission, their heroism in *spernere se sperni*, surpasses the virtues of all the saints. For two millennia an attempt was made to render them contemptible by treating them with contempt, and by barring to them the way to all honours and all that was honourable, and in exchange thrusting them all the deeper into the dirtier trades – and it is true that they did not grow cleaner in the process. But contemptible? They themselves have never ceased to believe themselves called to the highest things, and the virtues which pertain to all who suffer have likewise never ceased to adorn them. The way in which they honour their fathers and their children, the rationality of their marriages and marriage customs, distinguish them among all Europeans. In addition to all this, they have known how to create for themselves a feeling of power and of eternal revenge out of the very occupations left to them (or to which they were left); one has to say in extenuation even of their usury that without this occasional pleasant and useful torturing of those who despised them it would have been difficult for them to have preserved their own self-respect for so long. For our respect for ourselves is tied to our being able to practise requital, in good things and bad. At the same time, however, their revenge does not easily go too far: for they all possess the liberality, including liberality of soul, to which frequent changes of residence, of climate, of the customs of one's neighbours and oppressors educates men; they possess by far the greatest experience of human society, and even in their passions they practise the caution taught by this experience. They are so sure in their intellectual suppleness and shrewdness that they never, even in the worst straits, need to earn their bread by physical labour, as common workmen, porters, agricultural slaves. Their demeanour still reveals that their souls have never known chivalrous noble sentiments nor their bodies handsome armour: a certain importunity mingles with an often charming but almost always painful submissiveness. But now, since they are unavoidably going to ally themselves with the best aristocracy of Europe more and more with every year that passes, they will soon have created for themselves a goodly inheritance of spiritual and bodily demeanour: so that a century hence they will appear sufficiently noble not to make those they dominate *ashamed* to have them as masters. And that is what matters! That is why it is still too soon for a settlement of their affairs! They themselves know best that a conquest of Europe or any kind of act of violence, on their part is not to be thought of: but they also know that at some future time Europe may fall into their hands like a ripe fruit if they would only just extend them. To bring that about they need, in the meantime, to distinguish themselves in every domain of European distinction and to stand everywhere in the first rank: until they have reached the point at which they themselves determine what is distinguishing. Then they will be called the inventors and signposts of the nations of Europe and no longer offend their sensibilities. And whither shall this assembled abundance of grand impressions which for every Jewish family constitutes Jewish history, this abundance of passions, virtues, decisions, renunciations, struggles, victories of every kind – whither shall it stream out if not at last into great men and great works! Then, when the Jews can exhibit as their work such jewels and golden vessels as the European nations of a briefer and less profound experience could not and cannot produce, when Israel will have transformed its eternal vengeance into an eternal blessing for Europe: then there will again arrive that seventh day on which the ancient Jewish God may *rejoice* in himself, his creation and his chosen people – and let us all, all of us, rejoice with him! (*D*, §205)

Nietzsche's intention and tone are unmistakable. When he told the anti-Semitic Fritsch to read *Daybreak*, §205, as an illustration of his support and admiration for the Jews, he was pointing to a text that bears him out in both substance and emotion. *Nietzsche's admiration of Diaspora Jews is not capricious, since it is rooted in typically Nietzschean modes of evaluation.* The Jews were endowed with "psychological and spiritual resources"; they have historical depth, a diversified life experience, power, prudence, and have achieved self-overcoming; they have "courage," "liberality of soul," and other virtues of the nobler kind, by which they surpass all the Christian saints. Unlike other nations' ordinary folk, Jews do not retreat from distress into drunkenness and illusion; they are a sober people in both senses of the word. Above all, Nietzsche admires the Jews' affirmation of life in the face of an incessant journey of suffering and their capacity not to fall into despair but to make of their suffering the source of a more powerful existence which gives value to life while developing its depth.

These are all typically Nietzschean virtues. And it is on account of them, rather than of God's imaginary "election," that another trait which commands Nietzsche's esteem is warranted: the Jews' self-assurance and elitism. These Nietzschean virtues override the objectionable fact (to Nietzsche) that the Jews believe in a transcendent God, and insofar as they do, are mystified about the world and themselves. Even Jewish vengefulness, another Nietzschean vice which has survived in the Diaspora, he finds to have been mitigated by the Jews' experience and breadth of mind.

While the chilling tone of Nietzsche's prophecy about "the spectacles to which the coming century will invite us" derives in part from our memory of more recent events, it is still meant to produce a dramatic effect. Analyzing the Jews' situation, Nietzsche is not so wrong in observing the impasse into which modernity is driving the Jews, because on the one hand it makes their life in the ghetto no longer possible, and on the other hand it is producing a virulent political anti-Semitism which makes their life *outside* the ghetto equally impossible. In concluding that, as a result, the Jews must either "lose" Europe or become its "masters," Nietzsche is sending a grim warning[11] to Jews and non-Jews alike. Both must draw serious conclusions from the dark clouds gathering over the Jews' heads. In order for the Jews not to lose Europe – and for Europe *not to lose them* – it is imperative both to promote their integration into Europe and to accept their cultural ascent, and that the Jews themselves relinquish their secluded identity.

However, Nietzsche neither wishes nor thinks it possible that Jews will become passively assimilated and dissolve within Europe. Because of the Jews' special qualities, they are bound to produce outstanding men and deeds, which will enable them to influence Europe and come to its service. This, if we read the text carefully, is the exact meaning of the phrase: "Europe may fall into their hands like a ripe fruit." It means that they will attain leadership in European affairs so that "they themselves will determine what is distinguishing".

The two phrases creating the "startling sentence" thus have a specific Nietzschean meaning. "Losing Europe" means emigration or expulsion, and "mastering Europe" means that the Jews will influence the values that affect life in its *depth* (because they penetrate its instinctive base). Ancient Jews had the power to impose a decadent value system on the world in the form of Christianity; today it is time for the people of Israel to use the existential resources it has accumulated during centuries of exile in order to reverse the situation and become a dominant factor in creating the new post-Christian and Dionysian Europe, of which Nietzsche sees himself as the announcer.

Incidentally, Zionist leaders had also warned about the approaching "Jewish Rubicon," though they drew different conclusions. About a decade after Nietzsche, Theodor Herzl, the founder of political Zionism, expressed his acute sense of an imminent catastrophe; a similar feeling was voiced between the world wars by Vladimir Zabotinsky, the revisionist Zionist leader, among others. Nietzsche's position opposes Zionism (though from a Eurocentric, not a Jewish-centered standpoint), for should the Jews "lose Europe," then Europe will also lose *them* – which for Nietzsche would be a misfortune. On the other hand, the alternative – that the Jews will "master Europe" (in the nonpolitical sense already mentioned) – is welcome to Nietzsche, though he expects his readers to assume the contrary, and the rhetorical effect he seeks to produce is based upon this assumption. By *denying* it, Nietzsche surprises his readers and provokes the anti-Semites. His strategy, here again, is to play with his readers' expectations and prejudices, producing a surprise effect that reverses the anti-Semitic stereotype's intention and unsettles its owner.[12]

Of course, Nietzsche does not mean that the Jews should dictate their *old* values to Europe. He calls upon them to adopt *Europe*'s culture and make it their own. This may sound like Mendelssohn's ideal of *haskala* (see Introduction) or the call for Jewish assimilation, but actually it is very different from both. Nietzsche does not ask the Jews to copy the values of *existing* European culture or to passively allow themselves to be assimilated into it. His proposal can be called "creative assimilation." In adopting the culture of Europe, the Jews will at the same time go beyond it and be the standard-bearers of the new, nondecadent European culture that will grow from the negation of Christianity. The Jews are thereby called to give up their peculiar, separate historical identity and contribute their value-creating power to a common European effort, *no longer as members of the Jewish religion but as graduates of the Jewish existential and historical experience*. In this way, the tremendous wealth of growth and breeding, of experiencing and human richness, which, Nietzsche maintains, is stored up in present-day Jews, will no longer flow in its separate conduit but will help transform the European reality: "And whither shall this assembled abundance of grand impressions which for every Jewish family constitutes Jewish history, this abundance of passions, virtues, decisions, renunciations, struggles, victories of every kind – whither shall it stream out if not at last into great men and great works!" When this happens, the Jews too will be redeemed from their isolation and the remnants of *ressentiment* that still cling to them, and "Israel will have transformed its eternal revenge into eternal blessing for Europe." This is a key idea that fires Nietzsche's enthusiasm and sends him into a crescendo:

> Then, when the Jews can exhibit as their work such jewels and golden vessels as the European nations of a briefer and less profound experience could not and cannot produce, when Israel will have transformed its eternal vengeance into an eternal blessing for Europe: then there will again arrive that seventh day on which the ancient Jewish God may *rejoice* in himself, his creation and his chosen people – and let us all, all of us, rejoice with him!

This is an apotheosis. Nietzsche is rapturous. He is not only sketching a plan, but envisioning a new apocalypse – as if the world were born again – in a striking (though not surprising) resemblance to his twilight letter to Burkhardt![13] Meanwhile, until this vision comes about, Nietzsche addresses both Jews and non-Jews. To the Jews he says: Wait, but choose Europe; get out of your seclusion, marry into the Gentiles, rise high in European culture, and add your genius to the new European melting pot. Thus, the forebears of Christ will work in the service of the modern Antichrist (that is, Nietzsche–Dionysus), and thereby pay their debt to Europe which their ancestors helped corrupt. And to the non-Jews Nietzsche says: Accept the Jews, let your nobility marry them, encourage their exit not only from the physical ghetto but from lowly trades and professions and from their poor and meek manners; let them express their nobility in the European style too, including the use of arms, and eventually their presence among us will prove a blessing. Above all, he sees the Jews as allies and levers in the transition to a higher human psychology and culture. If the Nazis considered the Jews as *Untermenschen*, for Nietzsche they were a possible catalyst of the *Übermensch*.

It must be added that Nietzsche's enthusiasm for the vocation of modern Jews is not merely theoretical; it derives also from a classic problem confronting any revolutionary: Where is the lever *within* the existing system by which to revolutionize it? Who are the forces uncontaminated by the system? The existence, in the form of the Jews, of a human group he considers more powerful than any other, and free of Christian culture, is a practical asset which Nietzsche badly needs in order to make his revolution look less utopian in his and in others' eyes.

Nietzsche thus made himself an advocate of Jewish emancipation and creative assimilation, for reasons that have nothing to do with the liberalism of the Enlightenment, or with the Jews' own viewpoint, but rather derived from his own Dionysian philosophy of power and the project it dictates for Europe. The anti-Zionism implied in his pro-assimilation plan also derives from his wish to see the Jews "repay their debt to Europe." Nietzsche supports modern Jews for the same reason that he attacks their "priestly" ancestors: his concerns remain centered on Europe. The Jews corrupted Europe in the past; now they are needed to heal it.

In a certain respect, the Jews in Nietzsche's later thought assume the role which their arch-enemy, Wagner, had formerly filled. In the first edition of *The Birth of Tragedy* Wagner, through his music, was presented as the redeemer of European culture; now, most scandalously, he loses that role to none other than the Jews whom he hated and despised so much. Perhaps unconsciously, Nietzsche thereby gets even with his anti-Semitic former friend and master.

It was indeed (I think) Nietzsche's break with Wagner that opened the way to assigning a full-fledged redeeming role to his Jewish opponents. Both stories – the Jewish story and the one told in *The Birth of Tragedy* – have striking structural similarities, since both are stories of ancient corruption and modern redemption; but there is also a difference. Wagner was supposed to redeem Europe from a corruption perpetrated by *others* (Socratic Hellenism, Euripides), whereas the Jews are expected to redeem the evil they themselves (through their ancestors) have done.

Genealogy and uncommon psychology

Not pretending to be an empirical or scientific historian, Nietzsche took as many liberties with Jewish history as he did with ancient Hellenism.[14] His characterization of the three periods in Judaism is debatable. Yet it does tell us one crucial thing: that for Nietzsche there was no constant Jewish essence, attached either to "race" or to

any other eternal nature. Jewish history is a changing, evolving
entity; it has known radical shifts and several shapes, and is now
ready for a new transformation, perhaps its last. The metaphor of
genealogy, too, must not be taken as indicating an original, irre-
versible destiny; for genealogy is not a once-and-for-all hereditary
conditioning. Peoples and individuals can *overcome* the genealogical
traits that their earlier life manifests; they can evolve and adopt new
depth preferences and positions. Nietzschean genealogy points to the
psycho-existential ancestry of a person's or a group's life-form, not to a
historical or biological one – though the two may overlap on occasion. It looks for the *psychological* origin of our covertly preferred kind
of life, action, and thought, not for its literal genetic origin. Thus the
Jews too, while accumulating and transmitting many historical experiences, are not bound by a single genealogical pattern. Rather, the
psycho-existential (genealogical) pattern underlying their mind and
form of life has taken several turns in the course of their long journey – which also allows Nietzsche to judge it differently according to
its several shapes.[15]

From a systematic standpoint there is no contradiction between
the devastating critique of ancient Judaism and the no less devastating attack on modern anti-Semitism. The two positions are perfectly
compatible and even flow from a common genealogical origin. The
modern anti-Semite is the genealogical cousin of the Jewish priest,
so both must be rejected for the same fundamental reason: namely,
that both are driven by a weak personality, petty vengefulness, and
ressentiment. However, the anti-Semite is more despicable, because he
lacks the Jew's creative power and, especially, because he needs support from mass psychology to sustain his position.[16]

It follows that Nietzsche holds two perfectly compatible positions:
against modern anti-Semitism and against ancient priestly Judaism,
both of which stem from the same genealogical root, *ressentiment*.
Nietzsche's ambivalence depends on the combination of these two
positions. Although there is no logical contradiction between rejecting
both anti-Semitism and the moral message of ancient Judaism, this
combination creates a strong psychological tension which ordinary
people find hard to sustain – hence the need to transcend ordinary
psychology and cultivate an *uncommon*, noble character capable of
holding together the two positions despite the tension they create. In
other words, what is needed in order to maintain the two positions is
not only a systematic link between them (opposition to *ressentiment*)
but a special kind of *personality*, whose mental power allows it to maintain a stance of "nevertheless" and insist on the distinction it involves.

This is nothing new. Almost every important matter in Nietzsche calls for an uncommon psychology. This is true, above all, of *amor fati*, which draws creative power from hard truths and affirms life despite the demise of all "metaphysical consolations." Nietzsche is always pushing beyond the limits of ordinary humanity and human psychology, toward a goal which his rhetoric dramatizes under the name of *Übermensch*. Nietzsche's position on Judaism and anti-Semitism is no exception.

In a word, Nietzsche's ambivalence requires holding two (or more) differentiated positions that are logically compatible yet psychologically competitive and hard to maintain for the ordinary person. This analysis also helps to explain why Nietzsche's position has been so widely abused; for the mental revolution which he sought did not take place, while his ideas were generalized, vulgarized, and delivered to a public in which the old psychology prevailed.

A dangerous game

At times we have seen Nietzsche himself using anti-Semitic stereotypes, or playing with his audience's expectation that a hostile reaction will follow a certain description of Jews – and then he surprises us with the opposite reaction and turns the anti-Jewish image against the anti-Semites themselves. This, however, has a price: namely, that the argument's structure remains marked by anti-Jewish prejudice even though it has the reverse intention. Of course, Nietzsche exploits the latent (or overt) anti-Jewish prejudice of his readers so as to surprise or embarrass them, but thereby he seems to legitimize the use of an anti-Semitic stereotype. This is a sharp, sometimes efficient rhetorical/dialectical technique, but it can be dangerous. It is as if Nietzsche strikes at the anti-Semite from within the latter's own position, but thereby gives it the semblance of legitimacy.[17]

Nietzsche in these cases is playing with fire; his meaning can easily be twisted against his intention, his irony misunderstood, and his words taken to enhance what he actually opposes. The danger is that in speaking ironically to the vulgar, the speaker himself may end up the victim of an ironic reversal, by which his intent is undermined and his discourse is taken at face value. Nietzsche as a master of the art should have anticipated the ironic fate of ironizers.

It seems to me that Nietzsche uses varieties of this technique not for the sake of his readers only but also, to some degree, as a lever to override his *own* remaining prejudices. Earlier I stressed the *psychoanalytic* role played by Nietzsche's struggle with key figures in his life, including Elizabeth, Wagner, and possibly Burckhardt; now I should like to point out the role which *rhetoric* plays in the same process. In each case it is not the good liberal will which drives the process, but the anti-Semitic passion itself, or the affective relation to figures who bear and project this passion – they are the lever for self-overcoming. This is genuinely Nietzschean, as opposed to the "good will" of Kant and the Enlightenment. And it seems that here too, perhaps unconsciously, Nietzsche is a good deal more coherent than might be supposed on the basis of his fragmentary and apparently nonsystematic writing.

Our analysis has shown that Nietzsche's complex view of the Jews is far more closely linked to his philosophical thinking than is usually recognized. We have also found it to be more coherent than at first meets the eye. The Jewish issue is linked to two critical events in Nietzsche's narrative of European history: the rise of Christian decadence (which is one of the two sources of European decline, the other being Socratic rationalism) and the expected overcoming of this decadence in post-Christian Europe. Both the ancient slave revolution in morality and the curative revaluation of values expected in the future are crucial moments in Nietzsche's philosophical project, and both have the Jews playing a central role. The Jews who corrupted culture in the guise of (proto-Christian) priests must now help redeem it as secularized post-Christian new Europeans.

Nietzsche thus assigns a major role to the Jews *as Jews* within his new Europe. He opposes a nationalist (or Zionist) solution, because he wants the Jews to mix with the other European peoples, and because he opposes any kind of nationalism. At the same time he also opposes the usual, passive, imitative form of Jewish assimilation. His solution is *creative assimilation*, whereby the Jews are secularized, excel in all European matters, and serve as catalysts in a new revolution of values – this time a curative, Dionysian revolution – that will overcome Christian culture and the "modern ideas" born of it (the Enlightenment, liberalism, nationalism, socialism, etc. (and, if living to see it. fascism as well)). The Jews' role is thereby a transitory one, for it will abolish itself when successful.

Three further remarks are necessary. First, Nietzsche's admiration was not aimed at Diaspora Jews as bearers of a *religious* culture, but as a human group displaying the existential element which he thought necessary for his revolution. Nietzsche, of course, is as opposed to the Jewish *religious* message as he is to any other transcendent religion. The Jews' role is certainly not to "Judaize" Europe in a religious sense. But Nietzsche seems to believe that their existential qualities can be extracted from the Jews' experience regardless of the content of their belief. Nietzsche would rather expect them to *secularize* and practice creative assimilation in the framework of an atheistic Europe.

Second, we must emphasize that Nietzsche's pro-Jewish attitude does not derive from liberalism. Just as his attack on nationalism and racism comes "from the Right," so his defense of the Jews derives from his own Dionysian, anti-liberal sources.[18] Moreover, the Jews are supposed to promote that same Nietzschean philosophy of life – a task which many Jews, who were and are liberals, can hardly welcome. (See Epilogue.)

Finally, it is noteworthy that Nietzsche always attributes some decisive historical role to the Jews, whether negative or positive, corrupting or redeeming. In this ironic sense he continues to regard them as a kind of "chosen people" – or the secular, heretical Nietzschean version of this concept!

This closes the circle of our analysis. Nietzsche as anti-anti-Semite (and the "Dionysian" admirer of modern Jews) complements Nietzsche as critic of ancient Judaism, within the same basic conception and a single philosophical project. Using these distinctions, we were able to delineate the structure of Nietzsche's ambivalence toward the Jews and the relation between its ingredients. The analysis found a fairly consistent thought behind it. Beyond the contradictions, flashes of brilliance, dubious historical examples, and arbitrary statements which Nietzsche's pen often ejects, we discovered at bottom a uniform way of thinking, applied to a central philosophical theme.

Nietzsche and his abusers

Here the question must arise: Why has Nietzsche been abused more than any other philosopher? What was it that provoked his abusers? There seem to be at least four factors: his special mode of writing, the abnormal psychology required by his position, the "right wing" origin of his sensibilities, and his political impotence.

(a) Nietzsche's mode of writing is one major reason. His rhetoric is often deliberately wild and paradoxical, intended to arouse and provoke rather than to just argue and inform. It has a semi-prophetic tone at times, yet retreats from being didactic or authoritarian; so it plays games with the reader, uses masks, and often retracts its own claims – or veils them under a mask. Thus he speaks of a "superman" when he means a new man (or a new human psychology), and of a "slave morality" (or a "herd morality") when he means the morality of the mentally weak.

Another important element in Nietzsche's mode of writing is his often deliberate use of contradiction. Nietzsche notoriously contradicts himself, partly for the reasons mentioned above (irony, mask, esoterism, and retreat from authoritarianism), partly because he has not always made up his mind completely, and partly – this is typical of him – because he offers a new mode of philosophizing which he calls "experimental." Nietzsche was above all an anti-dogmatist; he was both seeking truth and shunning it at the same time (because he shunned its everlasting claim). This was perhaps the first contradiction in his philosophical personality, but it engendered many others. Such uses of contradiction, together with the other elements of rhetoric noted above, clearly open the way to much more misunderstanding and abuse than in the case of a more ordinary philosopher.

(b) Another reason for abuse is the inner tension involved in many of Nietzsche's complex positions. Nietzsche's philosophy puts a strain on ordinary mentalities and often breaks the ordinary "packaging" of intellectual stands; for it requires a person to hold *at the same time* positions which are usually considered mentally or psychologically incompatible. Thus, *amor fati* – rejoicing rather than despairing in a life and world which are inherently devoid of meaning – is opposed to ordinary human responses; so is the revulsion for both the anti-Semite *and* the ancient Jewish priest (and for the same deep reason), or the rejection of both altruism and utilitarianism. There is always some narrow path which Nietzsche traces within the cruder ordinary distinctions, a path which cannot always be defined conceptually but requires, he says, a certain *personality* to locate and identify. Such narrow paths are dangerous, however, in philosophy no less than in mountaineering; one can easily take a deep dive (deliberately or accidentally) and drag the author along.

(c) The fact that Nietzsche expressed sensibilities in which rightwing people could find a positive echo has also contributed to his abuse. Several of Nietzsche's feelings, judgments, criticisms, etc., when taken in themselves apart from the context, may invoke the joy of recognition in a rightist reader, who, because of the partial, local affinity he finds with a Nietzschean idea or sentiment, then sweeps the *whole* of Nietzsche into his own camp, no matter how many insurmountable obstacles he has to jump or ignore. This is bad, intellectually corrupt, historically unjust, but very common and all too human.

Today, there is also a new phenomenon – a *left*-wing abuse of Nietzsche. He is made the father of pluralism, even tolerance in a postmodern sense, the liberator from "hierarchic" rationalism and the "oppressive" Enlightenment. This abuse is no better, intellectually, than the right-wing one, though politically it seems less ominous. Nietzsche, however, would not have recognized himself in this new love of humanity masked as post-humanism; his thinking was far more cruel and daring – and it was impregnated with genuine right-wing motifs, though far from fascist ones. Thus it is another intellectual mistake to drag him into the camp of his fascist opponents (who represent everything he despises – they are nationalists, state-worshipers, racists, anti-Semites, "herd" leaders, and eaten by *ressentiment*), only because he equally opposes democracy and liberalism. From a philosophical viewpoint, Nietzsche deserves to – indeed, must – be understood as the specific, individual thinker he was, rather than classified by our ordinary distinctions, which he set out to abolish.

(d) Finally, Nietzsche attracted abusers because of what I call his political impotence – the vacuum he left in political theory, for which his philosophy does not provide any clear, or even possible, basis.

Nietzsche's Jewish admirers

No less significant is the question: What attracted *Jewish* intellectuals so much to Nietzsche? For it is a historical fact that he exercised a strong fascination on some of the greatest names in modern Jewish letters, especially among those engaged in the movements of Jewish Enlightenment, nationalism, and Zionism. Suffice it to mention names like Max Nordau, Hillel Zeitlin, Yosef Haim Brenner, Micha Yosef Berdytczevski, the young Martin Buber, David Frishmann, the young Haim Weizmann, and Vladimir Zabotinski, to name but a few, to realize not only the importance but also the *diversity* of Nietzsche's reception among modern Jewish writers and activists. (I have named only those who set out to revive Jewish life in some way, not Jewish intellectuals in general – in which case the list would be doubled or even tripled in size and would also include such names as Freud and Stefan Zweig.) Some of the people just mentioned were opponents of others on the list, which testifies to the range of Nietzsche's impact among the Jews; but of course this is to be explained by his mode of writing and the all-too-free approach which most of his readers have taken to his writings.

This book's focus is Nietzsche's attitude toward the Jews, not the Jews' attitude toward Nietzsche, however. So I cannot enter into the latter subject without starting a new book. I shall make only two points. First, the early Jewish fascination with Nietzsche shows how diversely he could be used, understood, and also misunderstood (the fascists have no monopoly in this domain). Jews have correctly perceived his opposition to anti-Semitism and his admiration for their own nation; they have often shared his admiration for the Bible and critique of the later (Talmudic) religion; and they have often misunderstood his anti-liberalism as a wilder form of the secular, anti-traditional revolution which started in the eighteenth century (and of which the Enlightenment, which Nietzsche rejected and they usually accepted, was not the only possible manifestation). They either did not realize the more ruthless potential latent in his philosophy or thought it, nevertheless, a welcome antidote to the humble, all-too-meek Jewish situation which they wanted to "cure" with an injection of new vitality. This indeed is my second point: Nietzsche was mainly perceived as the philosopher of vitality, of natural forces reasserting themselves in the face of a life of submission and from beneath mountains of petty religious ordinances and scholastic pedantry. Modern Jews usually had a far lower opinion of their Diaspora life than Nietzsche, and his philosophy, with all its excesses, seemed to some of them a source of new vitality, naturalness, and self-affirmation, which their lives badly lacked.

Epilogue

The Jews' ambiguous centrality

We have looked at the image of Judaism in the work of two of the most important philosophers of the nineteenth century. Our study found that the Jewish issue was far more important to both of them than is usually recognized. This was because, for better or worse, Hegel and Nietzsche saw European culture as profoundly Christianized, both in medieval times and, no less, in what appeared to be a semi-secular, post-Christian modernity; and Judaism was vital for interpreting the meaning and genealogy of Christianity. Hence, each philosopher needed to confront the "riddle" of the Jews and assess their agency in the formation and transformation of European culture – its leaps, corruption, redemption, or culmination, as the case may be. However, the Jews were seen as significant not in themselves, but because of the deeply Eurocentric perspective of both Hegel and Nietzsche, which made them grasp the Jews from the standpoint of what Christianity had done to Europe in the past, and what Europe will have to do with Christianity in the future.

From a broader perspective, the different assessments of Christianity and the Jews were linked to the conflicting philosophical goals of Hegel and Nietzsche. Briefly put, Hegel was a proponent of universal reason, and Nietzsche its opponent. Hegel was a Christian thinker (albeit a heterodox Christian), and Nietzsche a self-proclaimed

"Antichrist." Hegel strove to bring modernity to its climax, by transforming Lutheran Christianity into philosophical concepts and raising it to a rational theory (and practice) of freedom. Nietzsche, on the contrary, set out to undermine the modern world as he saw it coming and bring about an alternative modernity, to be effected through an anti-Christian, "Dionysian" revolution in values. These various considerations also affected their views of the meaning and status of Judaism, Christianity's longtime opponent and disavowing "parent." However, the Jews' crucial centrality was expressed by both philosophers with characteristic ambiguities.

Hegel

When the mature Hegel reversed his early claim that the Jews had contributed nothing worthwhile to humanity, the shift, as we saw, provoked a powerful inner conflict in him that paralyzed his pen and left a baffling hole in the *Phenomenology*. But when, years later, Hegel surmounted this block, he went so far as to attribute to Judaism one of the most consequential turning points in human history: the momentous discovery that absolute being is Spirit, not a natural substance, and that Spirit is higher and more actual than nature. Yet the Jews distorted and falsified their own revolution in the very act of performing it. The religion of the Spirit was initially offered as its own alienation, severed from God and built upon slavery, fear, and mechanical legalism.

Thus, in dialectical fashion, Hegel himself tacitly condemned the Jews in the act of praising them. The Jewish "religion of sublimity" is said to be afflicted with most of the ills which the young Hegel attributed to the religious phenomenon *in general*. Furthermore, unlike Nietzsche, Hegel denied post-Christian Jews any historical – and therefore any spiritual – significance. The Jews, in depriving themselves of the perspective of "absolute religion" that they had opened for Europe through Christ, aborted their own history and became, in their post-Jesus Diaspora, the empty shell of their former self.

This negative judgment, however, did not prevent Hegel from supporting political emancipation and social acceptance of the Jews – an unpopular position in Germany at the time. Hegel was ready to admit the Jews into the modern world as a leftover group that had inexplicably survived from antiquity and whose members' humanity must now be recognized. But because he continued to deny a living historical character to the Jews of the present – and regarded them as a religious denomination only – he could not find them a place in modernity *as* Jews; nor (contrary to Nietzsche) did he see the whole question as important.

Hegel hardly anticipated a serious and inevitable "Jewish problem" arising with the advent of modernity. Unlike Nietzsche, he failed to recognize the *nonreligious* creativity stored in the Jews, which was rife and ready to pour out in consequence of the political emancipation which he favored. Writing when most European Jews, even in the West, were unemancipated and not many lived in Germany, Hegel did not foresee the widespread role which secularized Jews, no longer confined to the ghetto, were to play in most branches of European society, or the bitter conflicts and passions this was going to arouse. To him, the "Jewish problem" consisted mainly in the need to grant civil rights, as individuals, to members of a marginal religious group that had long ago lost its historical vigor and creativity. Thus, ironically, the great philosopher of history and of European modernity was unable to identify the emerging *nonreligious* "Jewish problem" that was to become inseparable from the liberal modernity he was trying to conceptualize.

Nietzsche

Even more clearly, Nietzsche's grappling with Jewish topics was linked to some of the deepest issues in his philosophical program. Nietzsche assigns the Jews a cardinal role at the two main intersections on which his critique of life and culture evolves: ancient Jews helped to corrupt Europe (through Christianity); future Jews will help to redeem it. This corresponds to Nietzsche's unwavering distinction between his relation to contemporary anti-Semitism, which he fervently denounced, and to historical Judaism, which he treated heterogenously. Our reconstruction of his precise ambivalence toward the Jews found no contradiction between his profound admiration for the great figures of the Jewish Bible, his equally profound contempt for the Jewish priests in Jesus' time, whose creative *ressentiment* engendered Christianity, and his renewed admiration for Diaspora and contemporary Jews, in whom he placed great hopes for the future.

Diaspora Jews had made their rejection of Christ into a hallmark of their ongoing identity and turned their centuries-long suffering into a source of vigor. They had accumulated existential power and historical "breeding," and had arrived on the doorstep of the modern world mostly recovered from their ancestors' *ressentiment* which their enemies, especially the modern anti-Semites, now possess in abundance. Nietzsche wanted the Jews to become secularized, to mix with other Europeans, to excel in all European affairs, and eventually to set new values and standards for them. The Jews' existential vigor and anti-Christian disposition would then pour into Europe, promoting a Dionysian revolution of values. And this would close a historic cycle: the Jews are to act as catalyst in delivering Europe from the culture of decadence and *ressentiment* which their ancestors had inflicted upon it. Unlike Hegel, then, Nietzsche treats these Jews as an ethnic, historical human group and not primarily as a religion, and recognizes the nonreligious creativity stored in them. Also, again contrary to Hegel, he assigned them a modern role *as* Jews, even though this role is temporary and will abolish itself when successful.

But here was a paradox which Nietzsche could not resolve. In order for the Jews to participate in the creation of a Dionysian Europe that would overcome the effects of the Enlightenment, they had to rely on that same Enlightenment and its political fruits. The paradox is no less practical than conceptual. The Jews who emerged from the ghetto aspired to become part of a world dominated by the same principles of freedom and equality which had made their emancipation possible. Even Jewish revolutionaries (of which there were many, in most left-wing camps) adhered to those principles while giving them a radical interpretation. As a result, most Jews who engaged in European affairs as their own, as Nietzsche wished them to do, were potential opponents of Nietzsche's anti-liberal message. At the same time, many Jews were fired by another essential aspect of Nietzsche's Dionysian philosophy: his emphasis on power, vitality, and self-affirmation, and on rehabilitating nature and the body, in which Jewish intellectuals saw a necessary cure not so much for Europe as for *themselves* – for the meek, subdued mentality of ghetto life which caused them a complex of shame and sometimes even self-hate.

Opposing critiques of the Enlightenment

Both Hegel and Nietzsche criticized the Enlightenment, to which Kant had given powerful expression and which Hegel had espoused in his youth. But there is a world of difference between the two critiques. Nietzsche rejected the very ideal of a universal reason, which he saw as a falsifying illusion; whereas Hegel criticized only the abstract, merely universal concept of reason propagated by Kant and the earlier Enlightenment. Unlike Nietzsche, whose Dionysian culture was to be built on the ruins of Europe's Christian and rationalist traditions, Hegel wished to unite those two traditions by giving Christianity a modern rationalist-philosophical interpretation, and this he meant to do through a dialectical concept of reason that would preserve rationality but overcome the limitations of Kant and the Enlightenment.

In this respect Hegel rejoins Kant, and both oppose Nietzsche. Nietzsche rejects the concept of universal reason and the human equality it entails. A philosopher of Dionysian power, he distinguished between kinds of people according to genealogical characteristics – in other words, according to their inherent worth, as determined by psychological and existential factors – rather than by external universal criteria. Kant is the philosopher of the *critical* Enlightenment, based on the universal yet limited power of reason and the autonomous subject underlying it; and Hegel, though differently, also propagated a rational philosophy which preserves the principles of the Enlightenment in the special dialectical way of *Aufhebung*. This places Kant and Hegel among the founders of modern liberalism, albeit in different versions, whereas Nietzsche opposed all versions of liberalism, just as he also opposed socialism, nationalism, and other "modern ideas" which descended, he thought, from the marriage of his two chief opponents, Christian morality and universal reason.[1]

Nationalism, anti-Judaism, and self-overcoming

Hegel and Nietzsche were also human, all-too-human beings; and, as Germans, both lived within a psycho-political climate marked by strong or rising nationalist and anti-Jewish passions. Yet neither Hegel nor (certainly) Nietzsche was a nationalist. Nietzsche ardently opposed nationalism and saw German patriotism as boorish and "bovine." Hegel looked down on nationalism with a cool, ironic, remote glance which failed to grasp its dangers. True patriotism for Hegel refers to the state – its universality and institutions – rather than to ethnic and tribal components which the state is supposed to "sublate" (*aufheben*).

From early childhood, the two philosophers were exposed to anti-Jewish feelings and stereotypes that were pervasive in the education of most Christian youths. But there was a fundamental difference in the way each of them responded to that prejudicial input, and also in the *kind* of anti-Jewish environment in which they grew up. Nietzsche came to maturity in the second half of the nineteenth century amidst a wave of new anti-Jewish sentiment (specifically calling itself "anti-Semitism," to stress that it no longer depended on religion), which had a distinctly secular – racist and political – character. For a short time, Nietzsche says, he too "had resided in the zone of the disease" (referring to his association with Wagner, among others); but later he performed a powerful overcoming of that disease and became opposed to the anti-Semites with all the energy and passion of his soul.

Hegel's case and times were different. Born and raised in the eighteenth century, he was affected by anti-Jewish feelings and stereotypes that mostly emanated from the older Christian theology, primarily in its Lutheran version. Hegel was only marginally exposed to the secular anti-Jewish trend that had, paradoxically, arisen within the Enlightenment. That exposure took place in his youth, when Hegel himself was imbued with Enlightenment ideas, including Kant's attack on all historical religions, particularly Judaism. To some extent Hegel also overcame the harsh anti-Jewish stereotypes of his youth, yet both his effort and achievement in that battle were, as we saw, only partial. In the last analysis, the mature Hegel, no less than the old Kant, gave a systematic-theoretical expression to some of the anti-Jewish prejudices of his youth.

Critics of Judaism and anti-Semitism

When asking whether a philosopher who has criticized Judaism is anti-Semitic, two prior questions must be answered. (1) Does this person see contemporary Jews as a corrupting agent; does he or she feel threatened by them, hate or oppose them as a group, believe they will "contaminate" others? (2) Does he or she therefore wish to curb their freedom, deny them political rights, expel or eliminate them? The answers to both these questions are negative for Hegel and for Nietzsche. Each of them opposed anti-Semitic policies, and each actively supported Jewish political emancipation and social acceptance. Nietzsche also defended the Jews' emigration to Germany from the Eastern ghettos. On the other hand, if anti-Semitism is gauged by negative *private* feelings, residual stereotypes, betraying slips of the tongue or the pen – or biased contradictions between a philosopher's mainstream doctrine and what he says about the Jews – then such signals are amply present in Hegel, and to some extent even in Nietzsche. But the same can be said of many others who speak or write on Jewish subjects, including recognized philo-Semites and even Jews. The key concept – and test – remains self-overcoming; and this is a never-ending process, always open to slips and regression. In Nietzsche's case, despite the lapses, the process of self-overcoming was significantly achieved; not so in Hegel's case.

Still, the rather constricted question: Was so-and-so anti-Semitic, yes or no? cannot, I think, adequately encapsulate the task of understanding a philosopher's attitude to Judaism and the Jews. This all-too-narrow question is less concerned with genuine comprehension than with producing a shortcut verdict or label. True, a label or a verdict can be useful for some practical or emotional purpose; but the goal of philosophical understanding is better served by attending to the broader complexities of the issue and seeking (as I have tried to do in this book) to expound their diverse ingredients and relations – including their relation to the author's *other* philosophical views and commitments.

Reason and anti-Judaism: a disturbing compatibility

This broader perspective still leads to a disquieting result: a philosophy of reason and Enlightenment is unreliable as a barrier against anti-Jewish prejudices and publicly expressed sentiments. A priori – or, rather, superficially – one would expect philosophers of universal reason to be more sympathetic toward the Jews than a so-called irrational philosopher of power like Nietzsche. That this is not altogether the case aggravates present-day liberals and followers of the Enlightenment; yet their surprise is naive. The Enlightenment is known to have contained a distinct anti-Jewish tenet, especially among the opponents of historical religion (from Voltaire to Kant); and, as the present study shows, even a sober, "dialectical" rationalist like Hegel, who reinstated religion as a medium of truth, was far more ambiguous and unresolved about the Jews than the mature Nietzsche. So rationalism, whether "pure" or "dialectical," provides no immunization against anti-Semitism, just as Nietzscheanism does not necessarily lead to it. On balance, Nietzsche was far purer and more resolute in his overcoming of anti-Semitism than Hegel, whose mature system still betrays the anti-Jewish prejudices of his youth, now couched in systematic terms.

Embodied reason and the problem of the "multitude"

One might reasonably argue that Nietzsche rejects anti-Semitism because a philosophy of noble elitism involves inner restraints which cannot be universalized by the general public. So his philosophy suits people with an *extra*-ordinary psychology, who are capable of the kind of self-overcoming which Nietzsche advocates. Among the multitude, however, no genuine Dionysian position is conceivable, only its caricature or grotesque distortion. The person of the multitude is neither a Nietzschean "overman" nor a Kantian "universal man," but more often than not the passive object of manipulation by political demagogues and the moralists of *ressentiment*, including anti-Semites. By contrast, reason and the Enlightenment, even if lacking in power, at least set a *normative* barrier against discrimination and anti-Semitism (even if the philosophers personally sometimes transgress this barrier) and in this respect are useful as regulative ideas.

This is a valid argument, even if, to the persecuted Jew (or colored person, slave, foreigner, etc.), it hardly matters whether his or her suffering is caused by the "vulgarization" of a Dionysian vision or a "deviation" from a liberal one. Few great philosophers lived up to the implications of their own fundamental principles (even verbally, throughout their writings). In addition, most of them tended to ignore the dynamics by which ideas are realized and received by the larger public. They refused to acknowledge the problem of the multitude as a genuine *philosophical* problem, preferring instead to deal with the ideas themselves – be they rational, Dionysian, or anything else. Yet, in order to empower and reinforce the practice which an idea advocates, one needs political, institutional, and psychological vehicles, which do not function by pure reason alone. This was seen by Spinoza, who stressed the need to treat the masses (the "multitude") *as a problem in itself*. Kant failed to understand the problem of the multitude, and Hegel, who did understand it, was unable to cope with it. Both were prisoners of a teleological notion – the belief in historical progress that would eventually sweep the masses toward reason. Nietzsche, lacking that belief, had no guarantee as to what would happen to the masses, and most of the time did not seem to care. He despised the multitude and could bring himself neither to take it seriously nor to waste his mental powers on its account. Thereby he failed to address a most crucial aspect of the world in which he lived, and his opposition to modernity was, in that respect, rather *pre*-modern.

Occasionally, an opposite tenet appears in Nietzsche's thought, as when, without renouncing his elitism, he seems to call for a general Dionysian culture to be created. This may imply that the many must rise (or be raised) to the highest human level; but if so, the expectation carries the danger of distortion, grotesqueness, even terror. To mobilize the masses of ordinary people in the service of an ideal which they are inherently incapable of upholding is a prelude to tyranny. This is what the communists and also the fascists have done in our century, and before them the Inquisition, the Puritan witch-hunters, and others. The problem transcends a particular ideology. It concerns any practice of forcibly "elevating" the general public to something it does not want and cannot sustain. Did Nietzsche believe this could be done without despotism and political terror? If so, he failed to offer an alternative. How was the revolution in the foundation of culture to be propagated, and how was it to reshape the West? Even nontyrannical methods depend on persuasion, temptation, and other less-than-philosophical measures, which, however, need to be addressed philosophically, as part of the question of the multitude – the main problem not only in democracy, but in modern life generally. However, Nietzsche, who despised the masses, practically ignored their existence and the need for a philosophical theory that would address their limitations while also recognizing their rights and capabilities. Thereby Nietzsche missed a valuable lesson he could have drawn from a man he admired, Baruch Spinoza – namely, that democracy is important not because it is the mirror of pure reason, but because it is the domain of *semi*-rationality and less-than-philosophy.

Of course, no theory of the multitude – like no educational theory, however democratic – can avoid some manipulative element, because its principle must be based on rhetoric, trust, and examples, rather than on pure reason. However, if we suppose that rationality is common to all people, then using pre-rational means to help it evolve is not an arbitrary or deceptive maneuver, because its goal is to develop the rational (or *semi*-rational) capacity of those capable of it, and thus express recognition of them as persons. But in Nietzsche's case, what could be the intermediary factor which mediates and restrains a multitude of people who, by definition, have *no* potential for Dionysian nobility?

None, is the inevitable answer. It seems, therefore, that one should prefer a theory of the masses which is constrained by rational norms and serves as a vehicle for a semi-rational process to a theory of elitist mental nobility which has nothing to say about the problem of education and the ordinary public.

Of course the two are not necessarily incompatible: nobility as a mental attitude can complement the rational principle and mitigate its rigidity, rather than be its substitute. However – again learning from Spinoza (against Hegel, Marx, Nietzsche, and almost the whole of the nineteenth century) – one must not turn to politics, which is the domain of the multitude and of democracy, to achieve the goals of collective salvation, or to realize a high spiritual goal, be it rational, Dionysian, mystical, or semi-religious. In other words, politics as such cannot be made responsible for human elevation and ascent. The concept of collective salvation is theoretically false and practically dangerous; as the last century has demonstrated, it is the source of untold political and moral horrors. Human ascent, spiritual achievement – everything that can be thought of under the metaphor of "salvation" – must be sought and realized within the private or individual domain alone and is, in itself, apolitical and extra-political. Of course, it requires a political base in a regime of freedom and personal rights – a form of democracy; and such a regime is certainly not value-indifferent. On the contrary, it must embody universal value elements, but in a "thin" or minimal form, which cannot justify the claim that politics *itself* can lead to human ascent or salvation. In a word, on the social level (that of the "multitude") we need, *pace* Nietzsche, reason and democracy; and only in the domain of the individual is there room – and a call – to rise above the multitude in pursuit of higher human and spiritual achievements.

Returning to the Jews, one may argue that rationalist philosophy demands equality for the Jews as a matter of principle, whereas Nietzschean philosophy does so from a subjective (and therefore arbitrary) choice of values. But here we might learn from Hegel. An abstract principle is still nothing; as long as it has not been realized, *it is not even rational*. Only the principle's realization in life, feeling, social habit, and political institutions makes it actually rational (as distinct from an intellectual abstraction). Mere Enlightenment is in this respect an irrational position, which runs the risk of being transformed into its opposite, as has been proved more than once. A principle which cannot be sufficiently actualized within the existing or expected state of the world is not truly rational; it justifies nothing and guarantees even less. The Enlightenment abounded in anti-Semitic expressions, some rather fierce (Voltaire, Fichte), others milder (Kant). Likewise, Locke outlawed atheists (and Catholics, too); the writers of the American Bill of Rights accepted slavery and discrimination against women; Spinoza, Kant, and Freud (among many others) made anti-feminism remarks; and Descartes bowed to the theological authority which his *Meditations* undermines. As long as we build only on people's pure intellectual recognition, it is quite easy to devise exceptions to it, reverse its meaning and even use it to rationalize prejudice – as the historical material proves time and again. More important is to study how a theoretical recognition turns into an affective power – into an "instinct," as Nietzsche puts it. And to do this, we need philosophers like Spinoza, Marx, Freud, or Nietzsche himself, to help correct Kant's abstract vision. We likewise need a dialectician like Hegel to explain that rationality resides within the particular, historical facts – and also within the powers of life, feeling, and imagination – whereas a "pure" abstraction devoid of life *is not rational*.

In the end, universal reason is to be preferred, but only when human rationality is construed in an empirical and pragmatic sense, the sense of flesh and blood. This requires giving up the Kantian dream of *pure* reason. Only as *impure* reason can human rationality be accessible and even redeeming: that is, only as finite, incomplete rationality, open-ended, embodied in life and real experience, yet always also transcending its embodiment in the form of a demand and of self-dissatisfaction. The complex structure of this embodiment, as "impure universal reason," makes the fissure between reason and the world immanent to the world itself. It also accounts for the fact that the philosopher's biases and prejudices often lag behind the universal norms he or she implies or overtly declares in theory. There is nothing fatal in that inconsistency: it does not, as some think, spell the doom of rational philosophy but is, rather, the normal case, which highlights the finite human condition and the fact that human reason is always situated. Philosophers are real, historically placed persons, whose flesh and blood and *Zeitgeist* embody and constrain the outreach of their own rational principles, however advanced they may be in theory. At the same time, to be truly rational, their thinking must also transcend its placement and embodiment in the mode of *self-dissatisfaction* – it must be aware of its present shortcomings and defects (as measured in its own terms) and be driven to overcome them.

This dynamic seems to enable slavery to be abolished, women to gain voting rights, and Jews to be emancipated, long after the norms for these actions have been declared, and despite the anti-Judaism, anti-feminism, or racial prejudice of the great philosophers who had advanced those principles and lagged behind them.

In conclusion, what seems to be needed is a theory and practice of *finite* rationality, which spells out the conditions for reason's embodiment in the living, historical world, its never-ending work, and its partly subversive role with respect to existing reality. This would replace Kant's dream of pure reason and Hegel's illusion of providential teleology and "absolute knowing," without renouncing the value of (noninstrumental) reason itself. And, among (many) other things, a view of embodied rationality must recognize – and entail – the *philosophical* import of historical processes and the problem of the masses – and therefore of rhetoric, mass communication, psychology, prejudice, public habits, social and intellectual fashions, and so on – as the embodying, constraining, and also protest-provoking conditions of rationality. Without this, abstract enlightenment has no advantage and, as Nietzsche's case demonstrates, may be inferior to its opponents.

Notes

Preface

1 See pp. 17, 22–3.

2 See ibid.

3 Among the refutations of this belief see Arthur Hertzberg's well-known *The French Enlightenment and the Jews* (Columbia University Press, New York, 1968) and also Hannah Arendt's instructive words on the anti-Semitism of the Left in *The Origins of Totalitarianism* (Harcourt, Brace Jovanovich, New York, 1973), Part I; the present study also leads to qualifying this belief.

4 This sentence already entails a criticism of Nietzsche.

5 The latest example is Sarah Kofman's book *Le Mépris des juifs: Nietzsche, les juifs, l'antisémitisme* (Galilée, Paris, 1994).

6 Thus, Nachman Krochmal (Ranak) argued (in his *Guide of the Perplexed of the Time: Moreh Nebukhe ha-Zeman*) in *The Writings of Nachman Krochmal* (Hebrew), ed. S. Rawidowicz, 2nd edn (Ararat, London and Waltham, Mass., 1961) that in Hegelian terms it is, rather, Judaism which should stand at the top.

7 Actually Hegel opposed nationalism, he would have rejected communism, and there is no basis for assimilating him to fascism; yet political passions are more powerful than complex philosophical ideas, so Hegel *malgré lui*, served them all.

8 E.g. Y. Yovel, "Hegels Begriff der Religion und die Religion der Erhabenheit," *Theologie und Philosophie*, 51 (1976), pp. 512–37.

9 Y. Yovel, "Perspectives nouvelles sur Nietzsche et le Judaïsme," *Revue des études juives*, 138 (1979), pp. 483–5.

10 Michael Duffy and Willard Mittelman, "Nietzsche's Attitudes toward the Jews," *Journal of the History of Ideas*, 49 (1988), pp. 301–17.

11 See n. 5 above.

12 Weaver Santaniello, *Nietzsche, God, and the Jews* (SUNY Press, Albany, NY, 1994).

Chapter 1   Hegel and his Predecessors

1 See *inter alia*, Yaakov Goren, "The Image of the Jew and Judaism in Protestant Bible Scholarship from the Middle of the 18C to the Thirties of the 19C" (Hebrew), Ph.D. thesis, Hebrew University, Jerusalem, 1975.

2 See Y. Yovel, *Kant and the Philosophy of History* (Princeton University Press, Princeton, 1980).

3 I do not discuss here the Protestant theological sources – this topic would require a separate discussion.

4 Meaning that no qualitative progress was possible any more – no advance in the epistemic status of these sciences, although quantitatively their history is open-ended.

5 Spinoza, *Theological-Political Treatise*, B. Spinoza, *Chief Works*, tr. R. H. Elwes (2 vols, Dover, New York, 1951), ch. 17, pp. 219–20. For an elaboration, see my "Epilogue: Spinoza and His People," in *Spinoza and Other Heretics*, vol. 1: *The Marrano of Reason* (Princeton University Press, Princeton, 1988).

6 Spinoza, *Theological-Political Treatise*, ch. 3, p. 56.

7 Ibid., ch. 3.

8 Ibid., ch. 17, pp. 219–20.

9 Ibid., ch. 19; Yovel, *Spinoza and Other Heretics*, vol. 1, ch. 6.

10 One of the more reluctant converts was his son Abraham, father of the composer Felix Mendelssohn-Bartholdy, who probably did it for the sake of his son's career.

11 Actually, *both* of Mendelssohn's claims are questionable. Jewish religion was not voluntary in the sense in which modern political theories use this concept. It contained an element of coercion, of legal sanction, banning the rebel and subjecting the members of the congregation to rabbinical authority. This was usually done by decree of the Christian authorities. It was a kind of tolerance, or privilege, which the Jewish congregation enjoyed, but within the community it imposed the authority of a religious law and a semi-theocratic government of the kind which Mendelssohn opposed. Mendelssohn's words were intended for the non-Jewish world and are flawed with apologetic imprecision. As for his other claim, that Judaism is but a "revealed constitution," although it too is historically imprecise, it is not so far-reaching as is commonly thought. Mendelssohn does not deny that there are cognitive truths in Judaism; what he denies is that Jews are required to believe them on the strength of revelation and as a condition of salvation. The question is not whether there is a cognitive element in Judaism but what its *origin* is, and what *depends* on it. Mendelssohn says that in Christianity the cognitive element is "revealed"; that is, it originates in external authority and is a condition for salvation. Not so in Judaism, where the equivalent of "salvation" (success in attaining religious worth) depends only on fulfilling the commandments.

12 I. Kant, *Religion within the Boundaries of Mere Reason*, tr. Allen W. Wood and George di Giovanni (Cambridge University Press, Cambridge, 1996), p. 176.

13 I have done so in Yovel, *Kant and the Philosophy of History*, ch. 8.

14 In this respect there is an ironic similarity between Kant's anti-Jewish preju-

dices and the views of some fanatic religious Jews today (e.g. "Gush Emunim" in Israel and other tribal views of Judaism), which deny that Judaism expresses any universal morality, thus justifying Kant's bigotry.

15 What it tells is that the barriers of civility have weakened – in other words, there were only weak liberal barriers of civility: "external" in Kant's own sense, a case of mere *Legalität*.

16 Kant, *Anthropology from a Pragmatic Viewpoint*, tr. Mary Gregor (Nijhoff, The Hague, 1974), p. 17.

17 Kant, *The Conflict of Faculties*, in his *Religion and Rational Theology*, tr. and ed. A. W. Wood and G. di Giovanni (Cambridge University Press, Cambridge, 1996), p. 275.

Chapter 2   The Young Hegel and the Spirit of Judaism

1 Karl Rosenkranz, *G. W. F. Hegels Leben* (Berlin, 1844), p. 49; quoted by Otto Pöggeler, "Hegel's Interpretation of Judaism," *Human Context*, 6 (1974), pp. 523–60, at p. 525.

2 According to Hegel, a dialectical negation abolishes the inadequate form of an idea while preserving its true content and elevating it to a higher form of expression. This is also called *Aufhebung* – sublation.

3 Hegel, *The Life of Jesus*, quoted by Walter Kaufmann, *Hegel: Reinterpretation, Texts, and Commentary* (Doubleday, Garden City, NY, 1965), p. 61.

4 Even though such a claim is logically possible in Hegel's system. History is not totally deterministic in Hegel; its necessity is teleological in the Aristotelian manner, that is, determined after the fact, from the standpoint of the telos backward, and, a priori, leaves room for failures and deviations. Moreover, the existence of its contingency is itself dialectically necessary. However, Hegel knows he cannot explain Judaism as such a deviation, for its case is too important in world history. The Jews are not like the Kurds or the Assyrians, who have also survived from the ancient world. Judaism stands in permanent conflict and challenge to Christianity: subjectively at least, from their own viewpoint, the Jews defy Christianity's claim to have sublated them, so their continued presence is too problematic to be dismissed and too problematic to be accounted for.

5 I thus dissent from Pöggeler's view that Hegel tried to find a place for the Jews in the framework of a pluralistic world. (See Pöggeler, "Hegel's Interpretation of Judaism," p. 523: "The significance of Hegel's lifelong efforts to interpret Judaism was that already he was trying to help discover a way into the new world civilization for that people." The mature Hegel was an early pluralist who stressed the link between the individual and his or her historical community; but as we shall see, in the case of the Jews there were only individuals; Judaism as such had no history and no further contribution to make.

6 Herder was a disciple and opponent of Kant, one of the first philosophers of history and language in Germany, who stressed the weight of local culture, language, nation, the spirit of a people, etc. – and not only universal reason – as determining historical development and the "education of the human race."

7 Hegel, "Fragmente über Volksreligion und Christentum," in *Werke*, vol. 1: *Frühe Schriften* (Suhrkamp, Frankfurt, 1971), p. 45. This fragment is not included in *Hegels theologische Jugendschriften*, ed. H. Nohl (Tübingen, 1907, repr. Minerva, Frankfurt, 1976).

8 "Statutory commands" (or laws) is an expression used by Kant to designate unfree religious commands imposed by the will of an external master. This is the mark of a "heteronomous" religion.

9 Hegel, "Die Positivität der Christlichen Religion," in *Hegels theologische Jugendschriften*, ed. H. Nohl (Mohr, Tübingen, 1907); tr. as "The Positivity of the Christian Religion," in *Early Theological Writings*, tr. T. M. Knox and R. Kroner (University of Chicago Press, Chicago, 1948 (6th edn, University of Pennsylvania Press, Philadelphia, 1988), pp. 68–9.

10 Ibid., p. 69.

11 Hegel, *Jugendschriften*, p. 33. The allusion is to John 15: 5 ("I am the vine and you are the branches"). Later, in "Positivity", §§10–12, Hegel elaborates the comparison with much more moderation toward Jesus.

12 "Positivity," p. 146.

13 Ibid., p. 147.

14 Ibid., p. 149.

15 Ibid., p. 147.

16 Hegel's warning also sounds valid for Wagner, who ended up creating engaging stories and music but not a real mythology. The Nazi attempt to make it a popular mythology was forced and artificial – with disastrous consequences, to be sure, but without success.

17 Abbé Grégoire, *Essai sur la régéneration physique, morale et politique des juifs* (1789) (Stock, Paris, 1988). The book's title already indicates what we have said. One chapter speaks of the "danger in tolerating the Jews as they are now, because of the revulsion they feel toward other people." Other passages express similar ideas.

18 C. W. Dohm, *Concerning the Amelioration of the Civil Status of the Jews*, tr. H. Lederer (Hebrew Union College Institute of Religion, Cincinnati, 1957), p. 18 (and *passim*). A similar charge recurs in Kant, in one of the fiercest anti-Jewish passages he ever wrote. Kant clearly knew Dohm and did not say more than Dohm did, yet Kant's words were received by Jews as anti-Semitic while Dohm was seen as a philo-Semite. Descriptively speaking, Kant and Dohm had the same view of the Jews, which expressed the spirit of the time. Actually, Kant too favored an improvement in the Jewish situation – let all of them be like his distinguished friends, Mendelssohn, Herz, and Lazarus Bendavid! The difference between Kant and Dohm – which is immense – is one of attitude: Dohm was pained by the Jews' state and indulgent regarding their flaws, whereas Kant reproved them from a superior standpoint. Also, Kant attributed some of their flaws to the moral indifference of their laws, but Dohm to their situation in exile.

19 Hegel, *Jugendschriften*, p. 27; quoted by Kaufmann, *Hegel*, pp. 58–9; see also Kaufmann, *From Shakespeare to Existentialism* (Doubleday, Garden City, NY, 1960), p. 134; Pöggeler, "Hegel's Interpretation of Judaism," p. 537.

20 Hegel, *Jugendschriften*, p. 22; I use Kaufmann's translation (*Hegel*, p. 59).

21 More accurately, the fragments which Nohl arranged under that title in Hegel, *Jugendschriften*.

22 As too in a few unfinished drafts and in "Entwürfe über Religion und Liebe."

23 This indicates an early diagnosis of Judaism as the religion of "sublimity" rather than beauty.

24 "The Spirit of Christianity," in *Early Theological Writings*, p. 209.

25 Ibid., p. 211.
26 Ibid., p. 212.
27 Jacques Rivelaygue, *Leçons de métaphysique allemande* (Grasset & Fasquelle, Paris, 1990), vol. 1, pp. 270ff. Rivelaygue's illuminating analysis is given in a section on the young Hegel in Frankfurt.
28 Hegel at this point is not yet the "historical" philosopher he would later become.
29 For the whole section see the "Spirit of Christianity," pp. 182–6; quoted on p. 186.
30 Ibid., p. 182.
31 Ibid., p. 190.
32 Jacques d'Hondt, *Hegel secret* (Presses Universitaires de France, Paris, 1986), pp. 184–200.
33 The image of disease, we may remember, had already been used in describing the spirit of Second Temple Judaism," of which Jesus was miraculously free."
34 "Spirit of Christianity," p. 191.
35 Ibid., p. 192.
36 Ibid., pp. 197–8.
37 Ibid., p. 192.
38 Ibid., p. 193.
39 Actually, according to Josephus, the room was not empty but contained the golden candelabra, the instruments for dispensing incense, and a big monetary treasure which Pompey did not touch; but this imprecision is not Hegel's failure here.
40 "Spirit of Christianity," p. 194.
41 We found a variety of this prejudice in Kant, who also denied Jews any spirituality: i.e. a moral spirit, and saw their religion as merely political, and thus concerned with this-worldly external matters.
42 "Spirit of Christianity," pp. 204–5.
43 However, there seems to be another reason: Hegel has defined "Fate," the topic of the essay, as spirit falling into the service of "alien forces" – which is repeated here with reference to both the Jews and Macbeth. So Jews have Fate, but not Tragedy.
44 "Positivity," pp. 158–9.
45 Ibid., p. 159.
46 Ibid.
47 This shows that Hegel saw Diaspora and contemporary Jews as mentally corrupt – as opposed to sublated; see Epilogue.
48 Judging not by his emotions, but by his opposition to anti-Jewish policies and support of Jewish emancipation.
49 Pöggeler, "Hegel's Interpretation of Judaism," p. 530. This important essay, by an expert who knows Hegel's works of all periods, was written with much good will. After the German genocide of the Jews, Pöggeler seeks to resume the good relations between the two peoples and cultures. His attitude to Hegel is somewhat apologetic. He downplays (mentioning, but not quoting) Hegel's venomous texts against the Jews, and argues that the mature Hegel overcame his youthful position. The first point I make amends for in this essay, the second I shall reconsider. Nevertheless, Pöggeler's study helps to identify nuances in Hegel's development (not only at a later age but even in his youth) by putting

them in a broader context.

50 "Positivity," p. 98.

51 Mendelssohn confuses Judaism as he wants it to be with the way it actually is. Actually, the Jewish congregation in the Diaspora enjoyed much coercive power with respect to its members, usually anchored in legal privileges. (Even in today's "voluntary" orthodox communities that power still exists.) Mendelssohn draws an ideal, though inexact, picture of the Jewish *mohel* (circumcision officer) to stress that religious officers are volunteers, which is rather rare.

52 That too is historically incorrect. Jewish texts are full of cognitive claims which the believer is required to accept as true. Maimonides, the greatest interpreter of Diaspora Judaism, makes knowledge of God the top religious command; even knowledge of physics – God's creation – has religious weight. Mendelssohn, as reformer, describes the kind of Judaism he *desires* as if it were historically the case. His division between knowledge and law is useful for the purposes of the Enlightenment, but artificial and incompatible with the historical texts. (The same can be said of the late Yeshayahu Leibowitz's position, which was "neo-Mendelssohnian", and for similar reasons.)

53 Mendelssohn had not said anything of the sort. There is nothing in Mendelssohn's position which denies the moral nature of many Jewish commands; but what give Judaism its distinctive character are neither its true beliefs nor its moral insights (which are universal), but the specific customs and ceremonies which the Jews were ordered to keep, and in which their fidelity to their identity is centered.

54 "Spirit of Christianity," p. 196.

55 Hegel was known to be a wine-lover. In Tübingen he took part in wine contests, and later his salary included wine supplies (see Franz Wiedmann's popular biography, *Hegel: An Illustrated Biography* (Pegasus, New York, 1968), p. 19). This may be the reason for the present example. Wine is the fruit of civilization, and the excise taxes weigh heavily on it; likewise, Christian theology weighs on free truth. (The racism we may discern in this example should not, however, be judged in contemporary terms.)

56 There is, indeed, another text, a revision of "Positivity of the Christian Religion" written in 1800; the revision concerns not his view of Judaism, but his view of human nature, which is no longer seen as a constant essence (p. 169). The human spirit expresses itself in a variety of manifestations which transform themselves into one another over many centuries until they become crystallized in "the unity of certain universal concepts." This is the beginning of the revolutionary view that will be announced in *The Phenomenology of Spirit*. Yet no change is discernible concerning Judaism. Hegel repeats the harsh words of the first edition, attacks the arrogance, slavery, etc. of the Jews, repeats that Jesus' appearance was a sudden revolution, which owed nothing positive to the Jews. Jesus' spirit was (rather miraculously, but isn't religion built on miracles?) free of his people's servility, prejudice, and attachment to trivia – on which Hegel remarks: "Such religious purity is of course wondrous in a Jew!" Hegel now exempts Jesus from the charge that he himself started the positivity of Christianity. The blame is now shifted to the first Christians, who, unlike Jesus, were not free of Jewish faults. Above all, Hegel maintained his view that Judaism was only the negative background against which Jesus' leap took place, and that it contributed noting valuable to world history.

57 G. E. Lessing, *Nathan der Weise*, Act 2, sc. 7 in *Lessings Werke* (Volksverlag,

Weimar, 1963), vol. 2, p. 54 (my tr.).
58 This demand is powerfully present in the USA today, despite semi-official pluralism. Napoleon's example was: Let the Jews renounce their being a nation and be redefined as a mere "religion." This redefinition, which renounces a major aspect – the "people" aspect – of Jewish identity, is still powerfully ingrained in French and American political culture and in French and American Jews' self-perception.
59 Lessing, *Nathan der Weise*, Act 4, sc. 7, p. 117.
60 But what is a "person" – a concrete human person, as distinguished from the abstract "man as man" – if not someone whose very humanity is wrapped in more particular identity features, such as ethnic people, religion, sex, etc.?

Chapter 3   Jena and the *Phenomenology*: A Telling Silence

1 Hegel, *Phenomenology of Spirit*, tr. A. V. Miller (Clarendon Press, Oxford, 1977), p. 11. Hereafter, page references to this edition will be given in parentheses in the text.
2 Hegel may be thinking of the Stoic's submission to fate – which gives the philosopher a sense of selfhood. (This association is made more explicit in *Lectures on the Philosophy of History*.)
3 I bypass the second reference (p. 202), which seems marginal for our purpose.
4 The division will be modified and expanded in *Lectures on the Philosophy of Religion* (see next chapter).
5 This may be an allusion to the wantonness and illegality attributed to Rome in Nero's day.
6 Seen in this way, we can cast the three periods in terms of immanence and transcendence as follows. Natural religion is a religion of immanence, but also of substance; the absolute is not a person. Judaism makes God both personal and transcendent, severed from the world. Hegelianism (*aufgehoben* Protestantism) makes God personal too, but immanent again, though in a new, dialectical way.
7 Hegel also uses the term "manifest religion" with a polemical tinge, against Mendelssohn, who argued that Judaism was not a "revealed religion" but only a revealed law. Hegel agrees, but interprets this claim to Judaism's discredit.

Chapter 4   The Mature Hegel: The Sublime Makes its Appearance

1 If Rosenkranz is right that he was "always" concerned with the Jews, this is not visible in his publications of this period; yet this omission is not as remarkable as the "silence" in the *Phenomenology*, because in this period Hegel worked mainly on his less historical works, notably the first and second volumes of *The Science of Logic* and the first version of the *Encyclopedia of Philosophical Sciences*, both highly systematic and speculative.
2 With the qualification in mind that the *Lectures on the Philosophy of History* has not been critically edited.
3 *Vorlesungen über die Philosophie der Geschichte*, in *Werke* (Suhrkamp, Frankfurt, 1970), vol. 12, p. 272; *The Philosophy of History*, tr. J. Sibree (London, 1857; repr. Dover, New York, 1956), pp. 195–6. In Lasson's edition this section is called "Die Israeliten"; see *Vorlesungen über die Philosophie der Weltgeschichte*, ed.

G. Lasson (Meiner, Leipzig, 1919), vol. 2, p. 453. Hereafter page references to Sibree's English translation will be given in parentheses in the text.

4 Also, here it is the Jews who drain the natural world of its divinity, whereas in the *Phenomenology* this occurred out of the inner evolution of the pagan world itself.

5 On the radical change in Hegel's view of Judaism in these *Lectures* see Hans Liebeschütz, *Das Judentum im deutschen Geschichtsbild von Hegel bis Max Weber* (Mohr, Tübingen, 1967), p. 34; Steven B. Smith, "Hegel and the Jewish Question," *History of Political Thought*, 12/1 (1991), pp. 87–106.

6 Hegel, *Vorlesungen über die Ästhetik*, in *Werke* (Suhrkamp, Frankfurt, 1970), vol. 13, p. 467; tr. T. M. Knox as *Aesthetics: Lectures on the Fine Art* (2 vols, Clarendon Press, Oxford, 1975) vol. 1, p. 363. Hereafter, page references to the English translation will be given in parentheses in the text.

7 Hegel (vol. 1, p. 371), mentions Angelus Silesius (pseudonym of Johannes Scheffler, 1624–77). He might have included John of the Cross. On the other hand, the definition of sublime art includes Judaism and Islam, just as the definition of "revealed religion" had excluded these two religions for the same reasons.

8 Herein lies the logical link between sublimity and creation. A God whose creation is accidental, not essential, drains the world of all divinity and draws it all into himself, while being infinitely remote from the world. This motif will become central in Hegel's Berlin *Lectures on the Philosophy of Religion*.

9 Kant, *Critique of Judgement* (*CJ*) tr. J. C. Meredith (Clarendon Press, Oxford, 1952), §§29–32.

10 Kant also distinguishes between utilitarian fear and aesthetic (and metaphysical) dread. "We may look upon an object as fearful, and yet not be afraid of it," he says (*Critique of Judgement*, §28). True religion also involves a kind of awe and dread of the sublime, whereas "superstition" (= the Enlightenment name for popular religion) is based on utilitarian fear only.

11 See "General Remark on the Exposition of Aesthetic Reflective Judgements," in *Critique of Judgement*, §29, p. 120.

12 I. Kant, *Critique of Practical Reason*, tr. L. W. Beck (Bobbs-Merrill, Indianapolis, 1956), p. 156. Kant has not yet used the word "sublimity" in the second *Critique*, but the meaning is the same; and in the *Critique of Judgement* he already says explicitly: "we call the sight of the starry heaven *sublime*" (General Remark, pp. 121–2).

13 *Critique of Judgement*, §28. Kant – like Hegel – was still living in an era when nature seemed a powerful opponent, to be combated and conquered. In our age, of course, the perception has been dramatically reversed.

14 Ibid., p. 114.

15 Ibid., pp. 111–12.

16 Yirmiyahu Yovel, *Kant and the Philosophy of History* (Princeton University Press, Princeton, 1980).

17 Hegel accepted this goal from Kant and placed it at the center of his system, but he abolished the moralistic and utopian character it had in Kant and replaced it with a realistic, dialectical outlook. In Hegel the historical goal loses the "sublime" character it had in Kant and is mediated by real, empirical history with all its setbacks and limitations, and especially its lack of purity. Kant, on the other hand, projects the goal into some infinite future and defines it as absolute purity; he also inserts the sublime element into history itself.

Chapter 5   Sublimity is not Sublime: *The Philosophy of Religion*

1 Each of the several editors who tried their hand at it had to pay a considerable price for every improvement. The early editions (especially that of Karl
Hegel, 1840) compiled materials from different years and produced a fairly flu-
ent and significant, but uncritical, text. Lasson (1927) distinguished between the
various source materials at his disposal, but patched them up too liberally in a
cumbersome mode of his own. The two recent editions (those of Ilting, 1978 (of
Hegel's 1821 lecture notes), and Jaeschke, 1983–5 (3 vols, containing all the
available material), are incomparably more careful; they separate the materials
according to sources and dates, and offer scholarly sound texts; yet, because of
the nature of their materials, they are fragmented and lack integration.
Jaeschke's edition was published in a 3-vol. English translation, as *Lectures on the
Philosophy of Religion*, tr. R. F. Brown, P. C. Hodgson, and J. M. Stewart, ed. Peter
Hodgson (University of California Press, Berkeley, 1984). The same publisher
also brought out the lectures of 1827 in a separate single volume which inatten-
tive readers may take to be an abridged version of the whole text; yet in what
concerns the topic of Judaism, this version is unrepresentative (see later).
2 Hegel, *The Science of Logic*, tr. A. V. Miller (Allen & Unwin, London, 1969),
p. 50.
3 *Hegel's Logic*, tr. W. Wallace, 3rd edn (Clarendon Press, Oxford, 1975), vol. 1,
p. 3.
4 Hegel, *Introduction to the Lectures on the History of Philosophy*, tr. T. M. Knox and
A. V. Miller (Clarendon Press, Oxford, 1985), p. 124.
5 Ibid., p. 141.
6 Hegel, *Lectures on the Philosophy of Religion*, ed. P. C. Hodgson (University of
California Press, Berkeley, 1984), vol. 1, pp. 152–3.
7 Ibid., pp. 182–3.
8 One should not construe this parallelism too mechanically, as if every religious form corresponds to some specific philosophy. What is crucial for Hegel is
the principle that Spirit must be historicized and assume a series of finite forms,
including lower mental forms. That accounts for the difference between philosophy and religion, both in terms of their mental forms (imagination versus the
concept) and their changing historical configurations. But nowhere does Hegel
put forth a simplistic symmetry, for the good reason that according to his dialectic, contingent elements must always affect every form of history and the spirit.
9 Introduction to the *Lectures* 1827, pp. 145–6.
10 Ibid., p. 198, and see the note which reproduces the text of the 1840 *Werke*.
In the latter, ed. Bruno Bauer (and also in the current Suhrkamp edition which
is based on the older *Werke* – see vol. 16, p. 82), the text even says explicitly that
a justification of older religions is involved. Jaeschke's edition, on the contrary,
stresses that "being reconciled" (*versöhnen*) does *not* entail justifying (*rechtfertigen*);
and in the English edition Hodgson accepts this nuance but concedes that the
text, or rather the punctuation, also lends itself to Bauer's reading. I don't think
the issue is crucial, because everyone agrees that the context stresses the human
and basically rational nature of all religions; so even the weaker reading of our
quote – that a philosophical study reconciles us to the horrible and arbitrary side
of past religions without justifying them – is distinctly Hegelian, and contains a
weak form of theodicy. Hegel wanted to say that the philosophy of religion
makes us see (and accept) the basic rationality of historical phenomena despite

the fact that they contain so many objectionable elements that must today be rejected; this is perfectly compatible with his dialectical *Aufhebung*, which abolishes the contingent and arbitrary element yet recognizes the rational essence and so accepts the lower form as a "moment" of the higher. (This is the deeper sense of theodicy in Hegel: the irrational element is negated as such, but recognized as a historically necessary moment of the rational.)

11 Ibid., p. 187.

12 See the 1840 *Werke*, vol. 16, p. 83. In light of this analysis, Feuerbach's famous claim that religion is the alienated self-projection of the human image into God is a one-sided interpretation of Hegel. Though in Hegel God's image is indeed a mediated self-image of man, it is not necessarily a false image; in religion man becomes aware of his infinitude, of his own unique status in being, and this is the meaning of Christianity. Man does not take God's place in Hegel, as Heine, Feuerbach, and other left-wing Hegelians thought, but rather mediates God's existence, and is mediated by God.

13 When no true mediation between man and God is available, one must inquire whether that religion lacks the principle of mediation altogether or only misrepresents it in its cult and institutions (as does Catholicism).

14 The appellation appears in the early lectures only; later, the term (though not the idea) is dropped.

15 Curiously, this is also Hegel's critique of Spinoza: in *this* sense ancient Judaism is more advanced than the latter-day Jew Spinoza, who reverted to the religion of nature (of substance). On another occasion Hegel attributes an "oriental" background to Spinoza's thought.

16 The concept of "subject" has a logico-structural meaning in Hegel, prior to indicating a mind or a person. A "subject" is a certain dynamic relation between a universal principle and particular items, which constitutes a dialectical totality. The latter is a circular, organic system in which the universal element exists through its particularization, and each particular component exists only through its universalization (return to the universal principle). A system like this performs the action of self-totalization and constitutes its own identity as a *result* of that action. By contrast, a substance is a static, inert, finished system whose identity is given at the outset, and the particular item is unilaterally subordinate to the universal. A substance is therefore a false totality, whereas a true totality is a subject-like system.

17 See Preface to *The Phenomenology of Spirit*, p. 10. It is also the most crucial point in *Science of Logic*, the turning point from "Objective Logic" (world reason as object) to "Subjective Logic" (world reason as subject, and eventually spirit). This important transition leads from orthodox metaphysics to Hegel's objective idealism and his category of *Begriff*. In the history of philosophy, this is the most important step in modernity, leading from Spinoza through Kant to Hegel.

18 We already met this idea in *Lectures on Aesthetics*. The notion of creation, as "negative sublimity," stresses the contingent character of a world drained of its divinity, which is relegated to an external God. The notion of creation thus implies in Hegel a sharp critique of Judaism, which we shall meet again at center-stage of the 1827 lectures.

19 This quote is from Hegel's notes in the manuscript of 1821, as published by Ilting (p. 317). A similar passage in the 1824 lectures: "In this fear of the Lord, everything that belongs to our earthly nature, everything ephemeral and contingent, is given up. Hence it is the absolute negativity, it elevates us to the level of

pure thought which surrenders all else," (*Philosophy of Religion*, vol. 2, p. 443).
20 Also "Fear of the Lord is the absolute religious Duty. To regard myself as nothing, to know myself only as absolutely dependent – the consciousness of the servant vis à vis the master; it is this fear that gives me absolute justification in my re-establishment" (Ibid., vol. 2, p. 155; Ilting, p. 323).
21 Hegel's notes to *Lectures* 1821, ibid., vol. 2, p. 155; Ilting, p. 372. Spinoza too mentioned this hatred (in *Theological-Political Treatise*), but added to it the hatred which the nations have for the Jews. This, says Spinoza, is a major power which helps the Jews survive and maintain their identity. Hegel stresses only the Jews' hatred of the Gentiles (whom he designates in his notes by the Hebrew-Yiddish word *Gojim* (ibid.).
22 *Philosophy of Religion*, vol. 2, p. 158; Ilting, p. 325.
23 "The origin of property is personality, the individual's freedom. Man, in so far as he is a person, essentially has property" (*Lectures* 1824, ibid., vol. 2, p. 448).
24 1840 *Werke*; *Philosophy of Religion*, vol. 2, p. 159.
25 Hegel's notes to *Lectures* 1821, *Philosophy of Religion*, vol. 2, p. 160; Ilting, p. 329.
26 *Lectures* 1824, *Philosophy of Religion*, vol. 2, p. 450.
27 1832 *Werke*, *Philosophy of Religion*, vol. 2, pp. 684–5.
28 In a *Rechtsstaat* (state of right, as distinguished from mere law), the laws are supposed to express a reciprocity (at least a latent one) between the rulers and the ruled, of the kind which had existed in an immediate, unconscious way in the Greek polis and was later lost in medieval times. This reciprocal relation must be restored and actualized on a higher level by the modern, post-Napoleonic state, as it overcomes the one-sided flaws of the French Revolution. The modern state will create an explicit, self-conscious synthesis of individual freedom and community: this is Hegel's brand of liberalism, as distinguished from those of both Kant and Mill.
Hegel opposes the "neutral-state liberals" in maintaining that politics (and the state) do have a spiritual significance: actually, the state is the highest form of *Sittlichkeit* (embodied morality) and thus of "objective spirit." Hegel's view is a secularization of the Protestant idea that the state has religious significance – as does also the family. However, the family is a lower form of *Sittlichkeit*. In the family, the individual is a mere "member," not a free person (*Philosophy of Right*, §158); the individual overcomes his selfish isolation by renouncing his or her independence to some other, specific person(s) on the basis of love and natural kinship. In the state, by contrast, the individual overcomes selfish isolation by submitting to a universalized, reciprocal principle which is mediated by law rather than love, and by reason rather than sheer nature.
29 By this I mean that they do it just from the standpoint of Hegel's own dialectics. One cannot charge him with violating his own system on this count (as some, including myself in an earlier version of this study, have done or tended to do). However, as I shall argue in my concluding remarks, the dialectical system itself is unjust to Judaism, since it entails a patronizing appropriation of its message.
30 Pöggeler, "Hegel's Interpretation of Judaism," p. 550. Pöggeler is a major Hegel scholar and editor who seeks to reconcile Jews and Germans after the Holocaust, and tends to stress Hegel's positive remarks about the Jews. His testimony here is therefore of particular significance.

31 See Liebeschütz, *Das Judentum*, p. 34, and Nathan Rotenstreich's chapter about Hegel in *The Recurring Pattern* (Weidenfeld and Nicolson, London, 1963); see also Rotenstreich, "Hegel's Image of Judaism," *Jewish Social Studies*, 15 (1953), pp. 33–52.

32 Hans Joachim Schöps, "Die ausserchristlichen Religionen bei Hegel," *Zeitschrift für Religions und Geistesgeschichte*, 1 (1955), pp. 1–34, at p. 28.

Chapter 6   Hegel and the Jews: A Never-Ending Story

1 Still, I think Peter Hodgson, editor of the English translation of these lectures, exaggerates their pro-Jewish content, perhaps because he underestimates the negative significance which Hegel attached to the Jewish idea of *creation*, which stands at the center of these lectures. See his preface to the English translation of the 1827 lectures in G. F. W. Hegel, *Lectures on the Philosophy of Religion*, 1-vol. edn, *The Lectures of 1827*, ed. Peter C. Hodgson (University of California Press, Berkeley, 1988), pp. 55–7. Hodgson speaks of "this notably sympathetic phenomenology of the Jewish representation of God," meaning Hegel's depiction of this God as the creator whose glory the whole universe is telling; but on my reading, these characteristics are basically *negative*. As we see in the *Aesthetics*, the Jewish idea of creation introduces a break between the finite and the infinite and drains all worth from the world and human life; and Jewish religious poetry which tells of God's glory also expresses the nullity of man and of nature, whose whole purpose is the glory of the sublime God. The change in the 1827 lectures lies in their moderate tone, which testifies to an emotional overcoming, but not so much in their content. For this and other reasons mentioned above (viz., that the 1827 lectures provide a duller, more fragmented text than the previous ones), the editor's decision to publish the 1827 lectures separately, as if they constituted *the* volume representing Hegel's philosophy of religion to the large public, is problematic. At least in what concerns Judaism, this may cause misunderstanding.

2 Hegel, *The Lectures of 1827*, p. 364. Hereafter, page references to this volume will be given in parentheses in the text.

3 This is a Kantian idea from the *Critique of Practical Reason*. It is interesting that Hegal again, as in his youth, attributes to Judaism an idea from Kant's moral doctrine.

4 In the extant version, Hegel starts the discussion of Jewish cult, but then the text stops abruptly. Probably he delivered (or intended to deliver) this part of the lecture too, but the student notes are missing.

5 Regarding Jewish law, Hegel seems to revert to the issue of "positivity." "The laws do not yet appear as laws of reason but as prescriptions of the Lord, and in that connection all manner of political prescriptions enter in, down to the smallest detail, in external categories" (*Philosophy of Religion*, vol. 2, p. 742). It seems that Hegel reattributes a political character to Judaism after having denied it several times. Maybe he means theocracy. In any case, he stresses that Hebrew law confuses moral and ceremonial commands to such a point "that the eternal laws of right and ethics which subsist in and for themselves, stand on a par with laws relating to blue and yellow curtains" (ibid.). This legalistic uniformity derives from seeing God as a Lord in whose worship "the subjective spirit does not attain freedom," so no distinction can exist between the human and the

divine law. This is also the last explanation Hegel gave of the Jewish "formalism of constancy" (the persisting fidelity to their identity), the enigma he did not succeed in solving.

6 Including a special chapter he assigns to Maimonides in his *Lectures on the History of Philosophy*. He also uses Maimonides' classic, *The Guide of the Perplexed*, as source for information on the Arab *Kalam* philosophy (which Hegel, curiously, calls by its Hebrew name: Philosophie der "Medaberim").

7 See Yirmiyahu Yovel, "God's Transcendence and its Schematization: Maimonides in Light of the Spinoza–Hegel Dispute," in *Maimonides as Philosopher*, ed. S. Pines and Y. Yovel (Martinus Nijhoff, Dordrecht, 1986), pp. 269–82.

8 Incidentally, a similar position was held by Spinoza, whom Hegel knew and specifically attacked on that point (viz., Spinoza's denying that is a subject). I have reconstructed Spinoza's response to Hegel in *Spinoza and Other Heretics*, vol. 2: *The Adventures of Immanence* (Princeton University Press, Princeton, 1988), ch. 2. The main difference between Maimonides' and Spinoza's responses is that Spinoza's God is immanent and the same as the infinite universe, but the universe as such is devoid of the human image and of all moral or teleological patterns.

9 Concluding sentence of his *Ethics*.

10 There is a hint of Maimonides that even prayer, like the ancient practice of sacrifice, might be eliminated when the religious mind becomes more mature.

11 Hegel, *Lectures on the History of Philosophy*, tr. E. S. Haldane and F. H. Simson (Kegan Paul, London, 1894), vol. 2, p. 387. Hereafter, page references to this edition are given in parentheses in the text.

12 He thereby follows a Jewish (rather uncritical) convention which attributes the *Zohar*, the Cabbalah's major book, to Rabbi Shimeon Bar-Yokhai who lived in that era.

13 Hegel mentions Herrera's book, *The Gates of Heaven* (*Porta Caelorum*) by both its Latin and its German titles, but misspells the author's name (Irira instead of Herrera): *History of Philosophy*, vol. 2, p. 395. The book was published in Amsterdam in the seventeenth century and influenced later scholars; see Gershom Scholem, *Abraham Cohen Herrera, Author of the Gates of Heaven* (Hebrew) (Bialik, Jerusalem, 1978); tr. as *Das Buch Shaar ha-Shamayim oder Pforte des Himmels* (Suhrkamp, Frankfurt, 1979).

14 The text of the *Lectures on the History of Philosophy* from which I quoted appears in the second edition (1840) of Hegel's *Werke*, which is composed of materials from different periods. A new critical edition has not yet appeared.

15 On Hegel and the *Burschenschaft* in general see Jacques D'Hondt, *Hegel en son temps* (Editions Sociales, Paris, 1968). On Carové, Hegel and the Jews see Shlomo Avineri, "A Note on Hegel's Views on Jewish Emancipation," *Jewish Social Studies*, 25/2 (1963), pp. 145–51.

16 Shlomo Avineri, "Note on Hegel's Views," p. 147; see relevant documents in J. Hoffmeister (ed.), *Briefe von und an Hegel* (Meiner, Hamburg, 1953), vol. 2, pp. 455ff.

17 Kuno Fischer, *Hegels Leben, Werke und Lehre* (Winter, Heidelberg, 1911), pt. 1, p. 321; mentioned in Franz Wiedmann, *Hegel, An Illustrated Biography* (Pegasus, New York, 1968), p. 57.

18 Actually Cousin got much more from his visit, for he set up a connection and then a correspondence with Hegel.

19 Although the Rheinland Jews were emancipated by Napoleon, when Prussia

later annexed the Rheinland, they lost their rights, and Jewish lawyers were forbidden to continue practicing. (I owe this reminder to Shlomo Avineri.)
20 Hegel, *Philosophy of the Right*, tr. T. M. Knox, 3rd edn (Clarendon Press, Oxford, 1969), p. 134.
21 Ibid., p. 169.
22 This goes against nationalism, ethnicism, etc. Hegel concedes that a stable society needs commonality, but this is based not on a common race, ethnic group, religion, etc., but on equal citizenship, the translation of abstract humanity into a *civic* community.
23 *Philosophy of Right*, p. 169n.
24 Hegel could not have meant a "melting pot," whose unity is too "abstract" (in his terms) and therefore oppressive, nor a batch of ethnic and cultural ingredients merely coexisting alongside each other (whose unity is that of an "aggregate" rather than a "totality"). He meant a dialectical whole which both retains and transcends its particular ingredients. In Hegel's *Philosophy of Right* this is performed by the "universal," i.e., nonsectarian, nondenominational power of the state. Today, however, after the ambivalent performance of the nation-state and its enfeeblement by global forces, one might think of going beyond the single state toward a lean but powerful regional confederation – a kind of "democratic empire" – that allows for greater autonomy and diversity on the level of groups, localities, and minorities, while also providing objective unity and safeguards at a trans-state level.
25 Before his death in 1831 Hegel again lectured on the philosophy of religion, including Judaism. Of these lectures there is only a summary by David Friedrich Strauss. In the 1831 lectures the order of religions is radically changed. Judaism comes after Persian religion and before Phoenician and Egyptian religion; the latter serves as a bridge to the Greek religion "of beauty and freedom" and the Roman religion of expediency. Thus Judaism is here pushed way back – even preceding two oriental religions – yet it continues to fulfill the crucial roles we know: (a) here for the first time the divine becomes subject, a person; (b) "here for the first time God is truly known as creator and lord of the world" (*Philosophy of Religion*, vol. 3, p. 739); (c) "here for the first time the question how evil has come into the world acquires a meaning" (vol. 2, p. 740). Hegel now stresses in particular the question of suffering – that is, of theodicy – and the book of Job's coping with God's justice and power. Concerning religious law Hegel seems to revert to the issue of "positivity" that occupied him in youth: "the laws do not yet appear as laws of reason but as prescriptions of the Lord, and in that connection all manner of political prescriptions enter in, down to the smallest detail, in external categories" (vol. 2, p. 742). It seems that Hegel again ascribes a political character to Judaism after having denied it several times in the past (perhaps he means theocracy). Yet Jewish law confuses moral and ritual commands, "so that the eternal laws of right and ethics ... stand on a par with laws relating to blue or yellow curtains" (ibid.). This uniform legalism arises from perceiving God as Master without distinguishing between a divine and a human law. This is also the explanation Hegel gave before his death to the Jewish "formalism of persistence" (their fidelity, steadfastness) – the riddle he could not solve.
26 I discuss this in my paper "Tolerance as Grace and as Right," abridged (Hebrew) version in *Iyyun*, 45 (Oct. 1996), pp. 482–7; complete version forthcoming in Social Research (1998).

27 Emil Fackenheim has aptly called this "the religious dimension in Hegel's thought" (see his book of that title (Indiana University Press, Bloomington, Ind., 1967)).

28 I do not mean that necessarily as a criticism.

29 Nachman Krochmal (Ranak), was a religious Jewish thinker influenced by Hegel, who identified Judaism rather than Christianity as "absolute religion," and therefore saw no change and evolution in it, but rather timelessness, since it has transcended history into eternity. On him and other Jewish Hegelians see Shlomo Avineri, "The Fossil and the Phoenix: Hegel and Krochmal on the Jewish Volksgeist," in *History and System: Hegel's Philosophy of History*, ed. R. L. Perkins (SUNY Press, Albany, 1984), pp. 47–64.

30 E. Fackenheim, "Hegel and Judaism: A Flaw in the Hegelian System," in *The Legacy of Hegel: Proceedings of the Marquette University Hegel Symposium 1970*, ed. J. J. O'Malley et al. (Nijhoff, The Hague, 1973), pp. 161–85, at p. 161.

Chapter 7 Nietzsche and the Shadows of the Dead God

1 This concept was used by some German philosophers, like Dilthey, to denote a direct, semi-empathic grasp of someone or something else's state of life – be it a person, an era, etc.

2 I use the word *idol* somewhat in Bacon's sense, as a fiction or distorting image.

3 On the question of whether there is "genuine truth" in his philosophy, see later.

4 Because their overall philosophies seem at first so remote, Nietzsche's affinities with Hume have not been sufficiently noticed.

5 Genealogy is the search for a person's biological-familial origins: Nietzsche investigates the psychological and existential origins of various life-forms, stands, and world images.

6 In this he comes close to Hume, Kant, and Wittgenstein – regardless of their material differences.

7 The metaphor of birth, the complement of genealogy, was a Nietzschean favorite since *The Birth of Tragedy*.

8 Freud said that because of that affinity he had stopped reading Nietzsche at an early stage, in order to avoid being influenced by "a speculative" philosopher in matters of "scientific" import. The statement is neither very credible nor adequately grounded; its full clarification must await the opening of all of Freud's papers. (See his letter to Lothar Bickel, 28 June 1931.)

9 Nietzsche, *The Gay Science*, tr. Walter Kaufmann (Vintage, New York, 1974), §109. Hereafter *GS* and section number will be given parenthetically in text.

10 Since Nietzsche is no dialectician in the style of Hegel, there is no synthesis here, no reconciliation of the contradiction, only a self-defeating ironic situation.

11 Cf. Nietzsche, *The Antichrist*, in *The Portable Nietzsche*, tr. Walter Kaufmann (Vintage, New York, 1954), §62. Hereafter *A* and section number will be given parenthetically in text.

Chapter 8   The *Anti*-Anti-Semite

1 Nietzsche, *Beyond Good and Evil*, tr. Walter Kaufmann (Vintage, New York, 1966), §251. Hereafter, *BGE* and section number will be given parenthetically in the text.

2 The letters were first published in *Festschrift zum fünfundzwanzigjährigen Bestehen des Hammers* (Hammer Verlag, Leipzig, 1920) pp. 77–9. The letters cited in what follows are published in Nietzsche, *Briefwechsel: Kritische Gesamtausgabe*, ed. Giorgio Colli and Mazzino Montinari (W. de Gruyter, Berlin, 1973–93); hereafter *BW*.

3 Ronald Hayman, *Nietzsche* (Oxford University Press, New York, 1980), p. 189.

4 Ibid., p. 195.

5 Nietzsche, *On the Genealogy of Morals*, tr. Walter Kaufmann (Vintage, New York, 1969), III, §14. Hereafter *GM* and essay and section numbers will be given parenthetically in text.

6 Nietzsche, *Daybreak*, tr. R. J. Hollingdale (Cambridge University Press, Cambridge, 1982). Hereafter *D* and section numbers will be given parenthetically in text.

7 Nietzsche, *Nietzsche contra Wagner*, essay 8, §1. In *The Portable Nietzsche*, tr. Walter Kaufmann (Vintage, New York, 1954).

8 Burckhardt's attitude toward the Jews has been discussed by, among others, Hans Liebeschütz ("Das Judentum im Geschichtsbild Jacob Burckhardts," in *Yearbook of the Leo Baeck Institute* 4 (1959), pp. 61–80), and by Jacob Talmon (in an introductory essay entitled "Jacob Burckhardt" which preceded the Hebrew translation of Burckhardt's *Weltgeschichtliche Betrachtungen*, Bialik Institute, Jerusalem, 1962; see esp. pp. 20–4, and in his lecture entitled, "Nietzsche's Jewish Aspects in Historical Perspective," given at the World Congress for Jewish Studies, 8 August 1969, and first published in *Ha'arez*, 12 Sept. 1969). In the former essay Talmon calls Burckhardt "a true anti-Semite, lacking any respect for the Jewish people and hastening to hurt them on every occasion" (p. 22), and in the latter he lists Burckhardt as the first of the major anti-Semites with whom Nietzsche had contact. The facts, however, seem to be somewhat more complex. As Liebeschütz shows, Burckhardt also expressed empathy for the Jews' suffering, though he saw them indeed as aliens to the true European culture (which was Christian) and justified their medieval persecution on historical, though not on moral, grounds. As a student he wrote (for a living) an anonymous novel on the theme of "the knight and the Jewess" – somewhat like Lessing's *Nathan the Wise*, but expressing more critical sentiments. In maturity he was an ardent conservative, indeed a reactionary, who cherished the former European culture of the Middle Ages and especially the Renaissance, and expressed deep suspicion and pessimism about modernity. He saw great catastrophes looming in a future dominated by the plebeian, barbaric culture of the masses – including industrialization and democracy. A symptom of that oncoming barbarism was the Jews' emancipation and social ascent, which he opposed.

Burckhardt also denied (or disregarded, which amounts to the same thing) the role of the Jews in world history and especially in shaping traditional European culture. Nor did he recognize (as Liebeschütz shows) the common biblical sources of Judaism and Christianity. While expressing empathy for the Jews' suffering, he defended their exclusion with the claim that they were the very opposite of the European culture, which he saw as essentially Christian. It is noteworthy that Nietzsche, who shared Burckhardt's patrician elitism and learned from him to place culture above everything else, praised the Jews (in *Human, all too Human*) for precisely that *same* reason: namely, their alienness and opposition to medieval Christian culture. And while Burckhardt all but denied the common heritage of Jews and Christians, Nietzsche stressed it for *one* period (that of "priestly Judaism") and denied it for another (post-Christian Judaism).

Liebeschütz writes that Burckhardt saw the persecution of the Jews as abominable from the viewpoint of the value of tolerance, but as justified from a deeper historical perspective, because it entailed the opposition of two antithetical "national individualities" ("Das Judentum," p. 67), which he later labeled also an "irreconcilable national antagonism" (ibid., p. 68). Though the Jews' suffering evokes his sympathy and respect, Burckhardt became hardened to it because he believed that great cultural achievements are bought with human suffering (ibid., p. 71). In any case, "the listeners to [Burckhardt's] Basel lectures could not doubt that, to him, European Jewry did not belong to the forces which have built the great European tradition" (ibid., p. 71). Nietzsche must have been aware of this view, but reversed its meaning and thrust. The early Jews were responsible for the decadent element in European culture (Christianity), and the later Diaspora Jews, indeed aliens to that culture, were thereby keepers of a promise of a cure. Nietzsche too saw culture as the most important consideration, but opposed Burckhardt's evaluation of both the essence of European culture and the Jews' role in it. He was also more nuanced than the famous Basel historian, and made more historical distinctions.

In his private correspondence Burckhardt made several anti-Semitic remarks, not destined for publication; but Nietzsche, his younger friend and protégé could easily have heard similar private remarks from the master during their association in Basel. It is noteworthy, in any case, that Nietzsche took the opposite view on all these issues. Thus, Burckhardt wrote to Friedrich Preen (2 Jan. 1880) that the "Semites" (meaning modern Jews) would have to renounce "their totally unjustified involvement in everything"; whereas Nietzsche (in *Daybreak*, §205) demands that they do get so involved, and that they excel in all European matters. Burckhardt also wrote to Preen (3 Dec. 1880) that European liberalism would eventually have to retract the full rights given to the Semites "even if it causes it heartbreak"; whereas Nietzsche (though not out of liberalism) wanted the Jews practically to "dominate" European standards and values. In another letter (23 Dec. 1882) Burckhardt attacked "the nine-tenths of German Journalism produced by Jews," wondered why so little was done about that nation, and predicted that a referendum in Germany might decide to expel all the Jews. Nietzsche too, in *Daybreak*, fears that the Jews might "lose Europe" as their ancestors lost Egypt, but sees this as a misfortune for Europe; and in *BGE*, §251, he suggested expelling from the country not the Jews but "the screaming anti-Semites."

On balance, and judged by the written evidence, Burckhardt seems to have been much less anti-Semitic than Wagner and his circle. But Nietzsche might have heard many oral remarks from him, and seems on the whole to have taken him to be a genuine anti-Semite, one whom over time he came to associate with Wagner and Elizabeth, though he continued to respect him in an ambivalent way. The main point, for us, is not what Burckhardt was "objectively," but the way Nietzsche perceived him. Whether he was, as Talmon says, a "true

anti-Semite" or not, Nietzsche seems to have been convinced that he was.
9 Nietzsche, *The Will to Power*, tr. Walter Kaufmann and R.J. Hollingdale (Vintage, New York, 1968). Hereafter *WP* and section number will be given parenthetically in text.
10 Nietzsche, *Thus Spoke Zarathustra*, tr. R.J. Hollingdale (Penguin, Harmondsworth, 1961), I, §1. Hereafter *Z* and section number will be given parenthetically in the text.
11 Nietzsche, *Ecce Homo*, I, §3. Hereafter *EH* and essay and section numbers will be given parenthetically in text.
12 Nietzsche, *Twilight of the Idols*, VIII, §1, in *The Portable Nietzsche*. Hereafter, *TI* and essay and section numbers will be given parenthetically in text.
13 Nietzsche, *Human, All Too Human*, tr. R.J. Hollingdale (Cambridge University Press, Cambridge, 1986), I, §475. Hereafter *HH* and section number will be given parenthetically in text.

Chapter 9 Nietzsche and Ancient Judaism: The Antichrist

1 "Why I am a Destiny," *EH*, §7.
2 By using such terms as "setback" and "retreat" I do not mean to attribute a view of historical progress to Nietzsche. Yet in terms of his own values, there can be, and have been, advances and retreats, even though no historical necessity or teleological pattern governs or is expressed in them.
3 However, it may be "good" in the sense of human worth, which Nietzsche upholds. He distinguishes between the pair "good/evil" and "good/bad"; the latter is meaningful, though not judged by obligations, but rather by the degree of human worth and Dionysian perfection attained. (In contemporary jargon, it belongs to an "ethics of virtue" rather than an "ethics of duties".)
4 Julius Wellhausen, *Prolegomena to the History of Israel* with a Reprint of the Article "Israel" from the Encyclopaedia Britannica (Black, Edinburgh, 1885) p. 77.
5 Ibid., p. 76.
6 Ibid., p. 90.
7 Ibid., p. 509.
8 Wellhausen's hostility to priestly culture may have been inspired in part by Reimarus, the Protestant philosopher who also influenced Paul de Lagarde, Nietzsche's anti-Semitic opponent. (See Goren, "Image of the Jew," pp. 105–6).
9 Is Nietzsche unwittingly speaking of his own future career?
10 Nietzsche's attitude toward Spinoza has similar traits: admiration for his person and for parts of his doctrine, yet rejection of other parts – the belief in eternal truths, reason, etc., which, according to Nietzsche's genealogy, ought to have cast a "decadent," petty shadow on Spinoza's personal character as well and have led to a very different ethics and way of life than those advocated (and seemingly followed) by Spinoza. This was not only a contradiction, but, as I have suggested in *Spinoza and Other Heretics*, vol. 2: *The Adventures of Immanence*, pp. 132–5, a "genealogical scandal" in terms of Nietzsche's own philosophy; yet it was also a fact that Nietzsche could neither shake nor explain. Similar cases are those of Jesus and, to a lesser extent, Socrates: in each case a person is admired despite his overt doctrine. A similar case can be made concerning Nietzsche's admiration (for different reasons) of biblical and Diaspora Jews. All this must serve as a qualification to his genealogical doctrine: admirable features

can exist in people holding "decadent" theories.

11 We shall see another ironic example later, concerning his latent heretical use of the idea of an "elect people."

Chapter 10   The Diaspora and Contemporary Jews

1 What he praises is the rationalist element in the critique of religion (which Nietzsche accepts and uses himself).

2 Though Spinoza was justly seen as a paradigm for many *modern* Jews, Nietzsche seems to view him as paradigmatic of *medieval*, Jewish scholars too, and this is imprudent. What can be said is that scholars writing in Arabic, mostly Muslim but including the Jewish thinker Maimonides (and his follows and off-shoots), bore the tradition of Greek philosophy before it was adopted by the Christian West.

3 He admires Spinoza's strictly immanent philosophy and other ideas, but rejects as "decadent" his belief in a rational world governed by eternal truths. (For a detailed comparison see Yovel, ("Spinoza and Nietzsche: *amor dei* and *amor fati*") in *Spinoza and Other Heretics*, vol. 2, ch. 5.

4 This obvious point has eluded a few authors who have taken Nietzsche's words as complimenting the Jews. Yet we must read him in terms of his own values, not ours; and it is inconceivable that Nietzsche would praise Jewish morality.

5 These texts contain both an attack on anti-Semitism and an admiration of present-day Jews, and since I made a distinction between the two, I had to use these texts in both chapter 8 and here.

6 Nietzsche's remark about the "purity" of the Jewish race seems to be a case of his still using an idea which he had abandoned. Though Nietzsche may think the Jews racially "pure" (because of their seclusion), he does not see this as an ideal, but, on the contrary, wants the Jews to come out of their seclusion and the new Europe to be a mixture of races, including especially a strong dose of Slavs and Jews. (This further explains his demand that "the Jews and the Russians" be taken into account "in all projects for the future" of Europe) (*BGE*, §251).

7 One who was so misled was the late Jacob L. Talmon – which shows how the emotional power of this uncritical reading is hard to overcome, even for major historians. Given such examples, I must expect other worthy scholars to object to my corrective reading, however fair and textually more adequate it may be.

8 Let us remember that the "loss of Egypt" was experienced by the Jews as a positive event, the liberation that founded the Jewish people.

9 I say "opposes" (in the present tense) because, although Zionism officially started after Nietzsche had gone mad, there already existed a proto-Zionist book in his time, Moses Hess's *Rome and Jerusalem*; and while we don't know if Nietzsche read it, his known view clearly rejects this idea (also because of its nationalism). In any case, the problem which Zionism addressed was also before Nietzsche, and he gave a different, incompatible answer, which is so explicit that he can be called an "anti-Zionist before the fact."

10 Not noticing this crucial point is one of the reasons for the grave misunderstandings to which this Nietzschean text has been subjected.

Conventionally, it would seem "obvious" that Nietzsche, when faced with such a dilemma, would – like any other non-Jew (and not only the anti-Semites) – prefer to see the Jews lose Europe rather than dominate it. Yet Nietzsche, once again, is unconventional: he opts for the other horn of the dilemma. Upsetting his readers' "obvious" assumption, he prefers the Jews to "dominate Europe" (in the cultural sense explained), and opposes anything on their or on the Christians' part that might lead to the crisis of their departure.

11 A warning describes the dangers inherent in a situation, but is not necessarily personal. A threat is a personalized warning: the danger is coming from me or from us.

12 We may summarize the issue by the following schematic analysis. There are three levels of reading: Nietzsche's own position, today's uncritical reader's interpretation, and the way Nietzsche expected the conventional reader of *his* day to react. Today's uncritical reader understands "losing Europe" as something close to Nazi policies, and "dominating Europe" as actual political and economic control by the Jews; moreover, he or she assumes that Nietzsche, like most Europeans, would be driven to the first option if no way existed between the horns of the dilemma. Nietzsche, however, understood "losing Europe" in terms of exile or emigration, and "dominating Europe" as setting its cultural values, and emphatically preferred the second option. He too expected the conventional reader of his time (including, but not only, the anti-Semites) to assume that the first option is naturally preferable – and then surprised the reader by opting for the second. Better have the Jews "dominate Europe" (in his sense) than leave. And still better, he said elsewhere, is to drive out not the Jews but "the screaming anti-Semites" (*BGE*, §251).

13 See ch. 8, p. 119 above.

14 Hellenism, like Judaism, has no fixed essence. Nietzsche divides it into Olympian, tragic, and Socratic (rationalist) forms and judges them differently.

15 This conclusion is dramatically reinforced by Nietzsche's sentence in his twilight letter to Burckhardt: "I had Caiaphas put in chains ... Wilhelm, Bismark, and all anti-Semites deposed". Speaking as a Dionysian "crucified," Nietzsche here lumps together a single family of his opponents, the anti-Semites, the Jewish High Priest, and the modern German nationalists – all have the same genealogical parent.

16 Of the writers who have addressed this subject, Eisen in particular has observed Nietzsche's use of anti-Semitic images and the extreme language he uses both when attacking the Jews or praising them. However, Eisen does not realize that Nietzsche is speaking of two different periods (or genealogical phases) of Judaism. See Arnold M. Eisen, "Nietzsche and the Jews Reconsidered," *Jewish Social Studies*, 48 (1986), pp. 1–14.

17 From the point of view of an aristocratic ethics of virtue and excellence and a Dionysian ethics of power.

18 While his sensibilities tended to the cultural Right, Nietzsche was not a conservative. There is almost nothing Nietzsche wanted to conserve. He was a cultural radical, a revolutionary, who wanted to uproot the rationalist and Christian culture of the West. His positive attitude to the Jews also stems, in great part, from this radicalism, from a provocative reversal of the common view about them, seeing them as an elite, and therefore as fit for a new elitist culture.

Epilogue

1 Still, Nietzsche has *drawn upon* the Enlightenment no less than he has rejected it; his relation to it was more dialectical than is usually recognized by facile categorization. He too was an offspring of the eighteenth-century revolution, though he proposed a radical alternative *within* it. That makes him a modernizer – albeit a different kind of modernizer – rather than anti- or post- modern as he is fashionably presented today.

Bibliography

Works by Hegel

Sämtliche Werke: Kritische Ausgabe, ed. Georg Lasson, Johannes Hoffmeister et al. (Felix Meiner, Hamburg, 1911–56).

Werke in zwanzig Bänden, ed. Eva Moldenhauer and Karl M. Michel (Suhrkamp, Frankfurt, 1969–72).

Hegels theologische Jugendschriften, ed. H. Nohl (Tübingen, 1907; repr. Minerva, Frankfurt, 1966).

Early Theological Writings, tr. T. M. Knox and R. Kroner (University of Chicago Press, Chicago, 1948; 6th edn, University of Pennsylvania Press, Philadelphia, 1988).

Die Phänomenologie des Geistes, ed. Johannes Hoffmeister, 6th edn (Felix Meiner, Hamburg, 1952; 1st pub. as part 1 of *System der Wissenschaft* (Bamberg and Würzburg, 1807)); tr. A. V. Miller, as *The Phenomenology of Spirit* (Clarendon Press, Oxford, 1977).

Wissenschaft der Logik (Nürnberg, 1812–16); tr. A. V. Miller as *Science of Logic* (2 vols, Allen and Unwin, London, 1969).

Encyklopädie der philosophischen Wissenschaften im Grundrisse (Heidelberg, 1817; rev. edn 1830); tr. W. Wallace as *Hegel's Logic*, as *Encyclopedia of the Philosophical Sciences*, part 1 (1830; 3rd edn, Clarendon Press, Oxford, 1975).

Aesthetics: Lectures on Fine Art, tr. T. M. Knox (2 vols, Clarendon Press, Oxford, 1975).

Introduction to the Lectures on the History of Philosophy, ed. P. C. Hodgson (University of California Press, Berkeley, 1984).

Lectures on the History of Philosophy, tr. E. S. Haldane and F. H. Simpson, from the 2nd German edn (1840) (3 vols, Kegan Paul, London, 1894).

The Philosophy of History, tr. J. Sibree (1899; repr. Dover, New York, 1956).

Vorlesungen über Rechtsphilosophie: "Die Rechtsphilosophie" von 1820, ed. K. H. Ilting (Frommann Holzboog, Stuttgart, 1976).
Philosophy of Right, tr. with notes T. M. Knox, 3rd edn (Oxford University Press, Oxford, 1969).
Religionsphilosophie, vol. 1: *Die Vorlesung von 1821,* ed. K. H. Ilting (Bibliopolis, Naples, 1978).
Vorlesungen über die Philosophie der Religion, ed. Walter Jaeschke, 3 parts (Felix Meiner, Hamburg, 1983–5).
Lectures on the Philosophy of Religion, ed. Peter C. Hodgson, tr. R. F. Brown, Peter C. Hodgson, and J. M. Stewart, from Jaeschke's edition (3 vols, University of California Press, Berkeley, 1984–7).
Lectures on the Philosophy of Religion, One-Volume Edition, The Lectures of 1827, ed. Peter C. Hodgson (University of California Press, Berkeley, 1988).
Briefe von und an Hegel, ed. J. Hoffmeister (3 vols, Meiner, Hamburg, 1953).

Works by Nietzsche

Werke: Kritische Gesamtausgabe, ed. Giorgio Colli and Mazzino Montinari (W. de Gruyter, Berlin, 1967–86).
Briefwechsel: Kritische Gesamtausgabe, ed. Giorgio Colli and Mazzino Montinari (W. de Gruyter, Berlin, 1975–93); abbreviated *BW.*
Basic Writings, tr. Walter Kaufmann (Random House, New York, 1968). Includes *Beyond Good and Evil, Genealogy of Morals, Case of Wagner,* and *Ecce Homo.*
The Portable Nietzsche, tr. Walter Kaufmann (Viking Press, New York, 1954). Includes *Thus Spoke Zarathustra, Twilight of the Idols, The Antichrist, Nietzsche Contra Wagner,* and an abridged version of "Homer's Contest."
Beyond Good and Evil, tr. Walter Kaufmann (Vintage, New York, 1966); abbreviated *BGE.*
Daybreak, Thoughts on the Prejudices of Morality, tr. R. J. Hollingdale (Cambridge University Press, Cambridge, 1982); abbreviated *D.*
The Gay Science, tr. Walter Kaufmann (Vintage, New York, 1974); abbreviated *GS.*
Human, All Too Human: A Book for Free Spirits, tr. R. J. Hollingdale (Cambridge University Press, Cambridge, 1986); abbreviated *HH.*
On the Genealogy of Morals and Ecce Homo, tr. Walter Kaufmann (Vintage, New York, 1969); abbreviated *GM* and *EH* respectively.
Thus Spoke Zarathustra, tr. R. J. Hollingdale (Penguin, Harmondsworth, 1961); abbreviated *Z.*
The Will to Power, tr. Walter Kaufmann and R. J. Hollingdale (Vintage, New York, 1968); abbreviated *WP.*

Other Works

Altmann, Alexander, *Moses Mendelssohn: A Biographical Study* (University of Alabama Press, Birmingham, Ala., 1973).
Arendt, Hannah, *The Origins of Totalitarianism* (Harcourt, Brace and World, New York, 1973).
Aschheim, S., *The Nietzsche Legacy in Germany* (University of California Press, Berkeley, 1992).
——, "Nietzsche and the Nietzschean Moment in Jewish Life (1890–1939)," *Leo*

Baeck Institute Year Book, 37 (1992), pp. 189–212.

Avineri, Shlomo, "A Note on Hegel's Views on Jewish Emancipation," *Jewish Social Studies,* 25/2 (1963), pp. 145–51.

——, "The Fossil and the Phoenix: Hegel and Krochmal on the Jewish Volksgeist," in *History and System: Hegel's Philosophy of History* ed. Robert L. Perkins (SUNY Press, Albany, NY, 1984), pp. 47–64.

Baron, Jonathan, "Nietzsche's Relationship with the Jews: Ambivalent Admiration," *Mosaic: A Review of Jewish Thought and Culture,* 11 (1991), pp. 17–27.

Bataille, G., "Nietzsche and the Fascists," tr. Lee Hildreth, *Semiotext(e),* 3 (1978), pp. 114–19; repr. in *Visions of Excess: Selected Writings,* ed. A. Stoekl (Manchester University Press, Manchester, 1985).

Baudis, Andreas, "Das Volk Israel in Hegels frühem Denken: Eine Studie zur Entstehungsgeschichte der modernen Dialektik" (Ph.D. thesis, Freie Universität, Berlin, 1978).

Bäumler, Alfred, *Nietzsche der Philosoph und Politiker* (Reclam, Leipzig, 1931).

——, "Nietzsche und der Nationalsozialismus," *Nationalsozialistische Monatshefte,* (1934), pp. 289–98; repr. in his *Studien zur deutschen Geistesgeschichte* (Berlin, 1937).

Bechtel, Delphine, "Nietzsche et la dialectique de l'histoire juive," in *De Sils-Maria à Jérusalem,* pp. 67–79.

Berl, H., "Nietzsche und das Judentum," *Menorah,* 10 (1932), pp. 59–69.

Biser, Eugen, "Nietzsche und Heine: Kritik des christlichen Gottesbegriffs," in *Nietzsche as Affirmative Thinker,* ed. Y. Yovel (Kluwer, Dordrecht, 1986), pp. 204–18.

Brinton, C., *Nietzsche,* 2nd edn (Harper & Row, New York, 1965).

Cancik, Hubert and Cancik-Lindemaier, Hildegard, "Philhellénisme et antisémitisme en Allemagne: le cas Nietzsche," in *De Sils-Maria à Jérusalem,* pp. 21–46.

Cohen, Hermann, "Inner Beziehungen der Kantischen Philosophie zum Judentum," in *Berichte der Lehranstalt für Wissenschaft des Judentums* (Mayer & Mayer, Berlin, 1910), pp. 41–61.

——, *Religion der Vernunft aus den Quellen des Judentums* (Fourier Verlag, Wiesbaden, 1978).

Coutinho, A., "Nietzsche's Critique of Judaism," *Review of Religion,* 3 (1939), pp. 161–5.

De Launay, Marc B., "Le Juif introuvable," in *De Sils-Maria à Jérusalem,* pp. 81–9.

De Sils-Maria à Jérusalem: Nietzsche et le judaïsme; Les intellectuels juifs et Nietzsche, ed. Dominique Bourel and Jacques Le Rider (Cerf, Paris, 1991).

D'Hondt, Jacques, *Hegel en son temps* (Editions Sociales, Paris, 1968).

——, *Hegel secret* (Presses Universitaires de France, Paris, 1968).

Dohm, Christian Wilhelm, *Über die bürgerliche Verbesserung der Juden* (F. Nicolai, Berlin, 1781); tr. Helen Lederer, as *Concerning the Amelioration of the Civil Status of the Jews* (Hebrew Union College Institute of Religion, Cincinnati, Oh., 1957).

Duffy, M., and Mittelman, W. "Nietzsche's Attitudes toward the Jews," *Journal of the History of Ideas,* 49 (1988), pp. 301–17.

Eisen, Arnold M., "Nietzsche and the Jews Reconsidered," *Jewish Social Studies,* 48 (1986), pp. 1–14.

Fackenheim, Emil L., "Comment on N. Rotenstreich's 'Sublimity and Messianism'," *Human Context,* 6 (1974), pp. 523–60.

——, "Hegel and Judaism: A Flaw in the Hegelian Meditation," in *The Legacy of Hegel: Proceedings of the Marquette University Hegel Symposium 1970*, ed. J. J. O'Malley, K. W. Algozin, H. P. Kainz, and L. C. Rice (Nijhoff, The Hague, 1973), pp. 161–85.

——, *The Religious Dimension in Hegel's Thought* (Indiana University Press, Bloomington, 1967).

Fischer, Kuno, *Hegels Leben, Werke und Lehre*, 2nd edn (C. Winter, Heidelberg, 1911).

——, *Immanuel Kant und sein Lehre*, 4th edn (C. Winter, Heidelberg, 1899).

Friedlander, D., *Beitrag zur Geschichte der Verfolgung der Juden im 19ten Jahrhundert durch Schriftsteller* (Berlin, 1820).

Gay, Peter, *Freud, Jews and Other Germans* (Oxford University Press, New York, 1978).

Gilman, S. L., *Inscribing the Other* (University of Nebraska Press, Lincoln, 1991).

Golomb, Jacob, "Nietzsche on Jews and Judaism," *Archiv für Geschichte der Philosophie*, 67 (1985), pp. 139–61.

——, *Nietzsche's Enticing Psychology of Power* (Iowa State University Press, Ames, 1988).

——, "Nietzsche's Judaism of Power," *Revue des études juives*, 147 (1988), pp. 353–85.

—— (ed.), *Nietzsche and Jewish Culture* (Routledge, London, 1997).

Goren, Yaakov, "The Image of the Jew and Judaism in Protestant Bible Scholarship from the Middle of the 18th century to the Thirties of the 19th century" (Hebrew), Ph. D. thesis, Hebrew University, Jerusalem, 1975.

Graupe, H. M., "Kant und das Judentum," *Zeitschrift für Religions- und Geistesgeschichte*, 13 (1961), pp. 308–33.

Abbé Grégoire, *Essai sur la régénération physique, morale et politique des juifs* (1789), préface de Robert Badinter (Stock, Paris, 1988).

Greive, Hermann, "Fortschritt und Diskriminierung; Juden und Judentum bei Georg Wilhelm Friedrich Hegel und Franz Joseph Molitor," in *Homburg vor der Hohe in der deutschen Geistesgeschichte: Studien zum Freundeskreis um Hegel und Hölderlin*, ed. Christoph Jamme and Otto Pöggeler (Klett-Cotta, Stuttgart, 1981), pp. 300–17.

Guttmann, J., "Kant und das Judentum," in *Schriften*, ed. Gesellschaft zur Forderung der Wissenschaft des Judentums (Leipzig, 1908), pp. 41–61.

——, "Moses Mendelssohns *Jerusalem* und Spinozas *Theologisch-politischer Traktat*," in *Bericht der Hochschule für die Wissenschaft des Judentums*, 48 (1931), pp. 31–67.

——, *Philosophies of Judaism* (Doubleday, Garden City, NY, 1966).

Hertzberg, Arthur, *The French Enlightenment and the Jews* (Columbia University Press, New York, 1968).

Hodgson, Peter C., Editorial introduction to *Hegel: Lectures on the Philosophy of Religion: The Lectures of 1827* (University of California Press, Berkeley, 1988), pp. 1–71.

——, "The Metamorphosis of Judaism in Hegel's Philosophy of Religion," *Owl of Minerva*, 19 (1987–8), pp. 41–52.

Hoffmeister, Johannes (ed.), *Dokumente zu Hegels Entwicklung* (Frommann-Holzboog, Stuttgart, 1974; 1st pub. 1936).

—— (ed.), *Briefe von und an Hegel* (Meiner, Hamburg, 1953).

Hyppolite, Jean, *Genèse et structure de la Phénoménologie de l'Esprit* (Aubier-Montaigne, Paris, 1946).

Kant, Immanuel, "Anthropologie in pragmatischer Hinsicht abgefasst" (1798), in *Gesammelte Schriften*, vol. 7 (Prussian Academy of Sciences, Berlin, 1917).
——, *Anthropology from a Pragmatic Point of View*, tr. Mary J. Gregor (Martinus Nijhoff, The Hague, 1974).
——, *The Conflict of Faculties*, in Kant, *Religion and Rational Theology*, tr. and ed. A. W. Wood and G. di Giovanni (Cambridge University Press, Cambridge, 1996).
——, *Critique of Judgement*, tr. J. C. Meredith (Clarendon Press, Oxford, 1952).
——, *Critique of Practical Reason*, tr. L. W. Beck (Bobbs-Merrill, Indianapolis, 1956).
——, *Religion within the Boundaries of Mere Reason*, tr. Allen W. Wood and George di Giovanni (Cambridge University Press, Cambridge, 1996).
Kaufmann, Walter, *From Shakespeare to Existentialism* (Anchor Books, Garden City, NY, 1960).
——, *Hegel: Reinterpretation, Texts, and Commentary* (Doubleday, Garden City, NY, 1965).
——, *Nietzsche: Philosopher, Psychologist, Antichrist*, 3rd edn (Princeton University Press, Princeton, 1968).
Kofman, Sarah, *Le Mépris des juifs: Nietzsche, les juifs, l'antisémitisme* (Galilée, 1994).
Kuenzli, R. E., "The Nazi Appropriation of Nietzsche," *Nietzsche Studien*, 12 (1983), pp. 428–35.
Lessing, G. E., *Nathan der Weise* in *Lessings Werke* (Volksverlag, Weimar, 1963), vol. 2.
Liebeschütz, Hans, *Das Judentum im deutschen Geschichtsbild von Hegel bis Max Weber* (Leo Baeck Institute, J. C. B. Mohr, Tübingen, 1967).
——, "Das Judentum im Geschichtsbild Jacob Burckhardts," *Yearbook of the Leo Baeck Institute*, 4 (1959), pp. 61–80.
Lonsbach, Richard Maximilian, *Friedrich Nietzsche und die Juden* (1939), ed. H. R. Schlette, 2nd edn (Bouvier Verlag Herbert Grundmann, Bonn, 1985).
Luft, Eric von der, "Hegel and Judaism: A Reassessment," *Clio*, 18/4 (1989), pp. 361–78.
Mann, Thomas, "Nietzsche's Philosophy in the Light of Contemporary Events," in his *Last Essays*, tr. R. E. C. Winston and T. E. J. Stern (Knopf, New York, 1959), pp. 141–77.
Matheron, Alexandre, *Le Christ et le Salut des ignorants chez Spinoza* (Aubier-Montaigne, Paris, 1971).
Meinecke, Friedrich, *The German Catastrophe: Reflections and Recollections*, 2nd edn, tr. S. F. Fay (Beacon Press, Boston, 1963).
Müller-Buck, Renate, "Heine oder Goethe? Zu Friedrich Nietzsches Auseinandersetzung mit der antisemitischen Literaturkritik des Kunstwart," *Nietzsche-Studien*, 15 (1986), pp. 256–88.
Nicolas, M. P., *From Nietzsche down to Hitler* (W. Hodge, New York, 1970).
O'Flaherty, J. C., Sellner, T. F., and Helm, R. M. (eds), *Studies in Nietzsche and the Judaeo-Christian Tradition* (University of North Carolina Press, Chapel Hill, 1985).
Peters, Heinz-Frederick, *My Sister, My Spouse: A Biography of Lou Andreas-Salomé* (Gollancz, London, 1962).
——, *Zarathustra's Sister: The Case of Elisabeth and Friedrich Nietzsche* (Crown, New York, 1977).
Pines, Shlomo, "Spinoza's *Tractatus Theologico-Politicus*, Maimonides and Kant," in *Scripta Hierosolymitana*, 20 (Magnes Press, Jerusalem, 1968), pp. 3–54.

Planty-Bonjour, Guy (ed.), *Hegel et la Religion* (Presses Universitaires de France, 1982).

Podach, Erich F., *Nietzsches Zusammenbruch* (Heidelberg, 1930); tr. as *L'Effondrement de Nietzsche* (Gallimard, Paris, 1931; repr. 1978).

Pöggeler, Otto, "Hegel's Interpretation of Judaism," *Human Context*, 6 (1974), pp. 523–60.

——, "L'Esprit du christianisme de Hegel," *Archives de Philosophie*, 33 (1970), pp. 719–54.

Rawidowicz, Simon, "Zur *Jerusalem* Polemik," in *Festschrift Armand Kaminka zum 70. Geburtstage* (Maimonides Institut, Vienna, 1937), pp. 103–17.

Richards, Wiley R., *The Bible and Christian Traditions: Keys to Understanding the Allegorical Subplot of Nietzsche's Zarathustra* (P. Lang, New York, 1991).

Rivelaygue, Jacques, *Leçons de métaphysique allemande*, vol. 1 (Grasset & Fasquelle, Paris, 1990).

Rose, G., "Nietzsche's *Judaica*," in his *Judaism and Modernity: Philosophical Essays* (Blackwell, Oxford, 1993), pp. 89–110.

Rosenkranz, Karl, *G. W. F. Hegels Leben* (Wissenschaftliche Buchgesellschaft, Darmstadt, 1971).

Rotenstreich, Nathan, "Hegel's Image of Judaism," *Jewish Social Studies*, 15 (1953), pp. 33–52.

——, *Jews and German Philosophy* (Schocken Books, New York, 1984).

——, *The Recurring Pattern* (Weidenfeld & Nicolson, London, 1963).

Santaniello, Weaver, *Nietzsche, God, and the Jews* (SUNY Press, Albany, NY, 1994).

Scholem, Gershom, *Abraham Cohen Herrera, Author of the Gates of Heaven* (Hebrew) (Bialik, Jerusalem, 1978); tr. as *Das Buch Shaar ha-Shamayim oder Pforte des Himmels* (Suhrkamp, Frankfurt, 1979).

Schöps, Hans Joachim, "Die ausserchristlichen Religionen bei Hegel," *Zeitschrift für Religions- und Geistesgeschichte*, 1 (1955), pp. 1–34.

Smith, Steven B., "Hegel and the Jewish Question: In between Tradition and Modernity," *History of Political Thought*, 12/1 (1991), pp. 87–106.

Sonnenschmidt, Reinhard, "Zum philosophischen Antisemitismus bei G. W. F. Hegel," *Zeitschrift für Religions- und Geistesgeschichte*, 44/4 (1992), pp. 289–301.

Spinoza, B., *Chief Works*, tr. R. H. Elwes (2 vols, Dover, New York, 1951).

Talmon, Jacob, "Jacob Burckhardt," Introduction to Burckhardt, *Weltgeschichtliche Betrachtungen* (Bialik Institute, Jerusalem, 1962).

Thomas, R. H., *Nietzsche in German Politics and Society 1890–1918* (Manchester University Press, Manchester, 1983).

Troeltsch, E., *Das Historische in Kants Religionsphilosophie* (Reuther & Reichard, Berlin, 1904).

Wellhausen, Julius, *Prolegomena zur Geschichte Israels*, 2nd end (G. Reimer, Berlin, 1883); tr. as *Prolegomena to the History of Israel*, with a reprint of "Israel" from *Encyclopaedia Britannica* (Black, Edinburgh, 1885).

Wiedmann, Franz, *Hegel: An Illustrated Biography*, (Pegasus, New York, 1968).

Yovel, Yirmiyahu, "God's Transcendence and its Schematization: Maimonides in Light of the Spinoza–Hegel Dispute," in *Maimonides and Philosophy*, ed. S. Pines and Y. Yovel (Martinus Nijhoff, Dordrecht, 1986), pp. 269–82.

——, "Hegels Begriff der Religion und die Religion der Erhabenheit," *Theologie und Philosophie*, 51 (1976), pp. 512–37.

——, *Kant and the Philosophy of History* (Princeton University Press, Princeton, 1980).

———, "Nietzsche and the Jews out of the Ghetto," in *Nietzsche and Hebrew Culture*, ed. J. Golomb (Hebrew), (Magnes Press, Hebrew University, Jerusalem, forthcoming).

———, "Nietzsche, the Jews, and Ressentiment," in *Nietzsche, Genealogy, Morality*, ed. Richard Schacht (University of California Press, Berkeley, 1994), pp. 214–36.

———, "Nietzsche ve-Zilleli ha-El ha-Met," Postscript to the Hebrew translation of W. Kaufmann, *Nietzsche: Philosopher, Psychologist, Anti-Christ* (Schocken, Tel Aviv, 1983), pp. 426–38.

———, "Perspectives nouvelles sur Nietzsche et le judaïsme," *Revue des études juives*, 138 (1979), pp. 483–5.

———, "La Religion de la sublimité," in *Hegel et la religion*, ed. G. Planty-Bonjour (Presses Universitaires de Paris, 1982), pp. 151–76.

———, "Spinoza and Nietzsche: *amor dei* and *amor fati*," in *Spinoza and Other Heretics*, vol. 2, ch. 5.

———, *Spinoza and other Heretics*, vol. 1: *The Marrano of Reason* (Princeton University Press, Princeton, 1988).

———, *Spinoza and other Heretics*, vol. 2: *The Adventures of Immanence* (Princeton University Press, Princeton, 1989).

———, "Tolerance as Grace and as Right," (Hebrew), *Iyyun*, 45 (Oct. 1996), 482–7.

Zac, Sylvain, "Essence du judaïsme et liberté de pensée," *Nouveaux cahiers*, 34 (1973), pp. 14–29.

———, *Spinoza en Allemagne: Mendelssohn, Lessing et Jacobi* (Meridiens Klincksieck, Paris, 1989).

Index